A HISTORY OF WEST BROMWICH.

BY MARY WILLETT.

1882.

PREFACE.

I WOULD hope to disarm some hostile criticism by acknowledging at once that I have no pretension to literary power, or to that faculty of putting together antiquarian matter which is so needful an art in the would-be historian.

My ambition has had no higher range than to gratify a natural love of antiquarian research, by collecting and recording all that I could find of interest in the past relating to my native parish. That I have done this imperfectly, and by no means exhaustively, I am aware, and am, moreover, prepared to find myself corrected on some points by those more learned than myself. But those on whose judgment I could rely advised me that what I had written from personal antiquarian interest would be not unwelcome to many inhabitants of West Bromwich, past and present. I have accordingly acted on this opinion.

I have not written "The" History of West Bromwich; that more ambitious undertaking I leave for some one with higher qualifications than myself. Such a work would no doubt contain much of the past that I have not been fortunate enough to discover, and would, moreover, include all that makes modern West Bromwich so deservedly conspicuous among her sister towns of the Black Country.

I have only written "A" History, *i.e.*, a history of all that I could find relating to ancient West Bromwich, not touching on modern subjects, except so far as they incidentally spring out of the past.

If I have saved one single fact of the far off past from being lost, or have thrown any light on that which was doubtful in our local traditions, I shall not have spent the time occupied in writing this record altogether in vain.

I have received great assistance, which I here thankfully acknowledge, from the Reverend T. Jesson, the Reverend J. C. Cox (the well-known author of "The Churches of Derbyshire"), Colonel the Hon. G. Wrottesley, from the William Salt Library at Stafford, W. H. Duignan, Esq., and several other friends.

THE VICARAGE,
  WEST BROMWICH,
    August, 1881.

CONTENTS.

	PAGE.
THE MANOR AND FAMILIES CONNECTED THEREWITH	1.
THE PARISH CHURCH, &c.	22.
THE STANLEY TRUST	77.
PARISH RECORDS	94.
SANDWELL	143.
MISCELLANEOUS—THE OAK, AND OTHER HOUSES AND FAMILIES OF INTEREST	160.
APPENDIX	201.

A HISTORY OF WEST BROMWICH.

THE MANOR.

IT is one of the functions of the historian to correct the errors of his predecessors; it does not of course follow that such correction is an adverse criticism of those earlier than himself in the field. Far from it; for each generation in history as in art, science, or physical progress, has its own peculiar advantages, and it is the privilege of any one who now ventures to write the records of the past, to reap the benefit of that wave of antiquarian lore and research which is such a characteristic of the last fifty years. Each new historian ought to know more than the last; and so, in our comparatively little sphere of parochial history, it is no reflection on the labours of worthy Mr. Reeves (hitherto, we believe, the sole local historian of West Bromwich) in attempting to place on record all there is to be known of the Parish, to correct at the very outset a statement of that respected writer.

Mr. Reeves states that West Bromwich is not mentioned in Doomsday Book, this is incorrect. In making this statement Reeves, no doubt, followed Shaw's History of Staffordshire, in the second volume of which the same mis-statement occurs. It is true that in the Doomsday Survey there is no mention of West Bromwich in the place we should expect to find it; still we can claim for our Parish a place in that ancient record, and we proceed to show how.

Thanks to Colonel Wrottesley's investigations, West Bromwich has been found in Doomsday Book, placed under the head of Northamptonshire, among other of the possessions of William Fitz-Ansculph, Baron of Dudley, a nobleman who owned property in several counties.

The enumeration of West Bromwich among Fitz Ansculph's Northamptonshire property no doubt happened in this way. According to Mr. Eyton,* the Doomsday Commissioners made their primary reports on loose leaves or rotulets, and the work was arranged according to counties and hundreds. In due course these leaves or rotulets were sent en masse to the King's Exchequer, there to be transcribed, condensed, or paraphrased; there, also, to be codified, not in sequence of hundreds, but of tenures. In their passage to, or on their arrival at the Exchequer, some of the rotulets became confused with the rotulets of another county of the same circuit.

Mr. Eyton further assumes that Northamptonshire was on the same Doomsday Circuit as Staffordshire; thus the rotulets would very probably get mixed up, and that on which West Bromwich was entered, separated from those of its own county, would quite naturally find a place with the estates of its owner in another county.

Mr. Eyton gives us in the "Addenda and Errata" at the end of his book the actual entry which relates to West Bromwich, copied from the Doomsday Survey. It is as

---

* "Doomsday Studies," by the Rev. R. W. Eyton.

The Manor.

follows:—" Radulphus tenet de Willelmo (filio Ansculph) 3 hides in Bromwic, terra est 3 carucis. In dominio est una (caruca) et 10 villain et 3 bordarii habent 3 carucas. Silva ivi j lenna longa et dimidia lenna lata. Valuit et valet 40 solidos. Brictuin tenuit." Of this entry Mr. Eyton gives the following emendation:—"Bromwic held in the time of King Edward by Brictuin, held in capite A.D. 1086 by William Fitz-Ansculph, underheld A.D. 1086 by Radulphus, containing 3 hides, and a wood of 720 acres, annual value of the whole £2."

Here we find not only the names of the Doomsday tenant in capite, and fee or possession, but also that of the Saxon owner in the time of King Edward.

After such evidence as this, there can be but one opinion as to the antiquity of West Bromwich; an antiquity which is further demonstrated as we should expect, by the Parish Church, which gives ample proof of the very early existence of West Bromwich as an inhabited place.

We shall endeavour to trace the History of the Manor from this mention of it in Doomsday Book to the present time.

After the death of Fitz-Ansculph the Barony of Dudley descended eventually to one Gervase Paganel. Regarding this transmission of the Barony, Nash, on p. 457 of Vol. I. of his History of Worcestershire, states that "On the death of Fitz-Ansculph it (Frankley, a village like West Bromwich, in the Barony of Dudley), descended with the rest of his lands to Gervase Paganel, whose mother was daughter and sole heir to Fitz-Ansculph." It must have been Gervase Paganel's grandmother who was Fitz-Ansculph's heir, as there exists undoubted testimony that Ralph and Fulk, the father and grandfather of Gervase, both held the

Barony. (See the History of Dudley Castle by Dr. Booker, page 136.)

For most of the following, which relates to the holding of the Manor of West Bromwich, under the Barony of Dudley after the death of Fitz-Ansculph, we are indebted to Col. Wrottesley's valuable paper in "Historical Collections," Vol. I. There is extant in the New Record Office, Fetter Lane, a MS., known as the Liber Niger Scaccarii, or Black Book of the Exchequer; in this book, among other matters, is a list of most of the knights' fees, drawn up in all probability in connection with the levy of scutage, which at this date (1166) had been substituted for personal service in time of War. Under the Barony of Dudley, then held, as we have said, by Gervase Paganel, is the following return—"Willielmus Filius Widonis, 3. f. m." These fees were Ellesborough in Bucks, and Sandwell, Wombourne, and West Bromwich, and portion of Handsworth in Staffordshire.

Circa 1155, Guido de Opheni,* and Christiana his wife, and William his son, with the consent of Walter, the Bishop, gave the Church of Wombourne to the monks of S. James, of Dudley. (Harl.: MSS., 3868.)

Circa 1180, William Fitz-Wido de Offini, with the assent of Juliana his wife, and Richard his heir, gave to S. James, of Dudley, the land near Wudeford. About the same date William Fitz-Wido founded the priory of Sandwell, and gave to it the Churches of Ellesborough and Handsworth.

Circa 1200, Richard, son of William, gave all his lands at Wombourne in frank marriage with Matildis his daughter.

It appears from a copy of the Pipe Roll, of 21 Hen. II., 1174-5 (page 74 of Hist. Coll.), that Gervase Pagnel had

* A Village in Picardy, in the Department of the Somme. The modern spelling is Offignies.

to pay a fine of 500 marks "pro habendâ benevolentiâ regis;" and from the notes to the said Roll it appears that he had defended the Castle of Dudley for the Empress Matilda in 1137, for which offence the Castle was ordered to be dismantled; and he again offended by joining the rebels in 1173-4. Gervase Pagnel compounded for his offences by the above-mentioned fine—but four of his Knights, and among them William Fitz Wido, were compromised. Their offences were visited in 1176 by the King in person, who traversed the realm and held everywhere a Forest Court, and fined all those, who, in the rebellion, had shown disaffection to the Crown.

Gervase Pagnel was succeeded in the Barony of Dudley by the De Someri family—his only son Robert having died in his father's lifetime, the Barony passed to John de Someri, who had married Hawise, the sister of Gervase.

Colonel Wrottesley also gives us the following information. "On the Coram Rege Roll of Michaelmas term 7, Henry III. (1222), Geva Basset, the widow of Richard Fitz-William, sues James Fitz-William for one-third of half a hide of land in Esselburgh as her dower." Richard, son of William Fitz-Wido (or Guido, or Guy), left a son William, who died s.p., and two daughters, eventual co-heirs of their brother—Sara, the elder, married Walter Devereux; and Margaret, the younger, married Richard de Marnham.

In the "William Salt Library" is another copy of the "Coram Rege Roll," 9, and 10, Henry III. 1224-5, relating to the same Geva, widow of Richard. "Geva, who was the wife of Richard, son of William, seeks against William de Bromwic the third part of four vivaries, three acres of land, one messuage, and a rent of four shillings in

Bromwic, as her dower; and William de Bromwic comes and renders to her the third part of all the said premises, and he is amerced for having unjustly detained them." She also seeks against the Prior of Sandwell the third part of one mile, and one virgate and a half in Bromwic.

The following is from Shaw, Vol. I, App. XVII.—
" Walterus de Everoos et duo participes sui tenent villam de Bromwich de dicto Rogero de Sumery et nunquam fuit hidata, et placitat omnia placita excepto nam vetito. Et habent visum franciplegii. Et dant Vicecomiti pro visum franciplegii 5s. Et debent sectain ad duo magna hundra per ann." (From the Tenure Roll of the hundred of Offlow in the time of Henry III, about 1255.)

In the "William Salt Library" is the following inquisition of 20, Edward I. (1291), stating that " Walter de Everoos (Devereux) held half of Bromwic by service of half a Knight's fee of Roger de Somery, and Richard de Marnham held the other half by the same service." This was on the death of the aforesaid Walter Devereux.

Also, "On the Quo Warranto Pleas of 21, Edward I., Walter de Evereus claimed view of frankpledge, infangthef, gallows,* and wayf at Bromwich, and stated that he held the manor conjointly with Margaret, the wife of Richard de Marnham, of the inheritance of one Richard Fitz-William, and that the above franchises had been appurtenant to the manor from time out of memory." Walter de Evereus also stated " that King Henry, father of the present

---

* Col. the Hon. G. Wrottesley, in a letter lately received by the writer from him, says "Guy de Opheni must have been a cotemporary of Henry I., and I think they must have been a family of some importance by their right of gallows in West Bromwich. This is a franchise usually associated only with Baronial jurisdiction, and it was disputed even in the case of some of the Barons."

The Manor. 7

King, conceded to Walter de Evereus his father, and his heirs, free Warren in all his Lordship and lands in Bromwich, in proof of which he produced the Charter of King Henry."

The history of the manor is thus traced from 1155, when it was held by Guido de Opheni, to the year 1292, when it was held by Walter de Evereus (Devereux) conjointly with Margaret Marnham; and we will again briefly trace its descent through these 137 years. Guido de Opheni held the manor in 1155. William Fitz-Wido, that is the son of Guido de Opheni, held it in 1166, and was succeeded by his son Richard, who was dead in 1222.* This Richard had an only son, William, and two daughters. William dying without heirs, the manor became the property of his two sisters—Sara, married to Walter Devereux, and Margaret, or Margerie, to Richard de Marnham. Walter Devereux died in 1291; and was succeeded by his son Walter, who, in the following year, made certain claims as before stated. Two deeds of the Marnhams are printed in the appendix, the originals of which are in the possession of the Reverend Thomas Jesson.† Three other deeds, in which members of this family are mentioned, are also inserted. Shaw says in his 2nd Vol., page 185, in his account of the manor of Oxley: "By the survey taken of the forests in the County of Stafford, in the 28th of Edward I. (1299), it was then certified that Richard de Marnham

---

* Richard, son of William Fitz-Wido, was probably surnamed Basset, as his widow is called Geva Basset; and this will explain, perhaps, Shaw's statement, see vol. II., p. 127. Richard Basset's name appears in two very ancient deeds printed in the app.

† In one of these deeds William Marnham is styled Lord of West Bromwich. Under the feudal rule when a manor is divided between two sisters, the issue of the elder succeeds as Lord of the Manor, so it would appear that Margerie de Marnham was the elder sister.

held Oxley of the Barony of Dudley; in which family it continued until the 2nd of Richard II. (1378), when John Marnham grants this manor of Oxley to Edward Atte Lowe; and after, in the 12th of Richard II. (1388), William Marnham of West Bromwich, brother of the aforesaid John confirmed it, which Marnham sealed with three lozenges."

An inquisition on the death of John de Somery, 16th Edward II. (1322), mentions Stephen Devereux and Richard de Marnham as holding lands in West Bromwich of the said John. In an inquisition on the death of Roger Hillary, 30th Edward III. (1356), mention is made of William Devereux, and one John of Alrewas, and Alianora, his wife, of whom Roger Hillary held lands in West Bromwich by military service, etc., the said John of Alrewas, possessing lands in right of his wife Alianora.

Memoranda of fines relating to the Manor of West Bromwich, County Stafford:—

"Trinity (11), Edward III. Between William de Marnham *plaintiff*, and William Blaunchard and Clemence, his wife, *deforciants;* of the third part of a moiety of the Manor of Bromwych, with the appurtenances, except two virgates of land and five marks rents in the same third part. To hold to Marnham and his heirs for ever."

"Michas. Term (4), Edward III. Between William, son of Richard de Marnham, and Alianora, his wife, *plaintiffs*, by Thomas de Aston, guardian of the same Alianora and Bertram de Marnham, *deforciant;* of the Manor of Oxeleye, with the appurtenances, except 100 acres of waste in the same manor, and of a moiety of the Manor of West Bromwich, except 100 acres of waste in the same moiety. To hold to the same William and Alianora, and the heirs of their bodies, to be holden of the chief lords of the fee by the services which pertain to the aforesaid manor, and the two parts aforesaid, for ever. And, moreover, the same Bertram granted for him and his heirs that the third part of the aforesaid moiety—which William Blaunchard, and Clemence, his wife, held as the dowry of the said Clemence—of the inheritance of the aforesaid Bertram, and which, after her decease, ought to revert to the said Bertram and his heirs, should, after her decease, entirely remain to said William and Alianora and their heirs aforesaid. To hold with the said manor and the two parts aforesaid of the chief lords of the fee, and in default of such heirs of William and Alianora, then to the right heirs of said William for ever."

An inquisition, 4th Henry IV. (1402), on the death of another Roger Hillary, mentions land held by the said Roger of the heir of John Deures, no doubt a corruption of Devereux.

By divers inquisitions in the reign of Henry VI., it appears that William Freeman gave the manor of West Bromwich to his daughter Alice, widow of William Freebody of Dudley, and that she had issue, William Freebody.

Close Roll, VI. Henry, 6th m., 20.—" By a charter dated on Monday after the feast of St. Michael the Archangel, 6th Henry VI., Alice, widow of William Frebody, released to John Leventhorp the younger, esq., and William Aleyn, their heirs and assigns, all her right in the Manor of *Westbromwyche*, Co. Stafford. Witnessed by Nicholas Thyknys, William Robyns, Nicholas Scoles, and others. Acknowledged by the said Alice, Nov. 12th. 6th Henry VI."

In the absence of any direct evidence, it may be surmised that William Freeman inherited the manor by will. There is no " Fine " relating to his possession of it to be found, as would have been the case had he obtained it by purchase. He may have been the heir of John Deures (Devereux) mentioned in the last quoted inquisition.

Shaw says (vol. II., app. 16), " Marnham's part of the manor, in process of time, came by an heiress to William Freebody." And it may, perhaps, also be surmised that William Freeman had married the heiress of the Marnhams.

The manor was at this time held of Sir Maurice Berkeley, as of his Castle of Weolegh, by knight's service, instead of being held of Dudley, as heretofore; and the following extract will show how this came about.

Johanna de Someri, sister and co-heir of John de Someri, Baron of Dudley, married Thomas de Bottetourt, of Weley Castle, Northfield, County Worcester,* and West Bromwich was among those manors which fell to the portion of the said Johanna or Joan de Bottetourt. She died in 1388.

In the year 1436 William Freebody was Lord of the Manor, as is proved from the following extracts, copied in the W. S. Library from "Inquisitiones Post Mortem," Hadfield MSS.:—

" 15th Henry VI., A.D. 1436: William Freebody held the Manor of West Bromwich, and advowson of Priory of Sandwell, of the king at the above date."

" 26th Henry VI. (1447): William Freebody held the advowson of the Priory of S. Mary Magdalen at Sandwell, and Manor of West Bromwich, a member of Weolegh Castle. . . . . . . He also held Thorp Mandeville Manor in Northamptonshire, and was warden of Dover Castle; died. William, his son and heir, twenty years of age."

---

* Harwood's Erdswick, page 336.

"27th Henry VI.: William Frebody, son and heir of William Frebody, of Thorp Mandeville, proving his being of age." The last named William Freebody died without a male heir, and the manor passed to his daughter Cicely, by whose marriage the parish is brought into connection with a family illustrious in this, as in many other counties of England—the Stanleys, of whom Camden says "They were of consequence half-a-century before the Conquest, and they have invariably held an eminent place in history." Cicely Freebody married John, son of George, son of Thomas Stanley, of Elford. The Stanleys of Elford were a branch of the house of Derby, another branch being the present house of Stanley of Alderley. The following extracts from further inquisitions relating to the Stanleys may find a place here :—

"26th Henry VIII.: John Stanley, Esq., died. He held at West Bromwich 17 messuages called Bondsthing, 40 acres, 10 acres meadow, 3 cottages with appurtenances, from Cecilia Stanley, as of her Manor of West Bromwich, by military service and by rent of 22 pence; value 30s. and 8d. Francis, his son and heir, aged 30."

"6th Edward VI. (1552): Cecilia Stanley died. Held half the Manor of West Bromwich, 2 messuages, 10 acres arable land, 60 acres pasture, 10 acres wood, 10 acres meadow, with appurtenances, of Richard Jervis, Knight, as of his Castle of Weoly, by military service and ¼ Knight's fee; worth £20."

"4 & 5 Philip and Mary, 1556-7: Francis Stanley, Esq. died. *George, his son and heir, aged 11, held the Manor of West Bromwich of Thomas Jervis, Esquire, as of his Castle of Wheoley by Fealty; value £8."

---
* Intended for Walter (?)

We append a short pedigree of this branch of the Stanley family, and by it will be seen that Cecilia and John Stanley had three sons and one daughter. Francis, the eldest son, married Winifred, daughter of Thomas Middlemore, Lord of Edgbaston; and their son Walter made his name famous in the annals of West Bromwich, by founding and endowing a lectureship in connection with the Parish Church, an account of which is given elsewhere.

Walter Stanley was only 10 years of age when his father died, and during his minority his mother was Lady of the Manor, as will be seen in several deeds to be found in the appendix.

The following notes from the will of Walter Stanley, which is at Somerset House, may be interesting to our readers:—

Walter Stanley died in 1615. In his will he directs a certain sum of money to be applied for the advancement in life of Richard Shilton, his sister's son. He also mentions his nephew Robert Shilton, and Charles, son of Roger Stanley of Horburne, and Thomas Stanley, of Bromsgrove; also his sisters, Jane Okell, and Frances, the wife of John Wolverston. To his son, William Stanley, among other things, he bequeaths a double gilt standing cup, his armour, furniture, and weapons of war. To his daughter-in-law, Mary Stanley, his son William's wife, he leaves another double gilt cup. He also leaves a sum of money to be applied towards the completion of the Bilston causeway, and the highway between Bilston and Tipton.

William Stanley, who succeeded to the Manor on the death of his father in 1615, mortgaged it (after barring the entail) heavily ; in part to his cousin, Sir Richard Shilton, who, eventually, in 1626, became possessor of the whole estate, on paying off the claim of Sir William Hewitt, who also held a mortgage on the property. Mary, the wife of William Stanley, had died in 1624, and left several young children. What became of William Stanley we cannot ascertain, but he must have been much reduced in circumstances, as Sir Richard Shilton made an agreement to pay him £100 a year out of the estates.

Arms of Stanley, "Argent on a bend azure, 3 stags' heads cabossed or, between 3 mallards azure, 2 & 3." Degge.

Burke, in his "History of the Landed Gentry," vol 1, p. 95, gives the following account of these arms:—"Sir William de Stanley lineally descended from Henry Stanleigh de Stoneley, who lived 40 years before the conquest, became possessed of the manor and bailiwick of Wyrall Forest, and thereupon assumed the armorial bearings since used by his descendents, viz., three stags' heads on a bend."

The burial place of the Stanleys was in a chapel situated on the north-east side of the church. An account of it will be found under the head of "The Parish Church."

The following extracts from the Parish Registers relate to the Stanleys :—

BAPTISMS.

Elizabeth, the daughter of William Stanley, gent., and Mary his wife was baptised the 12th of January, 1608-9.

Mary Stanley, the daughter of William Stanley, gent., and Mary his wife was baptised Anno Dom. 1610, the 1st September.

Francis, the son of Mr. William Stanley, Esquire, was baptised the 20th of February, and born the 1st of February, 1614-15.

Thomas, son of William Stanley, Esquire, was baptised the 20th of December, and buried the same day, 1618.

BURIALS.

Rychard Stanley, gent., was buried the 12 of March, 1611.

Elizabeth Stanley, the daughter of William Stanley, gent., was buried the 12 of May, 1612.

Walter Stanley, Esq., was buried the tenth of April, 1615; aged 68.

Marye Stanley, the wife of William Stanley, Esq., was buried the 29 January, 1623-(4).

(For Stanley pedigree see Appendix.)

Sir Richard Shilton, Knight, was the next lord of this Manor, as before stated. He was cousin to William Stanley, his mother being Walter Stanley's sister. Sir Simon Degge says of Sir Richard that he "was some time Solicitor-General to the King, but not being found so fit for that emyloyment, was displaced, and made of the King's Council Extraordinary"—Shaw, Vol.II., 127. Sir Richard Shilton married Lettice, daughter of Sir Robert Fisher, of Packington, in Warwickshire, but had no family by her.

The Shiltons were a Birmingham family, and Sir Richard's father was a mercer in that town. Sir Richard died in 1647 and was buried in the Parish Church, having survived his wife about 5 years. He devised the manor to his sister, Alice Lowe, for her life, and afterwards to his nephew John, son of his brother, Robert Shilton. John Shilton, or Shelton, died in 1665, and was succeeded by his son John, who was baptised at West Bromwich in 1659.

This last-named John eventually mortgaged the Manor heavily to several different persons, and, at length, the estates were sold under an Order of Chancery to Sir Samuel Clarke, Knight, about the year 1720. John Shilton died in 1714, leaving one son, named Joseph, and two daughters.

The family of Shelton has disappeared from the parish, unless, as some say, the Sheldons of this parish, and of Wednesbury, are their descendants. John Shelton was also lord of the Manor of Wednesbury, which his father purchased in 1663. He, however, sold it about 1710 to John Hoo, of Bradley.

The only gravestone now existing bearing the name of Shilton is in the belfry, it is in memory of Elizabeth, 2nd daughter of John Shilton; she died in 1701. The inscription formerly upon the stone (now only the name is legible) will be found in the account of the church.

The arms of Shelton were "Sable, three escallop shells, argent." Degge.

Family of Shelton, from the Registers:—

BAPTISMS.

Lettis, the daughter of Robert Shilton, gent., was baptised the 28th of September, 1631.

Elizabeth, the daughter of Mr. John Shilton, Esquire, was born the 30th March, 1654.

Sibill, the daughter of Mr. John Shilton, Esquire, was baptised the 16th of May, 1655.

Phebe, the daughter of Mr. John Shilton, Esquire, and Elizabeth, his wife, was born the 22nd of April, 1656.

John, the son of John Shilton, Esquire, was born July 22nd, 1659.

Katherine, the daughter of John Shelton, Esquire, was baptised October, 5th, 1661.

Mrs. Barbara, the daughter of Mr. John Shilton, Esquire, was baptised the 3rd of December, 1662.

Mr. Richard, the son of Mr. John Shilton, Esquire, was baptised the 5th of March, 1664-5.

MARRIAGES.

Mr. Robart Turton and Mrs. Sara Shelton were married the 21st of June, 1649,

Mr. John Simcox and Mrs. Alice Sheldon were married the 28th of November, 1663.

Mr. Walter Needham and Mrs. Elizabeth Shilton were married the 3rd of November, 1666.

BURIALS.

Mrs. Ann Shilton was buried March the 7th, 1631-2.

Mrs. Margery Shilton was buried August 27th, 1636.

Lettice Shilton, the wife of Sir Richard Shilton, Knight, was buried the 23rd of July, 1642.

Sir Richard Shelton, Knight, was buried 7th of December, 1647.

Mrs. Mary Shelton, the wife of Mr. John Shelton, Esquire, was buried the 19th of June, 1649.

Elizabeth, the daughter of Mr. John Shilton, Esquire was buried the 27th of April, 1654.

A Child of John Shelton Esquire, being still-born, was buried the 27th of July, 1661.

Mr. John Shilton, Esquire, was buried February 18th, 1664-5.

Mrs. Sheldon was buried the 11th of April, 1666.

Elizabeth, the daughter of John Shilton, Esquire, was buried the 10th of October, 1701.

John Shelton, Esquire, was buried 5th of November, 1714.

Mrs. Mary Shelton was buried the 25th of September, 1715.

(For Shelton pedigree see Appendix.)

FAMILY OF CLARKE, AFTERWARDS JERVOISE.

In 1720 Sir Samuel Clarke, Knight, purchased the Manor House and a portion of the estates. The remainder of the landed property was sold in lots, and among the purchasers thereof are the names of Josiah Turton, John Piddock, William Silvester, John May Smith, Joseph Worsley, John Mayoe, John Lowe, Thomas Dudley.

Sir Samuel Clarke, the first of his name who possessed the Manor, lived at the Manor House, known as "Bromwich Hall," of which house, Shaw, in his 2nd vol., p. 128, gives the following description:—

"The old Manor House, called West Bromwich Hall, stands about a mile northward from the Church, in a flat situation, but well wooded. Like many other ancient family seats still remaining in this county it consists of a large pile of irregular half-timbered building, black and white, and surrounded with numerous out-houses and lofty walls." It must have been in these and subsequent days a county house of some considerable reputation, the centre of many hospitable re-unions and social gatherings. The garden, surrounded by the "lofty walls" of which Shaw speaks, has, in a curious manner, become an historical one. That it was a most productive garden there can be no doubt, and in the days of Sir Samuel Clarke seems to have been in a most flourishing condition. There has been preserved, for what reason, or by whom, is not known, among the documents of the Church kept in the vestry, a MS. catalogue of fruit trees supplied for the Old Hall garden, and correspondence relating to it. To judge by the orders given to the Essex nursery-man for trees, it would appear that Sir Samuel Clarke and his successors were enthusiastic horticulturists. In the appendix is given a great portion of these very interesting records of the Hall garden to which we have alluded, and which will, we think, repay perusal.

Another subject, too, is opened up by Sir Samuel Clarke's garden. Without it being, apparently, anything unusual, the nursery-man supplied him, among other fruit, with vines, peaches, and figs, for cultivation in the open air. Such fruit is unheard of now, in any garden in the open air in this neighbourhood. What has happened since the occupation of Bromwich Hall by the Clarke family to cause this difference? Some great climatic change has evidently taken place; it is not a question of smoke only, though, of course, that would be detrimental to such fruits. But were there no smoke at all in the present day the ripening of these fruits in the open air would still be such an improbability that no one thinks of planting such trees.

We have heard it stated that the destruction of the timber with which the parish was at one time so extensively covered, might produce some change in the temperature. It certainly is an interesting fact that grapes,[1] peaches, nectarines, and figs, a hundred years ago ripened as a regular crop in the open air in this parish. When the country has again reverted to its former green nature, and the cinder heaps have been covered by woods, will fruit again grow and ripen as of old?

A further mention of this garden is contained in Mr. Reeves' book. Writing in 1836, he says, "Sixty years ago there was a hop yard near the Hall, in which was a well, the water of which was considered medicinal, and was regularly drunk during the summer season by three maiden ladies, then living at Charlemont Hall, Elizabeth, Mary, and Sarah Lowe." [2]

---

[1] About fifty years ago a vine grew and bore fruit on a house at Hateley Heath. [2] Reeves, page 40.

Sir Samuel Clarke was succeeded by his son Samuel, who married Mary Elizabeth Jervoise, the daughter of Thomas Jervoise, Esq., of Herriard, in the county of Southampton.—"A descendant of William Jervoise, mercer, of London, in 1551, and whose descendants enjoyed Weoley Castle, in Northfield, 274 years."

This Mr. Samuel Clarke took an active part in the dispute which arose during the incumbency of the Reverend Peter Jones, in 1746, relative to the "Stanley Trust." An account of the dispute will be found under the head of "The Stanley Trust." It was only a local storm, but it, nevertheless, led to a lengthy suit in Chancery, in which most of the inhabitants of the parish seem to have taken sides.

Samuel Clarke was succeeded by his son, Jervoise, who assumed the surname of Jervoise in addition to that of Clarke, under the will of his maternal grandfather.

Jervoise Clarke-Jervoise, Esq., was a man of some considerable celebrity, being Member of Parliament for Yarmouth. He was buried in January, 1808, in the family vault within the Parish Church (probably in what was originally the Stanley vault) at the north-east end. When the Church was taken down in 1871, it was necessary to ascertain the position of all the vaults which were in it. The Clarke vault was opened in the execution of this purpose, and the coffin of Jervoise Clarke-Jervoise, M.P., was a very conspicuous object in it. To judge from the coffin, which measured 6ft. 6in. in length and 2ft. 6in. across, its occupant must in life have been a very fine man. He was succeeded by his son Thomas Clarke-Jervoise, who becoming insane, the Manor House and Lands were sold by an order in Chancery. The former was eventually purchased by Mr. James Smith, and is now the property of the Dorset family.

The Earl of Dartmouth is, at the present time, nominal Lord of the Manor; the manorial rights having been purchased by his father. West Bromwich, however, is not any longer a manor, there being now no copy-hold property or "customs" of the manor.

In 1836 the old Manor House was inhabited by three families, among them that of the Reverend P. G. Harper, Curate of the Parish. At the present time only the roof and walls remain, the interior having been gutted, and then made to accommodate a number of families. There is still a curious window and part of an ancient roof remaining, the latter probably belonging to the hall, though said to be that of the chapel.

Family of Clarke from the Registers:—

Samuel, son of Samuel Clarke, Esq., buried 5th January, 1749-50.

Kitty, wife of Jervoise Clarke, Esq., buried 6th March, 1772.

Reverend William Somers Clarke, buried February 28th, 1773.

Mrs. Anne Clarke, widow, buried January 7th, 1782.

Mrs. Ann Clarke, sister of Jervoise Clarke-Jervoise, Esq., buried September 30th, 1802. Aged 71.

Jervoise Clarke-Jervoise, Esq., buried January 22nd, 1808. Aged 74.

(For Pedigree of Clarke see Appendix.)

The arms of the Jervoise-Clarkes, according to Reeves, are:—

"First and fourth sable, a chevron between three eaglets close, argent for Jervoise.

Second and third azure, 3 escallops in pale or, between 2 flaunches ermine, each charged with a cross pattée fitchée gules for Clarke."

With the Clarke family the history of the Manor ends. We trust our endeavour to trace its fortunes from 1155 to the present time, a period of 736 years, has not proved uninteresting to our readers.

(For descent of the Manor, see Appendix.)

THE PARISH CHURCH.

IT will be in the recollection of our readers that an allusion has been made to the Parish Church in proof of the antiquity of West Bromwich as an inhabited place.

The remains of a Norman Church discovered in 1871-2 prove beyond dispute its existence soon after the Conquest, but it is more than probable that there was a Saxon and even an early British Church here, built most likely of wattles, according to custom, before the use of stone was practicable. The grounds for this theory are derived mainly from the position of the Church. The Church stands upon a very commanding and prominent site; now it is a well-known fact that such positions were chosen, when available, by church founders in very early times, with the object of making the house of God not only the chief feature in the parish, but also a landmark in the surrounding country. This motive actuated the Norman, and we believe the Briton and Saxon who lived here before him. Our opinion is strengthened by the position of the church on a principal ancient road. In those uncivilised days the inhabitants of the country were scattered, and there were practically no roads in our modern experience of the word; there were only those few central highways which, of British origin, had been improved by the Romans, and along which the first missionaries must have travelled when they came to preach the gospel to Britain. The church therefore would intentionally be placed on one of these ancient highways that it might be of easy access for the sparse population on all sides.

That the highway on which our church is situated is one of these primitive thoroughfares is most probable; it comes from those ancient ways which traverse Sutton Park and Cannock Chase from the direction of Watling Street, and crossing Icknield Street near the present Streetly Station, it passes by the Horns of Quislett and the Scott Arms of our day (thus forming the division of two ancient Saxon parishes, Great Barr and Handsworth), and so on into the parish of West Bromwich.

One branch of the road passes by the Old Church, and traversing the town, leads by Oldbury and Halesowen into Worcestershire. The other branch, through Wednesbury leads to Wolverhampton.

It is thought the road we have described as coming into the parish from Great Barr is the "Blake Street" of the Romans.

The suitability of placing the church on this road in Saxon times is obvious, and there is no doubt in our own mind that this suitability caused a church to be erected here generations before the Norman invader. Of its Norman existence there is positive proof, however, as we have said.

In 1871-2 when the building of the present church was in progress, some pieces of Norman work were discovered, and on examination they proved to be portions of a Norman belfry window, consisting of a shaft and two capitals, one of which is double. The shaft was found built up in the south-west buttress of the tower, the capitals not far distant, in another part of the tower. These have been preserved by being built into the north wall of the belfry, together with some ancient floor tiles of the 14th century, which were discovered under the wooden floor of the late church. Some other tiles were discovered at the same time, each containing one capital letter, and they are placed together with those before mentioned. With regard to these latter, on being exhibited at a meeting of the Archæological Society, in Wolverhampton, some members present pronounced them to be of the 11th or 12th century, others said they were as late as the 17th.

The earliest written records of the church are, we believe, the following, taken from Thomas' "Survey of the Cathedral Church of Worcester." On page 31, he gives a list of various donations copied from the fifth window in the west cloister, among them is " Rex Henricus dedit Bromwich et medietatem Castri Wigorniensis." This donation of West Bromwich Church to the monks of Worcester must have been prior to 1125, as at that date Thomas further says, on page 110, "Simon Bishop of Worcester confirms this gift of the king to the Monastery." The deed of confirmation is published on page 9 of the appendix, and it states the Bishop confirmed the gift of " Ecclesia de Bromwic cum terra que ad eam pertinet."

It appears that this church was granted by the Monastery at Worcester to that at Sandwell. Shaw, on page 17 of the app. to vol. II., says ;—" William Prior and Convent of Worcester grant to William Prior and Monks of Sandwell their church of Bromwych with all appurtenances ad perpetuam firmam, for six marks a year, thus :—

" Hec est conventio fa'a'int' W. priorem et conventum Wygorn' ex una parte, et W. priorem et monachos de Sandwelle ex alt'a; videl', quod dictus prior et convent' Wygorn conceșserunt prefatis priori et monachis de Sandwelle ecc'am suam de Bromwych, cum om'b' p'tinent' suis, ad p'petuam firmam, pro sex marcis annuis ad quat'or t'minos solvendis, v'l qu'or t'inor Octob'; scil' in festo s'c'e Mariæ in marci' viginti' sol ; ad festum s'ci Joh'is Bapt' viginti sol ; sub hac condic'one, scil', nativus, et ad festum s'c'i Michael viginti sol', et ad festum s'c'i Andree Ap'li viginti sol'; sub hac condic'one, scil', quod si p'd'i monachi de Sandwelle defic'nt in soluc'one ad aliquem p'd'tor' terminor' dabu't p'dc'is monachis Wyg'orn ad unu'qucq' t' minum in quo defec'int a sol'one decem sol' no'ie pene: si vero ad finem anni a sol'one cessav'runt, liceat d'cis monachis Wygorn' possessione ingredi memorate ecc'e sue de Bromwych omni appl'one et condic'ne cessantib'; et nichilominus d'ci monachi de Sandwelle p'fatis monachi Wygorn' tam pona' quam firma' detenta' psolvent pr'i et monachis de Sandwelle p'd'ce ecc'e honeste facient deservire s' et libros et alt'a ornamenta eccesiastica invenient, et o'ia on'a p'd'ce ecc'e tam ep'alia q' archidiaconalia sustinebu't. Ad majore' sec'ritate ecc'e scil' Wygorn' et de Sandwelle ven'abil p'r nr' d'us A. tu'c Coventr' et Lich' ep's sigill'm suu' una cu' sigill' capit'lor' Wygorn' scil de Sandwelle huic co'vencioni apposuit. 2. Universis sc'e matr's eccl'e filiis p'sentem paginam inspect', Alex' miseracone divina Coventr' et Lichfield ecc'ar' minist' humil' et'na in D'no sal'm. Cum' dilecti in X'po filii p'or et co'vent Wygorn' ecc'am de Bromwych cu' pertinc' dilict's in X'po fil' priori et monach' de Sandwell ad firma' concesserunt p'petuam, nos eandem concessionem ratam et gratam ha'tes prout in instrumento inter di'os p'ores et monachos confecto plenius continetur, eam ep'ali authoritate confirmavim', et presentis scripti pro'cimo et sigilli n'ri appensione co'munim'; salvo nob' et successiorib' n'ris pr'pontificali et parochiali; salva ecc'a in o'ib Coventr' et Lich' ecc'ar aut'e Co' cessim' et d'cis priori et monachis de Sandwelle qu'od pp't sua pauptate' p'p'um capellanu' ecc' deserviri faciant auditte Valete in D'no. Dat' ap'd Ychinton qu'to non' Octobr' pontificat' n'ri anno Septimo.

" Universis sc'e Matris ecc'e filiis att quos p'sens script' p'ven'it, Fr' R' Cove'nt ecc'e prior humil' et ejusdem loci co'ventus sal'm in D'no. Lr'as ven' p'ris Alex' Co'ventr et Lich' e'pi inspexim' in h' verba. (*ut sup*) Dat' ap'd Ychinton, qu'to non' Octobr,' pontific' n'ri anno Sept'mo, etc., et sigill anno gr'e M° cc° XL. quinto. Universis, etc. Rad's decanus Lich' ecc'e ejusd'm canon' capital' salt' in D'no. L'ras (ut sup) inspexim' etc., Dat' ap'd Ychinton quinto non. Octobr' pontific' Q'anno septimo et sigilliu' capi'li nost' apposum etc. Anno D'ni M° cc° L° quinto. Hiis testib' **Mag'ro Thom'** de **Wynnchester** p'centor' ecc'e Lich', mag'ro J. de Kyrney cancellar'; mag'ro et de Attebg', Alex' Blundo, d'no Waukellini, d'no Thom' Succentor', et aliis.

" Martinus ep's servus servor' D'i, dilectis fil' priori et monach' de Sandwell, ordinis s'ci Bened'cti' Coventr' et Lich' dioc' sal'm et ap'licam benedictionem. Eaque udi'co concordia t'ment fi'ma debent et illibata p'sistere et ne in recidine concencoinis stipulu' relabat' aplico'o con'enit p'sidio conveniri.—Exhibita siqd'm nob'v'ra petic'o continebat quod cum olim int'p'ore' et conventu' Wygorn, et vos sup p'p'et'ate ecc'e de Bromwych' conventr' dioc', aut' te ordinaria questio vertere tandem super his media' tib'amicis de consensu ep'i et capell'i Cov' et Lich' amicabil' int' p'tes composico int'venit, viz., quod d'ci p'r

The Parish Church.

et conv'nt Wygorn ecc'am sua' p'am cu' omib' p'tine' suis p' q'dam su'ma p'cunie vob' p'petuo ad firma' concesserunt, etc.

"Nos igitur v'ris rla'is postuba nib', etc., confirmamus et p'sentes scripti pattinia com'unim', Nulli g° om'o hom' liceat ha'c pagina' r're confimacois infringer vl' ei vsu temeraria' conti're. Si quis aut' hoc attemptare p'su'pserit, indignationem o'ipotentes Dei et beator' Petr' et Pauli apo'lor, ei' se nov'it incurfur'. Dat' ap'd urbem vet'em, viii Kal' Marcii, pontificat' n'vi anno t'tio."

The Bishop here mentioned was Alexander de Stainby, who was consecrated April 24th, 1224, and died October 26th, 1238. In 1255 the Dean and Chapter of Lichfield confirmed this gift to the canons of Sandwell.

The canons at Sandwell thus being responsible for serving the altar in this parish, did as most monasteries did in those days, viz., appointed a vicar[1] to do their work for them, and thus ecclesiastical matters remained until the time of Henry VIII. In the events that preceded and were subsequent to the Reformation, the Parish Church followed the fortunes of Sandwell, and the great tithes of the parish finally passed into the possession of the Whorwood family, about the year 1609, and with them was vested the patronage of the church.

To return, however, for a moment to the Norman church of which we have briefly spoken. Relying on the valued opinion of an eminent architect, we believe this church to have been very small, consisting of a Nave and Chancel only, with a Tower at the West end, surrounded by a burial ground sufficiently large for the small village population at that time. As time went on, and the population increased,

---

[1] In this instance one of their own regular clergy.

greater church accommodation was needed, and a second church, built during the fourteenth century, and re-modelled in the fifteenth, occupied the site of the early Norman one. Portions of this second church still remain, the lower part of the tower, including the window and arch, belong to it, and, to judge by its few remaining architectural details, it must have been very beautiful. It existed until the year 1786. This church consisted of a Nave, Chancel, and a North Aisle, with a Chapel at its eastern extremity. The High Altar would stand, of course, in the Chancel, and there would be a second Altar in the Chapel, which, as we see further on, was the burial place of the Lords of the Manor. There has always been a tradition of two chancels in this church, one belonging to the parish, and the other to the monks of Sandwell.

It will be observed that our present church resembles this earlier one of which we are now speaking in its general architectural character, with this exception, that we have now a South Aisle and Chapel, and the Nave is on the North. The present Vestry, the "Whorwood Chapel," was built, as the date upon it bears witness, in the year 1619, according to the directions for that purpose in the will of Sir William Whorwood, who died in 1614. The Font is also a relic of this church. From Wyrley's "Church Notes," A.D. 1597, given by Shaw, vol II., page 132, it appears that the following arms were then in the windows:—

1.—Vairy, Argent and Sable, a Fess Gules.
2.—Gules a Fess between six cross-crosslets Or.
3.—Or, two lions passant Azure.
4.—Argent a Fess Gules, and three torteaux in Chief.
5.—Argent, a Saltire, ingrailed Sable.
6.—Azure, two lions passant Or.

7.—Or, a Chevron Azure, between three plates Azure, each charged with a Fess Argent, on which are three leopard's faces, between six cross-crosslets fitchée, Gules.

8.—Argent, six cross-crosslets fichée Sable, 3, 2, 1, on a Chief Azure, two Mulletts pierced Or.

9.—Or, a Saltire ingrailed Sable.

10.—Gules a Chevron Chequy Argent and Sable.

11.—Party per Chevron Argent and Sable, two birds seemingly cocks proper (Middlemore).

12.—The base part broken. In Chief Argent, three Martlets Sable, impaling quarterly Ermine and Gules, a border ingrailed Azure.

With regard to these arms we have been able, with the kind assistance of Mr. Sydney Grazebrook, of Chiswick, to assign them to the following families, and it will be observed that they are nearly all in connection with the Lords of the Manor.

No. 1.—Bracebridge

2.—Beauchamp Earls of Warwick—the same arms are in Lichfield Cathedral and Walsall Church.

3.—Somery—Barons of Dudley.

4.—Devereux—Viscount Hereford. Nash ii. App. 86.

5.—Intended for Botetourt? or Tiptoft, one of the Quarterings of the Barons of Dudley?

6.—Erdington—Nash ii., App. 86.

7.—

8.—Clinton, Earl of Huntingdon. Dugdale's Warwickshire, p. 709. Also one of the Quarterings of the Bassets of Drayton. Shaw ii. Plate iii. Nash ii, App. 86.

9.—Botetourt of Weoley Castle. Dugdale p. 734. Nash ii.—52.
10.—Boteler. Nash i. P. 465.
11.—Middlemore. Nash ii. App. 88.
12.—Berkeley of Weoley Castle (impaling?) Nash ii. App. 84.—The same arms were in Wednesbury Church.

We next give a list of the Ornaments belonging to this Church in the year 1552. For this information we are indebted to the Reverend Prebendary Edwards, Vicar of Trentham, who some few years since published a work entitled "Annals of the Diocese of Lichfield," and in it are lists of various ornaments belonging to Churches in this Diocese. Mr. Edwards says "The occasion of which the said Inventory was made is thus set forth by Fuller in his Church History—Bk. vii., § ii.

"Lately information was given to the King's Council that much costly furniture, which was embezzled, might very seasonably (such the King's present occasion) and profitably be recovered. For private men's halls were hung with altar cloths; their tables and beds covered with copes instead of carpets and coverlets. Many drank at their daily meals in chalices; and no wonder if, in proportion, it came to the share of their horses to be watered in rich coffins of marble. And as if first laying of hands upon them were sufficient title unto them, seizing on them was generally the price they had paid for them. Now, although four years were elapsed since the destruction of Colleges and Chantries, and much of the best Church Ornaments was transported beyond the seas, yet the Privy Council thought that this very gleaning in the stubble would be worth while, and that on strict inquisition, they should retrieve much plate in specie, and more money for moderate fines of offenders herein. Besides, whereas Parish Churches had still many rich ornaments left in the custody of their wardens, they resolved to convert what was superfluous or superstitious to the King's use. To which purpose commissions were issued out, to some select persons, in every county . . . . . In pursuance of these their instructions, the King's Commissioners in their respective counties recovered much, and discovered more of Church wealth and ornaments. For some were utterly embezzled by persons not responsible, and there the King must lose his right. More had been concealed by persons not detectable, so cunningly they carried their stealths, seeing every one who had limned a church bell, did not ring it out for all to hear the sound thereof. However, the Commissioners regained more than they expected . . . . . This plate and other Church utensils were sold, and advanced much money to the Exchequer. An author tells us, that amongst many which they found, they left but one silver chalice to every church."

The Commissioners for Staffordshire were Walter Viscount Hereford, Lord Ferrers, of Chartley, Sir Thomas Giffard, Sir Thomas Fitzherbert, Sir Edward Ashton, Edward Lyttleton, and Walter Wrottesley, Esquires. These seem to have begun their investigation in September, 1552 (6 Ed. vi.) and to have made their returns in April and May following.

"Westebromwych.

Fyrste, one challes of sylver parcell gylte with a paten.
ij copes one of blew velvet and the other of cremesyn crule.
ij vestements one of blew velvet, and the other off grene crule.

iij candlestyks of brasse, one pyxe bownde abowte with silver, one crosse of latten, iiij Alter clothes.

iiij towells, one crosse clothe off grene sylke.

iiij grete bells. M.D. that ther was ij Alter Clothes stolne owt of the Churche, by whome the kno not, and also ther was solde by the consent of the whole parishe iij candelstyks for the mayntenans of a bryge nyghe ye sayd towne.

M.D. delivered by the right honorable Walter Vicounte Hereford, Lord Ferers of Chartley, Thomas Fitzharbert Knight, and Edward Littelton Esquier, Commissionars for Churche Goodes within the countie of Stafford, to Edward Hering and John Hayteley Churchwardens there, on Chales of Silver with a Patent, ij Linen clothes for the Holli Communion Table, a Surples for the Curat to minestre with, and iiij bells in the Stepull safelie to be kepte untill the Kinges Majesties pleasure therein be furder knowen, In witenes whereof as well we the sayd Commissionars as the sayd Churchwardens to thes presents interchaungeabli have putto our hands the xiiijth of May, Anno Regni Regis Edwardi Sexti Septimo. Indorsed Westebromewiche."

This Church, as has been before stated, was in the gift of the Monks of Sandwell, or rather it would be more correct to say the Monks themselves served the parish. The Rev. J. C. Cox, of Lichfield, author of "The Chutches of Derbyshire," has most kindly searched the Episcopal Registers to endeavour to obtain information on this subject, he says in reference to it:—

"There are no pre-reformation institutions to the Vicarage of West Bromwich in the Episcopal Registers. It therefore follows that this was one of those very rare cases (there is not one instance among all the impropriated

Rectories of Derbyshire) in which the Monastic owners of the great tithes undertook to do the parochial duties through one of their own regular clergy. This would only be allowed where the religious house was in close propinquity to the impropriated Church."

Mr. Cox also says "The Valor Ecclesiasticus of Henry VIII. gives the value of the Rectory of West Bromwich £4. and mentions that it was then in the hands of the Royal College, Oxford, owing to the suppression of Sandwell."

In the British Museum are Letters Patent, dated 30th August, 28th Elizabeth, granting the Rectory of West Bromwich to Edward Holte for 21 years.

The Parish Church is now dedicated to All Saints. It may be here noted that Shaw's statement that the Church was dedicated to S. Clement, and Mr. Cox's opinion expressed in his small work "How to write the History of a Parish," respecting Pre-reformation dedications to All Saints, have led the writer to make inquiries on the subject. All endeavour to prove the ancient dedication from Wills has been futile, but Mr. Cox says, in reference to the matter, "In Ecton's 'Thesaurus Rerum Ecclesiasticarum,' 1742, I find the dedication of West Bromwich Church as 'S. Clement.' This book does not give all dedications, but I never yet have found it wrong; Ecton took all his statements from MSS. It is also 'S. Clement' in Bacon's 'Liber Regis,' 1786. It would require strong evidence to upset this. All dedications to 'All Saints' are suspicious, as so many were altered, temp. Henry VIII, in order to reduce the number of Wakes or Village Feasts.'"

In 1608-9 the Reverend Thomas Johnson was discharging the duties of Parish Priest. At this date the Parish

Registers begin. During the time of Mr. Johnson's Incumbency it was that Walter Stanley founded a Lectureship, which has ever since borne his name; as this Lectureship was to provide for the increasing spiritual requirements of the parish, West Bromwich had no doubt grown, as a village, to some considerable size.

The following extracts, relating to Mr. Johnson, are from the Parish Registers:—

Mr. Thomas Johnson and Maudlin Sibbes were married the 2th of November, 1635.

Mr. Thomas Johnson was buried November 9th, 1636.

Hannah, the daughter of Mr. Thomas Johnson, was baptized the 16th of February, 1636-7.

To what a tragic family history do these extracts point; married one year, and dead the next, his child born three months after his death, and his widow re-married within eighteen months as we see by the following:—

"William Allen and Maudlin Johnson were married April 28th," 1638.

Registers of an early date were not kept with much accuracy, and it is only now and then, at the foot of a page, that we find the Parish Priest's signature, and this is the only real evidence that we have that "Mr. Thomas Johnson" was the parish clergyman.

With regard to the residence of the Parish Clergy, Reeves says "At the time of the destruction of religious houses, in the reign of Henry VIII., a house, with its appurtenances, stood, part in the churchyard, and part adjoining on the south side. This house was occupied by the priest, who daily waited at the altar. It is very probable that this establishment went to decay soon after that period and that the Parsonage House at the Hall End was then founded." We do not know on what authority Mr. Reeves made this statement. In a deed dated 8th Henry VIII. (1516), printed in the appendix, "The Manse of the Vicar of West Bromwich" is mentioned, and from the description it is probable the house in Church Lane is the one alluded to. The registers are without any signature, after the death of Mr. Johnson, for many years, but in 1645-6 there are entries attested by "Edward Lane, Minister." One entry refers to Mr. Lane's own family, as follows:—"Mary, daughter of Mr. Edward Lane, Minister, was baptised the 27th of April," (1646). It is probable that Mr. Lane continued to discharge the duties of his office until the year 1648. At this date he seems to have had his share of the "Sufferings of the Clergy," caused by the almost universal bigotry of the Puritan sect. There is no entry in the register of Mr. Lane's death, but his place was occupied by a very pronounced Puritan, one Mr. Richard Hilton.

Mr. Hilton's first ministerial act was a baptism, on July 30th, 1648, and he remained in office till 1662, when he was suspended for non-conformity, and his place filled by the Reverend Samuel Addenbrook.

Mr. Addenbrook must have spent the greater part of his life here. He held, in addition to the Incumbency, the Lectureship under the Stanley Trust, though contrary to the directions given in that Trust. Mr. Addenbrook died in January, 1709-10, and was buried in the Chancel of the Church. His wife placed a stone to his memory, which is now preserved in the belfry.

The churchwardens' books containing accounts of vestry meetings for various purposes, &c., begin in the year 1678, which was during Mr. Addenbrook's Incumbency—and his signature frequently occurs—a chapter is devoted to extracts from these books and other church papers which are of interest.

The following extracts from the Registers relate to the family of Mr. Addenbrook.—

Jane the daughter of Mr. Addenbrook, Minister, was baptised May 24th, 1677.

John, the son of Samuel Addenbrook, Minister, was baptised June 13th, 1681.

Mr. Samuel Addenbrook, Minister, was buried February 1st, 1709-10.

Mr. Addenbrook has left a copy of the *Terrier*, dated 1693, and it will be found among the church papers.

The church as it was in Mr. Addenbrook's time, and as it continued until 1785, except for some slight alterations, is described by Dr. Wilkes, who was born in 1691, and died in 1760. The extract from Dr. Wilkes' MSS. is taken from "Shaw's Staffordshire," vol. II., page 132.

" In the South Chancel:—Two alabaster tombs close together within iron rails, on the Southmost a man on his back with a book in his left hand. At the feet of the first:—
' Here lyeth the body of Sir William Whorwood, Knt. He departed this life July 1st, and was buried the 2nd of August, 1614. And Ann, his wife, was buried October 22nd, 1599. They had issue thirteen children, viz.—five sons and eight daughters.'"

"On the other on the North side.—' Depositum Field Whorwood, arm. & senatoris Lond⁸ Fil natu 4ᵗ Willielmi Whorwood de Sandwel, in agro Staff., equitis aurati, qui sideratus apoplexiâ interiit Julii, 1658, æt. suæ 66. Spe communi Christianorum jacet œternitatis candidatum.

'Integer hic vitæ quam multos vixerat annos
Mercator Civis Larus in urbe tuâ,
Occubuit tandem morbo quasi sidere tactus,
Fulgure sic cecidit quercus amata Deo.'"

"On the Wall over them:—' This monument was erected for the memory of Sir William Whorwood, of Sandwel, within this parish, knt., and Ann, his wife, daughter and heir of Henry Field, of King's Norton, com, Worcester, esq., who lye here interred; by whom he had 5 sons, Thomas, William, Robert, Field, and John; and 7 daughters, Frances, Ann, Elizabeth, Isabel, Mary, Dorothy, and Magdalene; which monument was erected by the said Field Whorwood, being his executor.'"

"In the North Chancel:—On the floor five stones in a row. On the 1st—' Here lyeth the body of Mary Stanley, late wife of William Stanley, esq., lord of West Bromwich, daughter and heir of George Gray, Esq., which William had issue by the said Mary, 5 sons and 2 daughters. She departed this life 20 Jan., 1623' (4). 2nd, 3rd, and 4th not legible; 5th, ' Here lyeth the body of Ann Shelton, eldest daughter of John Shelton and sister of Richard Shelton, knt., sollicitor-general of our sovereign lord King Charles. She departed this life 5 March, 1631, and expecteth a joyful resurrection.'"

"In the East Chancel, within the rails:—'Here lyeth the body of Elizabeth Page, widow of Robert Page, of Leighton, com., Huntingdon, and one of the daughters of Richard Edwards, of Alsey, com., Bedford, esq., who died 21 July, 1665, and of Eleanor Turton, widow, relict of William Turton, of the Oak House, in this parish, and one of the daughters of the aforementioned Robert Page, and of Elizabeth, his wife, who died 19 September, 1696, æt 61."

"Near it, on a flat stone :—' P. F. Matilda Adenbrook l. M. Mœritissimœ conjugis Mti. Sam⁴ Adenbrook, hujus ecclæ non ita pridem Minri, qui ob. prid. non. Feb. A.D. 1709.'" "In the middle aile of the Church:—'Here lieth William Turton de la Oak, Gent., who departed this life the 27 July, 1682, in hopes of a joyful resurrection. In memoriâ æterna justus erit. Also in this grave lieth the body of John Turton de la Oak, Gent., eldest son of Mr. William Turton above named, who died 6 Dec., 1705, æt 45. Sancti cum Deo vivunt.'"

In this account Dr. Wilkes mentions three Chancels, East, North, and South. The East would be where the High Altar, of course, stood, the North would be the Stanley chapel, mention of which is made in the curious old manuscript of Simon Ryder as recorded in the appendix. The South Chancel was the Whorwood chapel, or present vestry. With regard to this latter in an account of a vestry meeting as to the proprietorship of the same, it is described as a "Chancel."

Tradition speaks of seven Whorwood monuments (five of which were destroyed), as originally in the chapel.

Dr. Wilkes further gives the following arms, "In the North Chancel window :—

1.—Per fess dauncette Argent and Or, 3 besants in chief, a crescent for difference.
2.—Argent, on a bend boided, 3 buck's heads of the 2d, a crescent for difference.
3.—Argent, 3 beaugle horns.
4.—Argent, a chevron between 3 hearts Or.
5.—Argent, 3 chevronels.
6.—Sable semi of cross-crosslets, 4 flowers de liz Argent, a Canton ermine.

The Parish Church.

7.—Argent, 3 lozenges in fess Or."

These arms are Stanley, and quarterings. Almost the same are on George Lyttelton's tomb in Bromsgrove Church (his mother was a Stanley), and are given in Nash, vol. i. page 162.

1.—No doubt intended for Lathom.
2.—Stanley—not correctly blazoned.
3.—Wyrley.
4.—Freebody.
5.—George Stanley and Eleanor Beaumont? Shaw, vol. ii., page 86. Or Clare?
6.—Hillary?
7.—Freeman. Nash, vol. i., app. 87.

We are indebted to Mr. Sidney Grazebrook for assistance in identifying several of the above. With regard to No. 4 he says, "It is, I feel sure, correct. Nash calls them 'hurts or,' and I find I have a MS. note, '2 hearts, Frebody. Stanley, of West Bromwich, married daughter of Frebody, who bore a chevron between 3 hearts.' No. 6 looks like Hillary, but a very similar coat (3 fleur de lis instead of 6) was quartered by Ruding for Watercroft. Wm. Clerke, of Dudley or Rowley Regis, married Prudence, daughter of the aforesaid Watercroft, and Ruding married the heiress of Clerke."

On the death of Mr. Addenbrook, in 1710, the Reverend John Rann was appointed to the vacant Living, and also subsequently to the Lectureship. As in the case of Mr. Addenbrook, this latter appointment was quite contrary to the directions given by Walter Stanley in his Deed of Endowment as to the election of a Preacher. No doubt the cause of this deviation was this. The Living was very poor—only £20 per annum being paid to the Incumbent by the Impropriator out of the tithes, and on this sum of money no man without private means could exist,—therefore, no doubt, the Trustees, to assist the Incumbent, had allowed him, from time to time, to hold the Lectureship also.

Mr. Rann's name is very much mixed up with the unfortunate dispute which arose between his son-in-law, the Rev. Peter Jones, and the Stanley Trustees. During the time of Mr. Rann's Incumbency it was that the Church was ceiled; this took place in 1713, thus, no doubt, spoiling the ancient roof; again, in 1716, we find the Church was, according to ideas of church decoration prevalent at that time, "Clean whitwashed and new butefied." The latter seems to have consisted in painting the Ten Commandments, the King's Arms, the Lord's Prayer, the Creed, Moses and Aaron, and six sentences in " oyle work only without gold." [1]

Mr. Rann married Damaris, daughter of John Dolphin, of The Moss, in the parish of Shenstone; at the time, however, of his daughter's marriage Mr. Dolphin was Clerk of the Peace at Stafford. This fact must have escaped the notice of those employed to find Mr. Rann's marriage certificate about the year 1815, when search was made in the registers of the principal churches in the neighbourhood, but in vain. To find this certificate was of importance to the parties concerned, as will be seen in the account of the Stanley Trust. Mr. Rann was married at Stafford. The entry is as follows:—" Aprilis. 1711. Matrim inter Joh. Rann, Cler. de West Bromwich et Damaris Dolphin—3." Saunders, in his History of Shenstone, says " Damaris Dolphin, 3rd daughter of John Dolphin, of The

---

[1] See Appendix.

Moss, was the wife of Mr. Rann, of Caldmore, Walsall, late of the Delves, and Minister of Wednesbury (?) yet Vicar of Rushall, in 1769. Aged 82. She is yet living, but advanced in years. Damaris, their daughter, was wife of Peter Jones, Minister of West Bromwich, and Prebendary of Wolverhampton."

The following entries from the baptismal Register relate to Mr. Rann :—

John, the son of John Rann, minister, baptized 11th March, 1711-12.

Joseph, the son of John Rann, minister, baptized June 26th, 1713.

Mary, the daughter of John Rann, minister, born June 10th, and baptized June 25th, 1714.

Sarah, the daughter of John Rann, minister, baptised Aug. 14th, 1715; born Aug. 8th.

Elizabeth, the daughter of John Rann, minister, born Nov. 8th, 1716; baptized 19th Nov.

Damaris, the daughter of John Rann, minister, born Nov. 20th, 1720; baptized Dec. 8th, 1720.

Mrs. Margaret, the daughter of John Rann, minister, born July 14th, 1722; baptized Aug. 3rd, 1722.

Richard and Henry, sons of John Rann, minister, baptized Sept. 4th, 1723.

In 1743, Mr. Rann then holding both the Incumbency and Lectureship, resigned both, and became Vicar of Rushall, where he died in 1771, aged 84. His wife survived him three years, dying in 1774, aged 83. [1]

Mr. Rann's son-in-law, the Rev. Peter Jones, was appointed to the vacant Living, and soon after to the Lectureship, not however unanimously, but by the major

---

[1] Shaw, vol. ii., page 68.

part of the Trustees, who at this time were reduced to only four in number.

Mr. Jones was, as is stated in the quotation from Saunders' History of Shenstone, a Prebendary of Wolverhampton.

The dispute between the Stanley Trustees and Mr. Jones, which has been already referred to, related to some land at Wednesbury, the property of the Trustees, but which had through great neglect on the part of these Trustees become mortgaged to Mr. Rann.

This mortgage Mr. Rann handed over to Mr. Jones on his marriage with his daughter Damaris.

Neither Mr. Rann or Mr. Jones appear to have come out of the transaction with much credit.

Perhaps the lengthy and painful lawsuit had something to do with the sad termination of Mr. Jones' Incumbency. A reference to the burials in the following extracts from the Registers will shew that he, his wife and two children all died in one year. Mr. Jones was buried in the Church; his gravestone is now in the belfry.

Mr. Peter Jones and Miss Damaris Rann were married February 23rd, (1743-4).

John, the son of Peter Jones, Minister, was born August 28th, and baptized October 29th, (1750).

Peter, the son of the Rev. Mr. Jones, was born December 16th, 1751, and baptized January 6th, (1751-2).

The Rev. Peter Jones died January 17th, buried the 21st day of January, (1751-2).

Peter, the son of Mrs. Jones, was buried the 8th day of May, (1752).

John, the son of the Rev. Mr. Jones, was buried June 7th, (1752).

Mrs. Damaris Jones was buried August 7th, (1752).

On the death of Mr. Jones, the Living was sequestrated, and the Reverend William Jabet (who was Lecturer) appointed to the charge of the parish. Mr. Jabet continued in office as Curate-in-charge for one year, and was then succeeded by the Reverend Henry Saunders, afterwards Curate of Shenstone, and author of the History of that Parish.

In January, 1757, on the Living being released from sequestration, the Reverend Edward Stillingfleet was appointed to the Incumbency; and in the following year to the Lectureship in the place of Mr. Jabet who had held that office since the year 1746. The following extracts from the Registers relate to Mr. Stillingfleet's family.

Margaret, the daughter of the Rev. Edward and Margaret Stillingfleet, was baptized the 9th Sep., 1764.

Elizabeth Sarah, the daughter of the Rev. Edward and Margaret Stillingfleet, was baptized Sep. 28th, 1766.

Mr. Stillingfleet held the living until 1782, when he was succeeded by the Reverend Abraham Elton. Mr. Elton also held the Lectureship, and he retained both offices till the year 1790, when, on succeeding to the Elton Baronetcy, he removed to the family seat—Cleeve Court, in Somersetshire. The following records of his family during his residence here are from the Registers.

Henry, son of Abraham and Elizabeth Elton, was baptized the 18th of August, 1786.

Frederick, son of the Rev. Abraham Elton, was buried the 10th day of August, 1788.

Mr. Elton's Incumbency was a memorable one in the History of the Fabric of the Church. In 1783 the question of repairing the Church was first mooted, and a faculty obtained to execute the same. The faculty, which is dated July 11th, 1786, thus describes the state of the Church—

"It is much dilapidated and in want of repair; the pulpit and reading desk are very inconveniently placed, and a gallery at the west end of the Church called a Singing gallery, as also another small gallery which is the property of Mr. Jesson, Miss Lowe, and others, are very incommodiously situated, as well as are certain seats or pews of Jervoise Clarke and William Whyley . . . . it had been determined to take off the present roof . . . . and to raise the same so as to be secure and substantial, and to take down the pulpit and reading desk, the above-mentioned two galleries, and the said seats and pews, and to re-erect and set up a new pulpit and reading desk, with handsome galleries on the north and south sides of the said Parish Church."

That not only the roof was taken off, but the walls of the Church almost entirely destroyed, the following items show.

The faculty being obtained, the work proceeded.

12th October, 1786.—Taking down the Church walls.

	£	s.	d.
To Babb and Labourer, 2¼ days to North wall..		11	3
(Several other days were devoted to this.)			
28th, To Parkes, 2 days; Labourer, 2½ days to gable wall		9	7
3rd Nov., To Babb and Labourer, 2¼ days to South wall		11	3
Cleaning materials of arch after falling, and weeling away the rubbish.. ..		8	8
1787, 13th October, To 2 men, 1 day each cutting away walls with Mr. Couchman		10	8

The Parish Church.

		£	s.	d.
13th Nov., To 2 men, ½ day each, to foundations			2	8
1788, 1st March, To taking up old floors and making good old wainscot, and putting up do.		1	18	6
To building the arch that fell down, 1¼ rods 42 feet of brickwork, lime and labour		3	12	6
To making center to gothick arch		1	0	0
1¾ rods of brickwork as was down and was re-built, lime and labour only		3	19	0
2 window arches and sills, and 12ft. of cornice that was broke to pieces and made good		2	6	0
To 72 rods 45 ft. of brickwork reduced to 1½ brick, with all materials		55	8	0
53 yards ¼ of rough cast walls		2	13	4
150¾ yards of walls, sett		5	0	6
654ft. of oak floor and sleepers		19	1	6
Elipses arch between Church and Chancel, with ventilators in center, and pricked caps and palasters, and other ornaments		20	7	2
A truss between Church and Chancel		11	13	0
By Vestry, as pr. estimate		45	10	0

From these items it would seem that an arch, doubtless the tower arch, had been injured by, we imagine, the removal of the old walls, at the so-called restoration of the Church, and fell. It must have caused considerable damage by its fall to the floor and surroundings. The rubbish was cleared away preparatory to the re-opening of the Church, in November, 1787, but the arch was not re-built evidently till the following year, when some further alterations seem to have taken place in the interior of the Church. There is a tradition that the masonry of the Church was so firm and compact that gunpowder had to be employed to demolish the ancient building; may be one of these explosions injured the tower arch. Portions of the east and west walls which were left at the time we are speaking of, and not entirely taken down until 1871, testified to the probability of this tradition; for it required the aid of a miner's shot to do what the pick by itself was unable to accomplish.

A sad amount of ruthless destruction of ancient tombs and windows appears to have taken place in the 1787 alterations. Shaw says, writing in 1801—after giving Dr. Wilkes' MS. notes on the Church, already quoted—"When the Church was repaired most of the above-described monuments were destroyed. In addition however to those inscriptions which we are happy thus to perpetuate, are the following, on a flat stone thus inscribed:—

> Here lyeth the body of Elizabeth Shelton
> Second daughter of John Shelton
> (lord of this Manor)
> and Mary his wife
> who departed this life
> October 8, 1701
> in the 2d year of her age.

Arms in a lozenge shield, two escallops in chief, and a mullet in base." This stone is now in the belfry, but only "Elizabeth Shelton" is legible.

Shaw also gives an inscripton on a stone to the memory of Margaret Stillingfleet, also now in the belfry.

In the *Gentleman's Magazine* for August, 1793, there is a drawing of the west front of the Church, in which there is just visible a north lich gate. A critical eye would at once notice that the window in the tower facing west is not in the centre; this one-sidedness of the window was intentionally reproduced in the restoration of 1872. Its irregular position may be thus explained: Up to the restoration of 1872 there was an excrescence resembling an enormous buttress against the north wall of the tower; its existence was owing most probably to the fact that the original builders of the tower began to build it much wider than they afterwards considered necessary, and so when they had attained a certain height, they contracted the tower to its present width The window would be in the centre of the original width of the lower part of the tower, but when the excrescence to which we have alluded, and which represented the additional width of the base of the tower, was removed, the window would then be nearer the north wall than the south.

Another tradition in the parish says that at the time of the taking down of the Church in 1785-6 there were seven Whorwood monuments, five of which were entirely broken up and burnt for lime, to make mortar. The two which escaped this fate were put out of sight in the lower part of the tower, where they lay for many years in this receptacle for dirt and rubbish of all sorts. Afterwards the monuments were removed from their concealment and placed one on each side under the galleries at the east end of the Church.

The tower and Whorwood Chapel were left fortunately untouched. Had they not been, to judge by the Church built at the time of which we are writing, every trace of its original ecclesiastical architecture would have been utterly destroyed.

The edifice, (though afterwards very dear to many an old inhabitant of this parish, was not really worthy the name of a Church,) when completed in 1787 was as follows:—A square barn-like building, with galleries at the West, where stood the organ, and half-way up the North and South sides (the continuation of these to the East end was a later addition), no Chancel, but where this should have been a moulding ran across the whitewashed ceiling. Another moulding ran horizontally from this sort of arch, thus equally dividing the Chancel space; this was to shew the two Chancels which are alluded to on page 28. The vestry was built at the East end of the Church, connected with it by a door where the Altar should have been. In the East wall were two windows; under the south-east window stood the Altar, where It had before stood in the former Church, at the end of the Nave. This Altar is now in the Chapel of the present Church. It is of oak, and has upon It the date 1626. In the north-east window was some very old stained glass, that mentioned by Dr. Wilkes, [1] and of which Shaw says, "This coat (of arms) is still remaining in the north-east window, but most of the quarterings transposed."

In 1854 a small Sanctuary was added to the Church. It was erected where the vestry before stood, and was the gift of the late Earl of Dartmouth. Several alterations were made at this time, and Lord Dartmouth gave up the Whorwood Chapel, which had been used as his family pew, to the purposes of a vestry. The new Sanctuary window was afterwards filled with stained glass, placed by the parishioners to Lord Dartmouth's memory, and the two east windows were built up. The ancient glass was taken to Sandwell by James Cashmore, who was beadle at the time, and appears, from subsequent inquiry after it, to have been lost. That this was the window of the Stanley

---
[1] page 38.

Chapel there is no doubt. A portion of the north-east wall of the Church had been left standing in 1786, and in 1871 when the Church was entirely taken down, (with the exception of the Tower and Whorwood Chapel), under the plaster on this wall were the remains of a text in fresco, a few words and letters here and there sufficiently legible to prove it had been " Blessed are the peacemakers, &c." In all probability this was a favourite text of Walter Stanley, for in his orders for the Preacher, he directs that " He shall be a peacemaker, or do his best endeavour from tyme to tyme in that behalf."

Also when the north wall was taken down, under the second window from the East end was a step on a level with the floor of the Church, where no doubt the door had been into the Chapel from the outside. These facts all prove that the Stanley Chapel stood at the East end of the aisle in the Church. The following interesting mention of it, copied from Simon Ryder's MS. may find a place here. "A note of Henry Tey his saying concerning the building of the new Chancel or Chapelle at West Bromwich. Item, the 29th day of January, 1575, Henry Tey, of West Bromwich, co. Stafford, weelwright, did say unto me, Robert Rider, that the new Chapel was made at the cost and charges of the whole parish, and that John Wilkes and William Emsworth were the greatest doers in it, and especially John Wilkes. And he said that some of the stone which did build it was got from Highfield, and some from Hampstead, and he said that the master's name was Harwell, and they that made the roof were called Warnoll and Hollies. And said that the first wardens that were after the Chapel was begun to be built were John Wilkes and William Emsworth; and the next year after

Roger Bate and Robert Hadley; and the next year after, Humphrey Walker and Henry Farre; and the next year after, Robert Rider and Thomas Partridge; in the next year it was finished as he said. And I, the aforesaid Robert Rider, asked him the question for this cause. Henry Partridge asked me at the church the same day whether I did remember that my father and his grandfather were churchwardens when the new chancel was in building or not; and I said that I could not tell, and then he wished me if that I had any books at whome to take them up, for he thought we should have need of them; and I said I think that I have some, and there were two or three more concerning the new chancel. Then Henry Tey spake these words aforesaid, the day and year first above-mentioned, in the presence of me, the said Robert Ryder, Joane Ryder my wife, Henry Corns, Simon Ryder, William Ombersley, and Agnes Hickmans; and the said Henry Tey said further that Maister Stanley made no more but glazed the windows in the east end of the chancel and his portion as other men did; and Maister Ludley and others made the north windows."

We have departed somewhat from our subject, the description of the church which existed from 1787-1871.

In the middle of the Church stood an erection now popularly known as a "three decker," which after the removal of the Altar into the new Sanctuary entirely hid It from the view of the greater part of the congregation. The floor of the church was filled with high pews, the greater number being square and allotted to the principal families, quite contrary to the true principles of the "common" worship of Almighty God, that is the worship of high and low, rich and poor alike together. The free seats were at the west end of the church under the galleries; the men sat on the south, the women on the north side.

The account of the first allotment of the pews in November, 1787, will be found in the app., among other extracts from the churchwardens' books.

The Rev. William Jesse succeeded to the Living and Lectureship vacant on the resignation of Sir Abraham Elton in 1790. Mr. Jesse remained at his post until his death in the year 1815. A tablet to his memory is on the south wall of the Church. The following extracts from the Registers relate to Mr. Jesse's family.

Elizabeth, daughter of the Rev. William Jesse and Sarah his wife, was baptized Sep. 12th, 1806, born May 13th.

Sarah Christiana, daughter of William Jesse, Junr., and of Sarah his wife, was born Oct. 8th, 1807, and baptised Dec. 26th, 1808.

William, son of William Jesse, Junr., and of Sarah his wife, was baptized July 7th, 1809.

Frances Margaret, the daughter of Edward and Matilda Jesse, was baptized Aug. 16th, 1811. Privately baptized by the Rev. Mr. Morse, May 11th, 1811.

Mary, daughter of the Rev. William Jesse, buried Oct. 27th, 1803; aged 25.

Richard, son of William and Sarah Jesse, baptised 29th April, 1815.

Matilda, daughter of the Rev. William and Sarah Jesse, baptised April 17th, 1825.

Mary Anne, daughter of the Rev. William and Sarah Jesse, baptised May 19th, 1826.

Fanny, daughter of William and Sarah Jesse, born and registered at Caen, Jan. 21st, 1823, baptised April 20th, 1827.

George Richard, son of William and Sarah Jesse, baptized May 1st, 1827, born and registered at Caen, April 19th, 1820.

The Rev. William Jesse, Minister and Lecturer of this parish for 25 years, was buried the 6th of January, 1815; aged 77.

It will be seen that most of the above Baptismal Registers relate to the grandchildren of Mr. Jesse: his son acted as his Curate during several years.

In 1815, on the death of Mr. Jesse, Mr. Townsend his son-in-law was appointed to the living, and eventually to the Lectureship. A reference to the account of the Lectureship will show that there was at this time considerable excitement on this subject, and after the lapse of many years a sudden interest taken in it by the parishioners. It will be also seen that in consequence of this agitation an Act was obtained in 1819 for regulating the revenues of the trust, and also to merge the Lectureship in the Living.

Mr. Townsend held the Living until 1836, when he resigned and was succeeded by the Rev. James Spry, who had been working with Mr. Townsend as Curate. In addition to this living Mr. Townsend was Rector of Calstone in Wiltshire. During Mr. Townsend's Incumbency Christ Church was built.

The following extracts relate to Mr. Townsend:

Chauncy Henry, son of Charles and Lucy Townsend, was baptized July 6th, 1816.

Elizabeth, daughter of Charles and Lucy Townsend, was baptized May 24th, 1818.

Louisa Joyce, daughter of Charles and Lucy Townsend, was baptized October 28th, 1821.

As we have said the Rev. James Spry succeeded Mr. Townsend in 1836; although incapacitated for many years latterly, he continued in this position until his death in 1865. Mr. Spry died at Clevedon, and was buried with his second wife outside the east wall of this Church. At the re-building of the Church in 1871-2 the Chancel was extended, and one of the pillars came exactly in Mr. Spry's grave. With the consent of his relatives his body and that of his second wife were removed and he was buried where he originally wished to be, in a grave within the Church which contained the body of his first wife.

The Old Church and her services in the time of Mr. Spry will be well remembered by many in the parish. The Church in those days was very slothful and dead, with hardly any glimmer of light about her—in saying this let it not be for one moment supposed that we intend the slightest disrespect to good, gentlemanly Mr. Spry. He acted up to his light and the traditions of his predecessors. The Church was closed during the whole week unless opened for a wedding, baptism, or funeral. The first service on Sunday was at 10-30 a.m., and consisted of Matins, Litany, Table Prayers, and Sermon, followed once a month by a Celebration of the Holy Communion. This service was the fashionable one of the day; at one time there were as many as twenty gentlemen's carriages waiting outside the Church gates at the close of the service. An afternoon service at three concluded the public worship of Almighty God for the day, and week too. The services we have mentioned were very long and dreary. No singing, except of a 'Psalm' before and after the sermon, which latter was preached in a black gown from the highest part of the 'three decker.' Reverence was, we are grieved to say, not the custom, and kneeling the exception.

A very important person in those days must not be

forgotten; the dread of little sleepy boys and girls, and older ones too, whom he considered as behaving ill in Church; we refer to the beadle, James Cashmore. Attired in a livery consisting of a blue coat, with brass buttons and red facings, blue waistcoat, and knee breeches, with shoes and silver buckles, he was no insignificant officer of the Church. In his hand he carried a long stick, which was frequently to be heard arousing some unfortunate sleeping member of the congregation. On one occasion just before the service began, a girl sitting among the other Sunday School children dropped her bonnet over the front of the gallery. The beadle perceiving this at once repaired to the spot where the bonnet lay, looked up at the owner, placed the end of his long staff in the article and hoisted it up to the little girl.

The parish during Mr. Spry's Incumbency was blessed with the labours of a very well-known and excellent assistant Priest, the Reverend Isaac Bickerstaff. He acted as Curate to Mr. Spry, and afterwards as Curate-in-charge for over twenty years; and he it was who first began a weekly service on Wednesday evening, in the Parish Church, and evensong every Sunday evening at the School in Hallam-street. He also introduced the weekly offertory in 1859.

In 1863 Mr. Bickerstaff was appointed to the Rectory of Bonsall, in Derbyshire, where he remained until his death in 1874.

On the departure of Mr. Bickerstaff the parish was served successively by the Revs. Kirke, Edwards, and Davis.

About the year 1862 the pews were lowered and the square ones divided, the "three decker" removed, and a reading desk and pulpit placed in a more suitable position. Mr. Spry died in the year 1865, and was succeeded by the Rev. Frederic Willett, the present Vicar. Daily services and weekly Communion were introduced by Mr. Willett; and in 1867 the first step was taken in providing the populous district of Swan Village with Church accommodation. A site having been kindly given by Mr. Jesson, of Oakwood, the foundation stone of a School Church was laid by Mrs. Jesson in July, 1867. The building was completed in November; it consisted of an infant school, which served as a Chancel on Sunday, girls' school, which formed the Transepts of the Church, and a boys' school, which formed the Nave. This School Church was dedicated to S. Andrew, and its opening on S. Andrew's Day, 1867, will ever be memorable as being the occasion on which the Right Reverend G. A. Selwyn, Bishop of New Zealand, who was in England at this time, preached his first sermon in the Diocese over which he was destined so soon to preside.

In the year 1868, the Vicarage House, which was nothing but an old-fashioned Farm House originally, was altered and enlarged. The previous Incumbents from the time of Mr. Stillingfleet had resided at Churchfields House, by the permission of the then owner, the Earl of Dartmouth, there being no suitable residence attached to the living. The old Vicarage in Hall End, together with the Schools being in a delapidated condition, the Earl of Dartmouth conveyed the present Vicarage (then only a Farm House) in lieu of the house in Church Lane, in the year 1854, and it became the residence of the Curate of the parish, Mr. Bickerstaff.

The Deed of Conveyance states that "A house, buildings,

yard, garden, and plantation, situate in All Saints' Street, opposite the Church, are given as glebe land in exchange for a house, school rooms, and land in Church Lane, sometimes called Vicarage Lane."

In the plan accompanying the Deed the Pound appears as occupying a part of the wide space of road between the present Vicarage gates and the Church; here also stood the Stocks and Whipping-post, under an old hawthorn.

The following extract from the *Parish Magazine* may find a place here.

THE VICARAGE OF WEST BROMWICH.

"Perhaps some of our readers may be interested to know the meaning of a notice which has appeared in most of the papers, stating that all 'Perpetual Curates' are henceforth to be 'Vicars.' When Christianity was firmly introduced into this country, good and pious men built churches, and gave land to support the clergyman who ministered in them; or sometimes the clergyman was supported by tithes, *i.e.* a tenth of the produce of the land. In time monasteries were built, in which several clergy used to live together; these monasteries used to undertake the charge of a parish, receive the tithes, and undertake to supply the duties of the parish, by employing a clergyman for that purpose, and because he worked, 'in the place of' 'instead of' other persons, he was called a 'Vicar.' At the Reformation these abuses were abolished. The system, however, was by no means even then in every case improved, for while the support of the clergy was indeed rightly taken from the monasteries, it was not always given back to the clergy, but taken away altogether from the Church and made a present of to Henry VIII.'s friends. Thus when the Church of England (the same Catholic

Church let us always remember as before Henry VIII.'s time, only relieved from the authority of Rome) was established as it is now, some parishes kept their tithes, others had none. In the parishes which retained all their tithes the clergyman was called a 'Rector;' in parishes where a portion only was retained, the clergyman was called a 'Vicar;' in parishes where none were retained the clergyman was called a 'Perpetual Curate.' It has recently been thought better to do away with the title 'Perpetual Curate,' and give all such parish priests the title of 'Vicar;' this has been done by an Act of Parliament passed during the late Session, which ordains as follows—

INCUMBENTS OF CERTAIN PARISHES, &C., TO BE VICARS.

'The incumbent of the church of every parish or new parish for ecclesiastical purposes, not being a rector, who is or shall be authorised to publish banns of matrimony in such church, and solemnise therein marriages, churchings, and baptisms, according to the laws and canons in force in this realm, and who is or shall be entitled to take, receive, and hold for his own sole use and benefit the entire fees arising from the performance of such offices, without any reservation thereout, shall, from and after the passing of this Act, for the purpose of style and designation, but not for any other purpose, be deemed and styled the vicar of such church and parish or new parish, as the case may be, and his benefice shall for the same purpose be styled and designated a vicarage.' Hence the Perpetual Curate of West Bromwich becomes 'The Vicar' of West Bromwich, and the house in which he lives 'The Vicarage.' We confess to liking the title 'Curate,' or 'Carer for souls,' best, but as no one would ever, as we wished, use this address, perhaps the new law is for the best. Some of our readers may wonder how the cleygyman of this parish is supported, if there are no tithes attached to this parish. In the year 1613, Walter Stanley, Esq., left lands in Aston and Sutton Coldfield, for the maintenance of the clergyman (the proceeds of this land is now divided with the Vicar of of Christ Church), and in the year 1843, the late Earl of Dartmouth gave £7481 to the Governors of Queen Anne's Bounty, in augmentation of the Perpetual Curacy of West Bromwich. It is well all parishioners should know these matters, not only out of interest in the parish, but also that they may see how utterly misapplied any such terms as 'a State-paid Church,' or 'State-paid Clergy,' are to the real facts of the case."

In the year 1870 Mr. Willett first mooted the subject of the re-building of the Church. The condition of the fabric at this date is described by Mr. Willett in the November *Magazine* as follows:—" The plaster is peeling off the walls, the rain pours in at the roof, the walls are mouldy and stained, the windows let in draughts on all sides, the floor is so damp that it is almost dangerous to kneel, the belfry is unsafe, the bells useless for ringing, the whole building is and must be damp, inconvenient, uncomfortable, dirty, and slovenly."

Mr. Spry had several years previously bewailed the state of the Church, and had given expression to his feelings in the following lines:—

THE WARDEN'S PETITION, OR THE LAMENT OF THE
MOTHER CHURCH.

Pity the sorrows of the poor Old Church,
   Whose slighted state has forced us to your door;
Oh! leave her not, we pray you, in the lurch,
   But grant your aid, and heaven will bless your store.

The Parish Church.

Those dirty walls our poverty bespeak,
   Those shattered casements your neglect proclaim;
Where many a crack and crevice, shame to speak,
   Have formed a passage for the wind and rain.

Those large high pews, so snug, like parlours, seem,
   Where oft, alas! a single head one sees;
Where giggling girls may laugh their fill unseen,
   Or drowsy worshippers may lounge at ease.

O sad abuse! this wanton waste of room,
   In Churches consecrated to God's name;
Where rich and poor, for prayer together come,
   And all alike the right to worship claim.

Go, walk around, and say if you have seen,
   In all its parts, within, without the same;
A Church so poor, undignified and mean,
   Unsuited to the honour of God's name.

Much do we wish this temple to restore,
   And pious offerings for this purpose seek;
Dismiss us not unaided, we implore,
   For this good work your bounty we bespeak.

With anxious care our dwellings we adore,
   And think no cost bestowed on them too great;
And shall the House of God be left forlorn,
   Nor rescued be from this its low estate?

Your Mother Church your warmest love should claim,
   Your fond remembrance, and your deep respect;
For there—you first received your Christian name,
   And numbered were among the flock elect.

There—too perchance you formed the nuptial tie,
   And still the Sacrament of love may share;
There too your parents, perhaps your children, lie,
   And you yourself may yet be buried there.

There—Gospel truths are faithfully enforced;
   And hundreds flock attentively to hear;
There—faith and practice never are divorced,
   But each its proper part is made to bear.

Structures 'tis true more comely to the eye,
  Like fair young daughters lately have appeared;
To these let each all proper aid supply,
  But ne'er forget the Church your fathers reared.
Yon hall* erected by the holy well,
  With certain promise drew us down the road;
For Piety has there long pleased to dwell,
  And Charity has found a sure abode.
There—the oppress'd, the friendless, and the poor,
  For counsel and for aid their footsteps bend;
No worthy object's driven from the door,
  The poor and wretched ever find a friend.
Nor vainly there, shall we make our appeal,
  Religion's cause is honoured and upheld;
No sordid thought forbids the heart to feel,
  No off'ring to the Church is e'er withheld.
On you we call who this world's goods possess,
  Some token of your gratitude to shew;
To Him who crowned your labours with success,
  To Him—to whom your very all you owe.
Pity the sorrows of the Mother Church,
  In whose behalf we now approach your door;
Oh! leave her not, we pray you, in the lurch,
  But grant your aid, and heaven will bless your store.

REVEREND JAMES SPRY.

The history of the actual re-building of the Church will be best told by the following extracts from the *Parish Magazine*.

THE RESTORATION OF THE CHURCH.

"The Executive Committee held its first meeting on Tuesday evening, May 23rd. It was agreed (i.) to use the malt house adjoining the new Clergy House as a place of temporary worship; (ii.) to accept the tender of Mr. J. Mallin to pull down the present Church; (iii.) that Sunday, June 25, should be the last Sunday in the present Church;

---
* The Seat of the Earl of Dartmouth.

The Parish Church.

(iv.) that the Vicar should endeavour to arrange for Special Preachers during June; (v.) that advertisements be inserted in the local papers for builders willing to tender for the erection of the new Church. However much we may feel the absolute necessity of a new Church, it cannot but be with very deep feelings that we come to the last service in the present building. However debased its structure may appear to many of us, who have grown up with only the pattern Church of revived knowledge of Catholic truth and energy as our ideal of what a church ought to be, there are very many to whom the destruction of the present Church is a very sorrowful necessity. They first learnt to worship God within its walls, they were baptized in its font, they were perhaps married at its altar. Its services and internal arrangements call up memories very deep and tender, and that would, indeed, be an unfeeling heart that did not enter into such reminiscences and respect them. With us all the present Church will ever be an integral portion of our religious life, and its demolition an era in our spiritual history. Bills, announcing the Special Preachers, will be printed. The Holy Eucharist will be celebrated (D.V.) on Monday, June 26, and thus the last service will be, as it ought to be, the highest act of religious worship."—June, 1871.

The Last Days of the Old Church.

" Our *Magazine* would not hand down a true record of our parish history, if it did not record the wonderful even-songs, and striking sermons with which the last Sundays of the present Old Church were marked. On the 18th, Mr. Twigg was unfortunately unable to preach through domestic trouble, and Mr. Bodington most kindly, at a few hours' notice took his place, and to a very large congregation preached on "Worship." On Sunday afternoon, June the 25th, the children of the Old Church, St. Andrew's, St. Michael's, and Hallam Street Schools were gathered together in the Old Church, and there is not much doubt but that the Old Church, as it has been, will be impressed indelibly on 600 at least of the next generation, who will tell their children of the last children's service in the Old Church before it was restored. In the evening, an enormous congregation filled the Church from one end to another. A more memorable service we can hardly imagine and as the last verse of the recessional hymn was ended, we could not help wondering if the new Church, with all its superior beauty, would equal the present structure in congregational singing. On Monday morning, the Holy Eucharist was celebrated for the last time, at 6·30, and many met their Lord and commended to Him the great undertaking we were that day to commence for Him. In an hour's time the work of demolition commenced, and before the day was over the interior of the Church was a wreck. Very many we think would like to have some reminiscence of the Old Church, and we have therefore undertaken to have some crosses made out of the stone of the Old Church, which will be sold for the benefit of the Restoration Fund. As soon as the Church is down, we trust the contract will have been made for the new Church, the rising of which we shall all of us watch with eager interest, and pray that not only in beauty, but in spiritual blessings, the glory of the latter house may infinitely exceed the glory of the former."—July, 1871.

THE RESTORATION OF THE CHURCH.

"The foundations of the New Church are progressing most satisfactorily. It is a very difficult, as well as a most important part of the restoration, and requires great labour and patience. The ground has to be excavated down to the solid, then some of the largest stones from the Old Church are put in as a base, and then the trench is gradually filled in with the old material, all being concreted together with mortar and water. We wish to bear testimony to the excellent conduct of the workmen, who seem never to forget that they are working on holy ground; they are most careful too, and reverent in treating with proper respect any relics of the dead that may be turned up in the excavation. We have to record this month the most kind compliance of Lord Dartmouth with the views of the executive committee, in consenting to forego his own wish, and in giving permission for the removal of the sanctuary of the Old Church."—September, 1871.

"On Thursday Evening, September 21, The Executive Committee met to open the tenders for the re-building of the Church. The meeting was adjourned to the following evening, when the tender of Mr. Burkitt, of Wolverhampton, was finally accepted to re-build the Church for the sum of £6,300, so that to complete the work it will probably be necessary to raise the sum of £7,000."—October, 1871.

During the necessary excavations for enlarging the Church at the restoration, a great many bones had to be moved—the ground was everywhere full of them—all were, of course, carefully re-interred. On one occasion a number of bones were found together, some of a very large size, evidently those of a large animal. Among the bones were some shoe strings. The most probable explanation is that in some pit in the parish there had been an accident, and by the time the bodies of those who had been killed were dug out, their remains, and those of some horses that were killed at the same time, were so intermixed that it was impossible to distinguish those of the men, and thus they came to be all buried together in the churchyard. Numerous pieces of scrap iron too reminded the observer of the time when it was put on the top of the coffins to prevent "body snatching."

The Church, when completed, was re-opened for public worship on Tuesday, October 29th, 1872, and an account of the services on that day, taken from the December *Magazine*, is here inserted:—

"The re-opening of the recently re-built Parish Church of West Bromwich (the foundation stone of which was laid in the beginning of the year), took place on Tuesday last, and was celebrated with high festival. This is the fourth Church which has occupied the same site, and the Church which has been demolished was originally erected about eighty years ago. The Church was inconvenient, out of repair, and inadequate for the requirements of the district; and hence, about the middle of last year, the restoration and enlargement was decided upon. The services of the day commenced at 6 a.m., at which hour the Vicar, the Rev. F. Willett, conducted a service of Purification. This was followed by Low Celebrations at 7 and 8-30, at which there were 250 communicants. At 9-45 a *Missa Cantata* was sung by the Rev. J. Wylde, assisted by a large and well-trained choir. Processions with cross and banners took place before and after the Service, and various hymns were sung during the Service. The music was Merbecke's. There was a large number of worshippers, fifteen of whom communicated. Matins was sung at 11-30, when the Lord Bishop of Lichfield preached. Previous to the commencement of this Service, a procession consisting of clergy and choristers was formed at the temporary church, from whence they proceeded to the Church carrying several large and handsome banners, and headed by the cross-bearer and two churchwardens, a second cross being carried before the clergy, and the Bishop's pastoral staff borne by the Rev. F. Willett, who acted as chaplain. As they passed through the streets the choir chanted a metrical litany composed for the occasion. Amongst those in the procession were the Lord Bishop of Lichfield, the Right Rev. Coadjutor Bishop Abraham, the Revs. F. Willett, Vicar of the Parish; J. H. Iles, R.D., Rector of Wolverhampton; R. Twigg, Wednesbury; the Hon. and Rev. A. Anson, Sedgley; C. Bodington, Wolverhampton; J. Bradshaw, Hixon, E. Grigson, J. Wylde, and A. G. Jackson, Curates of All Saints', West Bromwich; R. Hodgson, Christ Church, West Bromwich; J. Richardson and R. B. Stoney, Wednesbury; G. Tuthill, Hill Top; W. G. Box, Gold's Hill; E. L. Edwards, Wombourn; J. Douglas, Dr. Collis, G. Bailby, J. M. Davenport, F. Lloyd, — Fortescue, J. Seymour, — Mansell, W. Purton, R. Wylde, T. Ridsdell, G. W. Murray, H. Jesson, G. E. Shepherd, J. Addenbrooke, O. Mordaunt, J. S. Pollock, S. Potter, W. H. Kay, Crane, E. Heath, R. Ritchie, N. Madan, F. E. Ogden, Frere, T. Pollock, Roper, R. M. Grier, G. Young, Clark, Stanley, and Sheldon. The processional litany was "God of Glory, God of Might." The Psalms were xcv., xxiv., xlvi., and xlvii. The versicles and responses were sung to Tallis's Festal. The Rev. J. Wylde, Curate, intoned the prayers. The Rev. F. Willett, Vicar, read the first lesson, which was 2 Chronicles, vii., to verse 17; and the second lesson was read by Bishop Abraham, and was St. John, iv. 19—25. The anthem was "How lovely are Thy dwellings fair," from

Spohr, and the tenor solo was sung admirably. The congregation was very large, including many of the gentry of the neighbourhood and distant places. The music was everything that could be desired. "Doran and Nottingham's Directory" is in use at this Church, and the precision with which the Psalter was rendered was sufficient to decide for ever in the minds of many present the often-contested merits of Doran and Nottingham's system. Every available seat in the Church was occupied, notwithstanding that the weather was very unfavourable. The choir of nearly ninety members was composed from those connected with the Old Church parish, viz., All Saints' Church, St. Andrew's, St. Mary Magdalen's, St. Mary the Virgin's missions, and of Christ Church parish. At the conclusion between 200 and 300 persons partook of a luncheon provided in All Saints' Schools. The Lord Bishop presided, and the clergy already named were present. Amongst the laity were Colonel and Mrs. J. N. Bagnall, Miss Bagnall, Miss F. Bagnall, Miss E. J. Ward, Mrs. Bagnall, Mr. Charles Bagnall, Mr. Thomas Bagnall, jun., Mrs. Bagnall (Hamstead Hall), Mr. and Mrs. W. H. Bagnall, Mrs. Willett, Mrs. Abraham, Mr. Hodson, Mr. and Mrs. George Ward, Mrs. Iles. The High Sheriff was prevented from being present by indisposition. Mrs. W. Oakley, Mr. and Mrs. Jesson, Mr. Thomas Jesson, jun., Mr. William Willett, Mr. Mr. Alfred Willett, Mr. George Willett, Mr. and Mrs. H. Duncalfe, Mr. and Mrs. Thursfield, Mr. and Mrs. F. James, Mr. J. Slater, Mr. and Mrs. Hudson, Mrs. B. Hemming, Mrs. W. Evans, Mrs. J. W. Williams, Mr. P. D. Bennett, Mr. and Mrs. R. Farley, Mr. and Mrs. Fellows, Mr. and Mrs. Birch, Mr. Cotterill, Miss Cotterill, Miss Wylde, Miss G. Wylde &c. A children's service was held in the afternoon, the preacher being the Rev. J. H. Iles, rector of Wolverhampton; and at 7.30 Evensong was sung, the Rev. C. W. Furse, Vicar of Staines, being the preacher. The procession was similar to that at Matins, and the effect as it returned from the well-lighted Altar, with the "seven lamps burning before the Throne" (Rev. iv. 5), was such as is seldom seen, and certainly never before in the Black Country. Throughout the day the services were very well attended and the greatest interest manifested. The ground plan of the new building is somewhat of an unusual type, but is very similar to that of the Church which existed upon the same site previously to the ugly square box (it can rightly be called by no other name) pulled down during the past year. This older building was chiefly erected during the fourteenth and fifteenth centuries—as its architectural details proved—and consisted of a nave and chancel, with a north aisle and chapel at its eastern extremity. The tower stood at the western end of the nave. In the present Church the old tower has been retained, but now forms the extremity of the southern aisle. The general plan is very similar to that of the older building, saving that the single aisle is now on the south side instead of on the north. This arrangement was dictated by the comparatively small size of the tower. The nave is now of considerable size, viz.:—92 feet in length, and 30 feet in breadth. The chancel 46 feet wide and 43 feet long. The total internal length of the Church being 135 feet. On the south aisle of the chancel, but not extending its whole length, is a side chapel, forming a chancel to the south aisle, which is equal in length with the nave and 14 feet in width. This portion of the Church will be more particularly appropriated to the daily services.

As in the older Church there is an aisle on one side of the nave only. The western end of the south aisle is terminated by the old arch leading into the tower, an arch which was always intended to form a leading feature in the architecture of the building, but which in the edifice lately pulled down was almost invisible, having been cut across by the heavy western gallery and stopped up by a partition which was found to consist in part of the timbers of the screen belonging to the previous Church. The general architectural character of the new building is similar to that of the older one, which has been already described. An exact restoration would have been impossible, as all the main features of the previous work had been totally destroyed at the end of the last century, when the square galleried edifice—hitherto known as West Bromwich Old Church—was erected. Entering the Church by the porch on the south side, which occupies the site of its predecessor, the first feature of interest is to be found in the elaborate hinges and handles of the entrance door. These hinges, &c. are entirely of brass, very richly moulded, and have, with the rest of the brass work, been exceedingly well executed by Messrs. Thomason and Co. of Birmingham. Looking to the left, the old tower arch, previously mentioned, is visible, and to the right the whole length of the south aisle. Advancing a few steps the nave is reached. At its western extremety stands the old font which, cleaned from many coats of paint, is raised upon a platform, and presents by no means so poor an appearance as it used to do, lost under the capacious gallery of the Old Church. Above the font rises the west window of five lights. This has been filled with stained glass, most admirably executed by Messrs. Powell and Sons, of Whitefriars, and designed by

W. E. Wooldridge, Esq. It is the gift of Colonel and
Mrs. J. N. Bagnall, of the Moss, Shenstone, and is certainly one of the greatest ornaments of the Church. The
central figure—a crucifix—is admirably drawn. Looking
eastward, the chancel arch and rood screen are prominent
features. The screen is, however, but of a temporary
nature, and will be ultimately replaced by one of oak. It
is to be surmounted by a larged carved cross, richly decor-
ated—its place is now occupied by a simple one of deal.
The nave roof is panelled on the underside of the rafters,
the main timbers alone being visible. By this treatment
the barn-like effect, so often observable in open timber
roofs, is avoided, and a greater equality of temperature can
be maintained. Passing through the screen into the chancel, we find on the left a lofty and capacious recess for the
organ, occupied at present by the organ from the west
gallery of the Old Church. On the right, the chancel is
separated from the south aisle by two arches, in one of
which, raised once more upon an altar tomb, repose the
effigies of two members of the Whorwood family, of the
period of Charles I.[1] They are carved in alabaster, and
show the remains of painting in various parts. They were
left for many years in a coal hole in the Old Church, and
have suffered seriously from ill usage. The altar, promin-
ently raised upon a flight of five steps occupies the main
portion of the eastern wall of the sanctuary. It was vested
in a superb white lace frontal, entirely worked by Mrs.
Oakley, of Newland, Gloucestershire. The reredos, of
red sandstone, as is all the rest of the Church, is not at
present complete, but will ultimately rise to the sill of the

---

[1] The open beams of the Whorwood Chapel were richly carved.
One of them has been made to serve the purpose of a Lectern in the
Side Chapel of the present Church.

east window, at a considerable elevation from the floor, and be crowned by a row of niches, with figures and rich tabernacle work. The altar cross and candlesticks, the gift of Colonel and Mrs. King, of Monmouth, were especially designed for the Church by the architect, and executed by Mr. Thomason, as were the brass gas pendants which have, contrary to the custom in Churches, been provided with glass globes, shielding the eye from the cold and unpleasant glare of the naked gas jet. On the south side of the chancel are three single lights which have been filled with glass, the gift of Mrs. Edwyn Dawes, of Surbiton, designed by the same artist as the west window, and also executed by Messrs. Powell. Each light is filled with a single figure of a seraph upon blue ground, studded with suns. The design of these figures is in every way equal to that of the west window. The east window is filled with the stained glass which heretofore occupied a similar position in the Old Church, and was erected to the memory of the late Lord Dartmouth. It was executed some years since and was by no means up to the standard of the present day, but through the exertion of Mr. Jesson it has been re-erected with some improvement by Messrs. Camm, of Smethwick. The kneeling cushions for communicants have been worked by Mrs. J. N. Bagnall, Mrs. Jesson, Mrs. Fellows, and Miss Bagnall; the pede mats by Mrs. W. A. and C. V. Willett; and the mat for the litany desk by Mrs. Thomas Bagnall, jun. The litany desk itself has been given by Ann Riley, a servant girl, who has obtained subscriptions for it entirely by her own exertions. The vestments for the altar are exceedingly rich, and besides the frontal already mentioned, a most splendid piece of Indian work, from Bombay, with a burse and chalice veil, given by General Hough, of Her Majesty's Indian army, and a green silk frontal, burse and veil, given by Mrs. Willett, may be mentioned. The chalice is made out of that in use in the Old Church. It has been re-worked by Mr. Thomason, in parcel gilt, and set with pearls, opals, and garnets, the gifts of members of the congregation. In the south aisle of the chancel are two windows of three lights, one the gift of Mr. Charles Willett, in memory of his infant son; the other the gift of Mrs. Willett and her brothers and sisters, in memory of a sister who died young. These windows have been executed by Messrs. Hardman. The work has been carried out with great rapidity by Mr. Charles Burkett, of Wolverhampton. The architect is Mr. Somers Clarke, jun., 3, Delahay Street, Westminster. It is estimated that the new church will accomodate about 1,000 people. The total cost of the restoration will be £7,000, and towards this sum £5,000 has already been subscribed.

The octave of All Saints was kept with becoming dignity, the special preachers being the Right Rev. C. J. Abraham; Revs. R. F. Wilson, M. H. Noel, Hon. Augustus Legge, A. H. Ward, the Lord Francis Osborne, C. Parnell, and R. M. Grier. The offertories were very good, £70 being collected on the Sunday of the Octave.

On Wednesday, the day after the opening, there was a Special Service for the guilds of the neighbourhood, under the auspices of the Guild of All Saints, more than 400 members of whom, after tea in the school, marched in procession to the church, each guild being headed by a banner. It is hoped this will be an annual custom, and was done with a view to the ultimate confederation of the various guilds in the Black Country, of which there are a large number.

The Bells are not mentioned in this account of the Church, the fact being that to the great disappointment of all, the persons who undertook to have them re-hung in time for the opening of the Church, failed to fulfill their promise. The 5th bell, which was cracked, had to be re-cast. Soon after the opening of the Church the Bells were re-hung, and their tones again heard, to the great delight of the parishioners. The cost of repairing the Bells was borne by Colonel Bagnall, of the Moss, Shenstone.

The inscriptions on the Bells, eight in number, are as follows:—

1st Bell—"Thomas Mears, Founder, London,
All Saints', West Bromwich.
William Barton (Clerk).
James Cashmore (Beadle)."

2nd Bell—"Rev. C. Townsend, M.A., Perpetual Curate of West Bromwich, and Rector of Calstone, Wiltshire. Thomas Hood, James Dorsett, Churchwardens.
Taylor and Co. 1832. Founders."

3rd Bell—"Jesus be our speed, 1711."

4th Bell—"Glory be to GOD on high. 1711."

5th Bell—"William Blews & Sons, Founders, Birmingham. This bell was re-cast and the peal repaired, A.D. 1872. Frederic Willett, M.A., Vicar.
Henry Duncalfe,
John Nock Bagnall, } Churchwardens."

6th Bell—"God save His Church."

7th Bell—"Rev. C. Townsend, minister.
T. Hood, J. Dorsett, Churchwardens.
Glory be to GOD on high.
Taylor & Co. Founders.
1832.
Oxford."

8th Bell—"C. & G. Mears, Founders, London, 1848."

From these inscriptions it appears that the peal consisted at first of four Bells, then six, then eight, two being added, one at each end, in 1832, and two more in the same way in 1848.

The Lich gate leading to the south porch was built by the family of the late Mr. Jesson, of Oakwood, to his memory in 1874, from plans supplied by Mr. Somers Clarke.

During the re-building of the Church two Mission Chapels were built in the Old Church parish, one dedicated to S. Mary Magdalen, at the top of Stony Lane, and the other dedicated to S. Mary the Virgin, at Hateley Heath. These chapels were built to bring the services of the Church within reach of the population of the outlying districts of the parish. S. Mary's, Hateley Heath, was used as a school on week days until within the last year, when the population having very much decreased in this part of the parish the school was not needed and so was closed. There is still a Sunday School held in the morning of every Sunday. Since the re-opening of the Church two more windows have been filled with stained glass. One consisting of three lights on the north side of the Chancel, and corresponding in design with that on the south side, the gift of Mrs. Ward, of Rodbaston, and her sisters, to the memory of their father, the late Mr. John Bagnall. The other, the easternmost window in the south aisle of the Church, consisting of three lights, to the memory of Thomas Jesson, Esq., of Oakwood, whose name had been so long associated with the Old Church.

It is hoped all the windows in the Church will be filled with stained glass in time, the subjects being "All Saints,' commencing with the Patriarchs and closing with modern times. Among the Saints we trust "S. Clement," the Patron Saint of the Church, will find a place.

THE CHURCHYARD.

Originally this was small—its extent down the Barr Lane can be traced by the old stone foundation still remaining. In 1773, when the needs of the Parish were greatly increased, Jervoise Clarke, Esq., gave a piece of land for enlarging the churchyard, and a new wall was built to enclose the same at the expense of the Parish. Another addition to the Burial Ground was made in 1823. The Earl of Dartmouth sold an acre of his land at the east end of the church for £80 to the Parish. In 1859 the present Earl of Dartmouth liberally gave upwards of an acre of land to enlarge the Churchyard still further—this piece extends towards the south. Again, in 1875, Lord Dartmouth gave upwards of an acre to the east of the Churchyard for the purposes of a Burial Ground. This latter portion of the Churchyard has been conveyed to Trustees for the burial of parishioners only, with the service of the Church of England. A second lich gate, erected by the Revs. Henry and Thomas Jesson in memory of their sister, leads from the old to the new Churchyard. We must not omit to mention that in November, 1872, an improvement was made by rounding off the north-west corner of the Churchyard wall. The ancient pillion stone is in the west wall to the left of the north porch gate. This information was obtained from the writer's great-grandmother, who in former years, when riding to and from church, used this pillion stone.

The lich gate leading from the old Churchyard to the new Burial Ground was built by the Revs. H. and T.

Jesson, in memory of their only sister, who died in 1878.

In the Churchyard are some curious old tombstones, the oldest, which was until just lately sunk into the earth, to the right of the path leading to the south porch, bears the following inscription:—

"Here Lyeth
The Body of Jos-
eph, the Son of Joseph
Avern. He Dyed
the 26 of March,
1682."

Further up, on the same side of the Church, is another stone, bearing date of the same year, some months later:—

"Here lyeth the Body of
Elizabeth, the wife of John Marsh,
Shee Departed this life the 2d
of Desember, 1682. 'All you
that pass mee by, as you are so was I,
And as I am so must you Bee,
Remember your End and thi"ke
On Mee.'"

Another old stone is placed close to the west wall of the Churchyard, facing the tower. The inscription upon it is as follows:—

"Here lieth the Body of Mary,
Late Wife of Joseph Aughton,
Shee departed this life the 27th
Day of June, Anno. Dom. 1696.
'Stay, Reader stand, and spend a tear
Over this dust that slumbers here,
Consider now this state of mine,
For the next Summons may be thine.'"

It is scarcely necessary to add that the verse beginning
"Afflictions sore long time I bore"
is to be found here on several stones.

Mention of the building and opening of Christ Church will be found in the Extract from the Churchwardens' Books, also incidental mention of S. James', Hill Top. Holy Trinity and S. Peter's have been built in comparatively recent times. S. Andrew's, which is mentioned in the account of the Parish Church, is now a separate Ecclesiastical District, the Church having been consecrated in 1879. Another district has been also cut off—taken out of Christ Church Parish. The Church is dedicated to S. John. A mission chapel has been lately opened in this parish. Christ Church has a mission chapel, and so has also S. Andrew's, one lately built in Wood Lane. Of the mission chapels belonging to the Old Church mention has been made.

STANLEY TRUST.

WE have already, in writing the history of the Church, alluded to the munificence of Walter Stanley, Esq., who in the year 1613 gave a valuable estate, situated in the Parishes of Erdington, Sutton Coldfield, and Aston, for the maintenance of a Lecturer in the Parish Church of West Bromwich. This trust, apart from the purpose for which it was designed, was the origin of many interesting events in the history of the parish, which we now proceed to place on record. Subjoined is a Copy of the Original Deed creating the Trust. Also, Walter Stanley's Orders for the Trustees and the Preacher.

"A true copy of the Feoffment for the Preacher's Maintenance in the Parish of West Bromwich. Dated 12th March, 1613.—This Indenture, made the Twelfth Day of March, in the Year of our Lord God, One Thousand Six Hundred and Thirteen, and in the Eleventh Year of the Reign of our Sovereign Lord James, by the Grace of God, of England, France, and Ireland, King, Defender of the Faith, &c., and of Scotland, the Seven and Fortithe; between Walter Stanley, of West Bromwich, in the County of Stafford, Esq., on the one Partye, and William Stanley, Gentleman, Son and Heir apparante of the said Walter Stanley; Edward Grove, William Turton the Elder, William Turton, John Turton, and Thomas Turton, Sonnes of the said William Turton the Elder, Francis Simcox the Elder, William Simcox, Son of the said Francis, William Partridge the Elder, John Hayteley, George Partridge, Frances Partridge, John Jesson the Younger, William Hobbins, Simon Warde, Thomas Gretton, and Michael Poultney, of West Bromwich aforesaid, Yeomen, of the other Partye, Witnesseth, that the said Walter Stanley, for and in consideration of the Summ of Ten Shillings of lawful Money of England, to him the said Walter Stanley in Hand payed, and for diver and sundry good causes and Considerations him moving, hath given, granted, bargained, sold, enfeoffed, and confirmed, and by these presents doth give, grant, bargain, sell, enfeoffe, and confirm, unto the said William Stanley, Edward Grove, William Turton the Elder, William Turton, John Turton, and Thomas Turton, Francis Simcox, William Simcox, William Partridge, John Hayteley, George Partridge, Francis Partridge, John Jesson, William Hobbins, Simon Warde, Thomas Gretton, and Michael Poultney, their Heirs and Assigns for ever, All that Messuage or Tenement, with Apurtenances in Erdington, in the Parish of Aston, in the County of Warwick, wherein one John Ediall lately dwelled, with all Barns, Stables, Buyldings, Gardens, Orchards, Foldyards, Backsides, Easements, and Commodities to the same Messuage or Tenement belonging or appertaining: And also all those nine Closes, Pastures, or Parcells of Ground in Erdington aforesaid, called, or known by the several Names of the Sprigge and Toplande, now divided into two parts, the Hill Close, the Barn Close, the Broome Close, the Pease Leasow, the Old Field, the Studfolde, the Little Blacknolde, and the Laughton, and five acres of Arable Land, or field Ground, lying in the common Fields of

Erdington aforesaid, and one Parcel of Ground, called Piggehill, and one Day's Mathe and a Quarter of Meadow Ground, be it more or less, lying in a Meadow in Erdington aforesaid, called Bramford Meadow : And also all those Closes, Pastures, or Parcels of Ground, with their Appurtenances, in Sutton Colefield, in the said County of Warwick, called or known by the several Names of Shearnetshead, Broadfield, and the Hayes (which Hayes is now divided into two parts :) And also all those seven Pastures, or Closes of Land, with Appurtenances, called Deepings Fields, or by any other Name or Names, lying together at the Wilde, within the Mannor or Lordship of Sutton in Colefield aforesaid, and now in the Tenure or Occupation of one John Lane : And also all that Meadow, with Appurtenances, called the New Nymyings, alias Hemynges, lying, and being within the Mannor or Lordship of Sutton in Colefield aforesaid, and late in the Tennure or Occupation of the aforesaid John Edyall, or of his Assigns, which said seven Pastures, or Closes, and Meadow, called Nymyings, alias Hemynges, the said Walter Stanley lately purchased to him and his Heires of one Robert Briskoe, and Richard his Sonne : And all other Lands, Tenements and Hereditaments in Erdington and Sutton aforesaid, or in either of them, which the said Walter Stanley lateley purchased of the said John Edyall, Robert Briskoe, and Richard his Sonne, or any of them : And also all other his Messuages, Lands, Tenements, Meadows, Leasows, Pastures, and Hereditaments in Erdington, Sutton in Colefield, and Aston aforesaid, or in any of them, together with the Reversion or Reversions, Remainder and Remainders of all and singular the Premisses, together also with all Deeds, Evidences, Charters, Writings, Escripts and Munyments concerning only the Premisses, or any part thereof, to have and to hold the said Messuage or Tenement, Lands, Tennements, Meadows, Leasows, Pastures, and Hereditaments, and all other the Premisses with their Appertenances, to the said William Stanley, Edward Grove, William Turton the Elder, William Turton, John Turton, Thomas Turton, Francis Simcox, William Simcox, William Partridge, John Hateley, George Partridge, Francis Partridge, John Jesson, William Hobbins, Simon Warde, Thomas Gretton, and Michael Poultney, and their Heirs: To the use and Behoofe of him the said Walter Stanley, and his Assignes, for and during his natural Life, without Impeachment of any Manner of Waste; and after his Decease, then to the Use and Behoofe of them the said William Stanley, Edward Grove, William Turton the Elder, William Turton, John Turton, Thomas Turton, Francis Simcox, William Simcox, William Partridge, John Hayteley, George Partridge, Francis Partridge, John Jesson, William Hobbins, Simon Warde, Thomas Gretton, and Michael Poultney, their Heirs and Assigns for ever: And yet, nevertheless, upon special Trust and Confidence in them reposed, and it is the full Intent and true Meaning of the said Walter Stanley: And it is also concluded and agreed upon between the said Parties to these Presents, that all the Rents, Revenues, Issues, and Profits, of the said Messuage or Tennement, and of all other the Premisses, shall for ever, from and after the Decease of the said Walter Stanley, be wholly employed and bestowed from Time to Time to such Intents and Purposes, in such a Manner, Order, and Form, as in and by these Presents, by the said Walter Stanley, is declared, express'd, and appointed; that is to say, for and towards the Maintenance and finding of One Honest, Virtuous and Learned Preacher, to preach the Word of God in the Parish Church of West Bromwich aforesaid, according to the Doctrine and Religion now establish'd in the Church of England: And the said Walter Stanley doth also ordain and appoint, and it is also agreed between the said Parties, that all and every such Preacher for the Time being, shall, from Time to Time, for ever preach in the foresaid Parish Church of West Bromwich, once every Sabboth-Day in the Forenoon, and once every principall Feast-Day, as on the Feast of the Nativity, Circumcission, Epiphany, Passion, and Ascension of Christ; and shall Catechize every Sabboth-Day in the Afterndon in the same Parish Church; and shall be diligent to visit and exhorte all sick Persons within the said Parish, as well Poor as Rich, unless he have any lawful Lett or Impediment, through Sickness or otherwise, such as shall be allowed of by the said Feoffes and Churchwardens of the said Parish Church for the Time being, or the more Part of them: And also the said Walter Stanley doth by these Presents ordain and appoint, that every such Preacher shall be a Graduate in one of the Universities of Oxford or Cambridge, and a single Man unmaryed, and shall be nominated and chosen from Time to Time by the said Feoffees, (or such as shall be Feoffees of the said Premisses) and by the Churchwardens of the said Parish Church for the Time being, or the more Part of them: And for that the said Walter Stanley earnestly desireth that one of good Conversation and Carriage shall from Time to Time supply the said Place of a Preacher, he doth also ordain and appoint, and thereunto the said Feoffees do consent and agree, that if at any Time or Times hereafter, any Preacher chosen according to the Purporte or true Meaning of these Presents, shall be, or shall become to be, a Drunkard, or Haunter of the Alehouse, Whoremaster or Fighter, or known to have or use any such notorious Crime or Fault, and shall not upon Admonition thereof by the said Feoffees and Churchwardens for the Time being, or some of them to the Number of Four, within one Quarter of a Year after Admonition thereof, amend or reform himself, that then such Preacher shall by the said Feoffees and Churchwardens, or the more Part of them, for the Time being, from Time to Time, be displaced and another chosen and placed according to the Purport, Intent, and true Meaning of these Presents: And to the End such Preacher shall from Time to Time be diligent to preach sincerely, and truly, and carefull to live thereafter, it is the Mind and Desire of the said Walter Stanley, and so he doth by these Presents ordain and appoint, that no such Preacher shall have further Estate but from Year to Year upon his good Behaviour, and the Approbation and Allowance of the said Feoffees and Churchwardens for the Time being, or the more Part of them: And the said Walter Stanley doth also ordain and appoint, and so it is also agreed between the said parties, that the said Churchwardens of the said Parish Church for the Time being, shall, from Time to Time, receive and gather the Rents and Revenues of the Premisses, and shall, also from Time to Time, pay and deliver them to the said Preacher, for the Time being, as may best stand with their Receipts, and the Necessity of the said Preacher; And if any Receipt happen to be in Time of a Vacation, or Want of a Preacher, then the same to be from Time to Time reserved, and payed to the next that shall succeed in that Place: And that no Lease be made of the Premises or any Part thereof, but at Wille, or for One and Twenty Years or under, and in Possession, and no Fine to be taken for any such Lease, but a yearly Rent reserved, to the reasonable yearly Value as near as conveniently may be; And that the said Tenant and Tenants be bound to keep Reparations; And that the Ordering, Disposing, Letting, and Setting of the Premisses, be, from Time to Time, by the Direction of the said Feoffees and Churchwardens for the Time being, or the more Part of them: And that the said Churchwardens for the Time being, every Year when there shall be Election and Choice there made of new Churchwardens in West Bromwich aforesaid, shall make and give up a true and perfect Account and Reconing to the foresaid Feoffees for the Time being, their Heirs or Assigns, or to so many of them as shall be there present, what Rents, and how much they have received of the said Lands, Tenements, and Hereditaments, and how they have paid the same; And if upon their Accounts it shall appear that any of the said Rentes shall remain in their Hands, that then they shall pay the same to the next Churchwardens, immediately to be employed and bestowed to the Uses and Intents aforesaid: And also the said Walter Stanley doth ordain and appoint, and it is thought convenient by all the said parties, That if any of the said now Feoffees or Churchwardens, or any other for the Time being, be upon juste Occasion put to any Costs, Charges, or Expences, for the Levying, Gathering, or Injoying of the said Premises, That then the same shall from Time to Time, upon just Account and Reconing thereof to be made to the foresaid Feoffees and Churchwardens for the Time being, or the more Part of them, allowed and deducted out of next Receipte of the Rents, Revennues, or Profits as aforesaid. And for that it is thought convenient that Provision shall be made, that the Estate of, and in the Premises may from Time to Time continue in Persons fit and willing to make Performance of the Premises; Therefore the said Walter Stanley doth further ordain and appoint, and all the said Parties do thereunto consent and agree, that when the greater Part of the said Feoffees in these Presents named as Parties shall die, and no more but Four of them remain living, That then the said surviving Feoffees shall within one Month next after the Death of the Feoffee that last died, convey the said Premises discharged of all Charges and Incumbrances by them done, to the Use of other Feoffees, to the number of twelve at the least, and their Heirs, or to the Use of themselves and other Feofees to the like Number and their Heirs, being of the most honest and substantiall Inhabitants in West Bromwich aforesaid, to be for ever employed according to the Purport, Intent, and true Meaning in these Presents; And that such new Feoffees shall do the like, and so all other Feoffees hereafter to be named, appointed, or made according to the Purporte, Forme, or Effect of these Presents, shall from Time to Time do the like, as Time and Occasion shall require: And it is also covenanted, concluded, and agreed, by and between all the Parties to these Presents, That if any of the said Feoffees shall remove from the said Parish of West Bromwich, and dwell in any other Parish, then every such Person so removing, shall within six Months after such removing, by his Deed in Writing, release all his Right, Title, and Authority into, or concerning the Premises, to the Rest of the Feoffees for the Time being, and to their Heirs, to the Uses, Intents, and Purposes herein and hereby specified, intended, and declared: And nevertheless it is the true Intent and Meaning of the said Walter Stanley, and he doeth by these Presents further ordain and appoint, any Thing before in these Presents mentioned to the contrary notwithstanding, That if it shall happen at any Time or Times hereafter, that the Religion now established and alowed in the Church of England, shall be suppress'd, and any other Kind of Religion instead thereof shall be maintained by Law, or commanded by Authority, (which GOD forbidd) That then, and from Time to Time, during such Time only, and so long the said Feoffees for the Time being, or the More Part of them, shall or may imploy, bestow and distribute the yearly Rents and Revenues arising and coming of the foresaid Messuage, Lands, Tenements, Hereditaments and Premises in and upon, or towards any other godlie or charitable Use or Uses, to be made, done and performed in West Bromwich aforesaid, (other then the keeping or Maintaining of a Schoolmaster) as by the said Feoffees and Churchwardens for the Time being, or the more Part of them, in their good discretions shall be thought most meete, requisite and convenient. In Witness whereof the Parties abovesaid to these present Indentures, interchangeably have put their Hands and Seals, the Day and Year first above written."

ORDERS FOR THE PREACHER.

1. Hee shall be and cotynewe obedient and comformable to the Ecclesiasticall lawes of the realm.

2. Hee shall be a Peacemaker, or do his best endeavor from tyme to tyme in that behalf.

3. Hee shall himself be and contynewe of a quyet, patient and meeke behavior towards all poore and riche, old and younge.

4. *He shall not marry nor take upon him any other Cure or Benefice, during his abode there.*

5. He shall not at all medle with serving the Cure of West-Bromwiche, which belongeth to the farmer or proprietor of the parsonage, unless it be upon very urgent necessity, and that very seldome.

6. Hee shall visit the sick and needy, from tyme to tyme, yf it be not of the plague.

7. Hee shall be noe gamester, nor frequent the taverne, alehouse or any evil company, or any house or place of suspicion, or evill report.

8. Hee shall keepe noe common schoole nor practice phisick, nor chirurgery, for money or other reward.

9. Hee shall not meddle with making of bonds, bills, acquitances, conveyances or other writing of like nature, (wills, testaments and inventories onlie excepted.)

10. He shall keepe the house and all other things therein, (or thereto belonging, or therewith occupied, in sufficient reparations and in good order.)

11. He shall performe all other thing on his part to be performed, mentioned in a certyne feoffament, indented, made by the said Walter Stanley, dated the 12th day of March, 1613.

12. And to avoid all suspicion, *the said Walter Stanley earnestlie desireth*, that no such Preacher, shall keep in his house, any woman (except his mother or his sister).

A great portion of the following account is taken from a pamphlet published in 1815, entituled "An Account of the Lectureship in the Parish of West Bromwich," and from briefs, affidavits, &c., in the vestry.

Of the proceedings which took place in consequence of this Deed of Trust from its original date, during a period of 133 years, scarcely any traces are known to exist, an almost total dispersion, if not final loss of the most ancient writings and records connected with the endowment having taken place.

If however history is silent during all these years, subsequent events made up for the past oblivion.

In April, 1710, the Reverend John Rann, of Trinity College, Oxford, Incumbent of the Parish, was appointed to the Lectureship, but for some reason his appointment was cancelled, and the Reverend William Broughton appointed in his place. Mr. Rann must however have been eventually re-appointed to the Lectureship, as he was holding that and the Living in 1745, when he resigned, and was succeeded by the Reverend Peter Jones, who married his daughter Damaris. The election of Mr. Jones to the Lectureship was not unanimous, but by the major part of the trustees, who were about that time reduced to only four in number. The trustees appear to have been very loose in their conduct of the affairs of the trust, and to this want of faithfulness to their charge, the litigation and heart burnings which subsequent events caused are to be traced.

On the 29th of April, 1746, the four surviving trustees nominated Samuel Clarke, Esq., Thomas Jesson, Esq., and Jesson Lowe, Esq., among others to join them in the Trust. Immediately on their appointment the new trustees began a journal of their proceedings. This book begins with a copy of the Foundation Deed and Walter Stanley's Orders and Ordinances for the Preacher. The effect of fresh blood in the Trust was soon perceptible. The trustees appear to have thoroughly looked into the affairs of the Trust, with the result of finding much that was irregular and illegal. It would appear that in the year 1662 there had been a considerable fall of timber on the Stanley Trust Estate. With the money realised by the sale of this timber the trustees purchased a house and land in the parish of Wednesbury. This property, contrary to the express terms of the Trust Deed, had been let on a long lease of eighty years, to a man named Joseph Worsley. Worsley afterwards assigned the lease to one William Nicklin. This man Nicklin had some pecuniary dealings with Mr. Rann, not in his position as Lecturer, but in his private capacity. In the year 1736 Nicklin appears to have been unable to meet his liabilities to Mr. Rann, and to have given as security for his debt a mortgage of this property of which he held the lease. In 1743 Mr. Rann's daughter Damaris was married to the Rev. Peter Jones, and Mr. Rann gave to his son-in-law, no doubt as a dowry with his daughter, his mortgage on Nicklin's leasehold. Mr. Jones foreclosed the mortgage and thus obtained possession of the property. Once in possession, he soon began to open coal pits, and no doubt obtained considerable profits therefrom. In consequence of these illegal proceedings on the part of Mr. Jones, the trustees held a meeting in October, 1746, when it was decided to institute a suit in chancery against Mr. Jones, to oblige him to give up the land in question. A few days after the meeting already mentioned, viz. on October 29th, a second was held, when the trustees determined that notice should be given to Mr. Jones of the intention of the trustees to remove him from the Lectureship. On the 2nd of February, 1747, the trustees elected in Mr. Jones' place the Rev. William Jabet as Lecturer, but Mr. Jones refused to allow him to enter the Church; and the Vicarage House in Church Lane being declared to be the property of Lord Dartmouth, and not (as the trustees endeavoured to prove) belonging to the Stanley Trust, the question of Mr. Jabet's position in the parish must have been very perplexing. In Walter Stanley's Orders a house is mentioned as belonging to the Trust: perhaps this was lost owing to carelessness. The suit against Mr. Jones was indeed a lengthy and painful one. It was continued until his death in 1752.

Although, as we have before said, Mr. Jones did not seem to come out very well in this sad affair, yet he may at the same time have been a victim to the wrong doings of others, and he may have believed himself to be at liberty to work the mines under the piece of land at Wednesbury, the cause of all the trouble. He affirmed positively that the land had nothing whatever to do with the Stanley Trust. It seems that the difficulty which the Trustees experienced in their suit arose from an informality in the title deed of the property at Wednesbury upon which the trespass of Mr. Jones was committed. As we have said Mr. Jones died before the conclusion of the suit. On his death the Trustees proceeded against his widow for damage done by Mr. Jones, but on her death only a few months after her husband, they again had to obtain power to proceed afresh. This time it was against Mr. Rann, Mr. Jones' father-in-law. At last the proceedings were brought to a close, and Mr. Rann had to pay the sum of £91 to the Trustees, and, of course, restore the land to them. The land was eventually sold by the Trustees in 1849 to the South Staffordshire Railway Co. In the account of the Lectureship which we have before alluded to, it is stated that from the death of Mr. Jones for six years no election to the Lectureship took place, but as a matter of fact Mr. Jabet had been elected by the Trustees before Mr. Jones' death in 1746, and after that event in 1752 his name appears as "Curate under the Sequestration;" he held both offices for one year after the death of Mr. Jones. As we said in the account of the Parish Church the Reverend Henry Saunders succeeded Mr. Jabet as Curate, but the latter continued to hold the Lectureship by yearly appointment, as proved by entries in the Trustees' Journal, until the appointment of the Reverend Edward Stillingfleet to the post in 1758. When the Living was released from the Sequestration necessitated by the heavy costs of the lawsuit, Mr. Stillingfleet was appointed Incumbent; the statement that his appointment was on the resignation of Mr. Rann is a mistake. It is not likely (apart from facts) that after all that had occurred Mr. Rann would be very anxious to return to West Bromwich. As already stated, a year after Mr. Stillingfleet's appointment as Incumbent he was chosen to fill the vacant post of Lecturer; however, this election was not unanimous on the part of the Trustees.

In July, 1782, on the resignation of Mr. Stillingfleet, the Reverend Abraham Elton, the newly appointed Incumbent of the Parish, was chosen as Lecturer; and on Mr. Elton leaving the Parish in 1790, the Trustees appointed the Reverend William Jesse, who succeeded him in the Living, to the vacant Lectureship. On the death of Mr. Jesse in 1815, the subject of the Stanley Trust and Lectureship seems for the first time to have awakened an interest in the minds of the inhabitants of West Bromwich; copies of the foundation deed and orders were eagerly sought for and obtained. There was little doubt in the mind of anyone that Walter Stanley intended that there should be two Priests in the Parish—at the Parish Church—holding separate offices, not to interfere one with the other, and notwithstanding the almost universal custom of the previous Trustees, they could not legally elect either the Incumbent, a married man, or any Clergyman holding any other Cure or Benefice, as Lecturer.

This agitation began in consequence of the desire of the greater part of the Trustees to elect the Reverend Charles Townsend, he being a married man, the Incumbent of the Parish, and Rector of Calstone. A memorial, expressing the dissatisfaction of the inhabitants of the Parish at large at the previous arrangements, was extensively signed, and presented to Lord Dartmouth and the Trustees.

On the 21st April, 1815, the Trustees met in the Parish Church to choose a Lecturer. Six of the Trustees elected Mr. Townsend, but four others expressly dissented from this appointment on the ground of its illegality. The opinion of an eminent barrister was taken, which confirmed the illegality of the election. A lawsuit, however, would seem to have taken place in consequence of the dispute, and it was at this time that such urgent search was made for the certificate of Mr. Rann's marriage, to which we have before alluded. The object, of course, being to prove that although a married man, he, as also most of his predecessors and successors, held the Lectureship. Party feeling ran very high at this time, and an answer appeared to the pamphlet giving an account of the Lectureship, in which the writer states, among other things, that many did not believe the "Orders for the Preacher" to be genuine, or even authorised by Walter Stanley himself. However this was again replied to by the previous writer in a third pamphlet.

The only solution to the difficulty was to obtain an Act of Parliament, and as also about this time it was necessary to build a new Church, it was considered a favourable opportunity of obtaining power to alter the terms of the Trust to suit the requirements of the Parish.

An Act of Parliament was obtained, which received the Royal Assent July 6th, 1819, " For regulating the appropriation of the Revenues of certain Trust Estates, given by Walter Stanley for pious purposes; for effectuating in a more extensive and beneficial manner the general objects of the Trust; and making a provision for, and regulating the appointment of, a Minister of a New Church intended to be built at West Bromwich, in the County of Stafford."

The Act states several facts relating to the Trust which, having before stated we will not trouble our readers with again, and the Act then proceeds to say that the population of West Bromwich had greatly increased and was increasing, and was then estimated at about 9,000, and that the distance of many parts of the population from the Church rendered it necessary that additional provision should be made for the " performance " of Divine Service in the Parish. It further states that a subscription had been entered into by Lord Dartmouth and others for the erection of a New Church, and that His Majesty's Commissioners under the Act for building additional Churches in populous Parishes, had resolved to contribute so much of the expense as should be wanted; and whereas it was also desirable that as many free sittings as possible should be provided in the New Church, and on that account the income of the Minister of the New Church might be lessened, and also for providing an additional and permanent endowment therefore, it has enacted that one half of the rents or revenues arising from the Trust estates should be paid to the Minister of the New Church, and the other half to the Curate of the Parish Church, the latter taking upon himself all the duties of Preacher. With regard to the election of the Clergyman of the New Church, the Act says that the Earl of Dartmouth should submit the names of two Clergymen, graduates of Oxford or Cambridge, and of these the Stanley Trustees should select one. The Act further states that the Incumbent (or Curate) of the Parish Church must be a graduate of Oxford or Cambridge, and might be a married man.

The Act concludes with the following injunction:—That if either of the Clergymen before mentioned shall not be diligent to preach sincerely and truly, and careful to live thereafter, or shall be guilty of any notorious crime or fault, and shall not, on admonition of the Bishop, amend or reform, then it shall be lawful for the Churchwardens of the Parish Church, upon the order of the Bishop, to withhold from the party so offending the rents and revenues of the Trust estates to which he is entitled, &c., &c.

In the year 1840, thanks to the indefatigable exertions of Mr. George Wilmot and Mr. Thomas Jesson, of Oakwood, two of the Trustees, another Act was obtained to enable the Trustees to grant building leases on the estate extending to 99 years.

The leases, when they fall in, will considerably enrich the two Parishes for whose benefit they were made, that is to say if untouched by sacreligious hands before that time. May God, who put it into the heart of our pious benefactor, Walter Stanley, to endow the Lectureship for the religious good of the Parish, bless the increase thereof to His Honour and Glory, and the good of His Church.

PARISH RECORDS.

CHURCHWARDENS' BOOKS.

THE earliest entry in the first of these books is on November 15th, 1678.—Mr. William Turton, of the Mill, Humphrey Turton, William Turton, Thomas Jesson, Richard Sheldon, John Lowe, &c., were present at a Vestry Meeting on that day.

May 5th, 1682.—John Turton's name appears, also that of Nicholas Ryder.

In 1688, we find—Allowed Churchwardens for saying the office, 6/8.

Paid Thomas Hadley for catching sparrows, £1.

Nov. 4th, 1689.—Accounted then with William Underhill for 2 levies for the trained shoulders (soldiers), one at 1d. per £1, and 1 at 2d. (Underhill was constable.)

April 22nd, 1690.—John Turton, of Cop Hall, 1694; John Lowe, Junior.

The 11th of January, 1691—These inclosures underwritten were thrown open by us whose names are subscribed in the parish of West Bromwich, (then follows a list) by us, Henry Hunt, Richard Sheldon, John Stamps, James Cox, John Lowe, George Simcox, Josiah Simcox, Thomas Culwick, Thomas Jesson, William Sterry, William Turton, &c.

In the year 1691, Received for breaking the Church, 3/4.

In 1692, For Breaking up of the Church 5 times, 16/8.

The accompts of Mr. John Lowe, Junr., concerning the buying of nayles delivered to ye Parish Nayler in July, 1697,

	£	s.	d.
which come to	105	16	06
due to him for Nayle bags	000	12	08
due to him for Iron delivered to Nayler	000	04	07
due to him for Interest ye 26th July next	004	12	00
	£119	05	09½

In 1698, Benjamin Low was one Churchwarden.

On March 24th, 1698—A second mention of throwing down inclosures by freeholders in the parish, among these are John Lowe, and John Lowe. Junr.

March 9th, 1701.—We, the inhabitants of West bromwich whose names are subscribed, doe hereby unanimously agree, consent, own, and acknowledge that the Little Chancell that is on the South side of West bromwich church aforesaid, and all the propriety right, title, interest, claime, and demand whatsoever thereto belongeth to the Right Hon[ble.] The Lord Dartmouth, and soe to remain and continue to him and his heirs for ever, without any lett, trouble, denyale, interruption, molestation, or disturbance of us or any of us, Witness our names—Bayley Brett, John Lowe, Richard Sterry, George Simcox, Job Simcox, Richard Brooks, John Jesson, &c., &c.

1704, Received for breaking the Church for Hobbeage's grave, 3/4.

In 1704 appear the names of Nicholas Ryder, Josiah Turton, Samuel Lowe.

In 1706, John Blakmore, Edward Blakemore.

18th Nov. 1707.—Whereas a misunderstanding has happened betwixt John Hawkes and ye Widow Biggin and the parishioners, we had this day a publique acc^{t} produced, and by the perticulers on both side there appears due to the Widow Biggin eighteen shill. and elevenpence half-penny..

1710, Benjamin Lowe, John Lowe, Josiah Turton.

1711, John Rann, Minister.

July 17th, 1713.—It was then agreed upon by us whose names are hereunto subscribed yt ye Church of West bromwich should be ceiled.

March 9th, 1715-16.—Left out of the ungatherable out of Mr. Shelton's estate three pounds sixteen shillings and ninepence.

April 6th, 1716.—At a publique meeting, it was then agreed upon ... that the collectors of the land tax, overseers of the poor, and other officers of our parish of West bromwich, goe to Sergeant Hooe or some other counsell, to take advice how they may come into theire land tax and levies due from Bromich Hall and demean lands thereunto belonging, and that there be a guiney allowed from the parish for a ffee.—Signed by Thos. Scott for the Earl of Dartmouth.—Thomas Brett, Joseph Freeth, John Jesson, Josiah Lowe.

20th April, 1716.—There is due to the parish from the demeanes of Bromich Hall and the out ffarmes as followeth:

	£	s.	d.
ffor the Demeanes	09	4	0
ffor Ridgacres	00	4	0
ffor Wheeler's field land	00	1	4
ffor Bulls farme	00	4	0
ffor field gate	01	4	0
Mansell's ffarme	00	5	4
In all for ffour Levyes	12	5	8

July 11th, 1716.—It was then agreed upon that the Church of West bromwich should be clean Whit washed and new Butefied, by we whose names are subscribed.

August 31st, 1716.—The said day and year Robert Summerfield, of Woolverhampton, painter, for the consideration hereafter mentioned, doth covenant and agree with Jos. Ffreeth and Rich. Jesson, Churchwardens, and the rest of the inhabitants of West bromwich, whose names are subscribed as folleth. That he paint the Ten Commandments, the King's Arms, the Lord's Prayer, the Creed, Moses and Aaron, and Six Sentences, and to find cloth and fframes: the Churchwardens to be at the charge of the carriage from Woolverhampton and irons to set them up, and for the said work the said Robert Summerfield to be paid the sume of twenty pounds within the space of one yeare next after the date hereof, and it is agreed that the said work be done in oyle work only without gold, and the said Robert Summerfield doth covenant and promise to compleate and perfect the said work at or before Christmas next.—Witness our hands, Robert Summerfield, John Rann, John Baker, Richard Jesson, John Jesson, &c., &c., &c. . . . .

Oct. 8th, 1716.—At a publique meeting, We, Richard Sterry, Samuel Westwood, and Job Simcox, Trustees for the poores land in the occupation of Thomas Jesson, doe consent and agree that the parishioners doe erect houses upon partes of the said premises for the use of the poore of our Parish of Westbromwich. The day and year above written We, whose names are subscribed, doe mutually consent and promise to put the said work in execution as soon as conveniently may be, and to use all means that shall be thought requisite for the perfecting ye same.—

Thos. Scott for ye Earl of Dartmouth.—Jno. Lowe, Jos. Turton, Richd. Brett, Thos. Brett, Joseph ffreeth, Richard Jesson, &c., &c.

The same day and yeare it was agreed that the ringers be paid for ringing six shillings and eightpence a day by the Churchwardens for the time being, upon such days as shall be appointed them by the said Churchwardens, and to ring soe long or soe much as the Churchwardens shall think fitt, not demanding above 6/8 as above said, only Christmas Day and New Year's Day, they are to have 2 gs., according to the former custom.

March 21st, 1718.—The day and yeare above written it was agreed upon that there shall be only one shilling allowed to any officer going into a monthly meeting, and noe ale to be allowed upon any account whatsoever.

This 12th day of December, 1718.—Wee, the inhabitants of West Bromwich, being freeholders, did ride through the new incroachments of the Lords Wast, as our names are here subscribed—Paul Lowe, Josiah Lowe, John Turton, James Selvester, William Turton, William Turton, jun., Paule Cashmore, Ric. Partridg, Ann Thornton, Geo. Withers, John Turton, John Lowe, Joseph Worsley, &c., &c., &c. . . . .

ffeby. 3rd, 1719.—Agreed that these cottagers hereafter named be indited at the next Quarterly Assession for inhabiting, erecting, or selling cottages, or encroaching upon the Waste. [List of cottagers.]—Signed by John Turton, Josiah Turton, Thos. Jesson, &c., &c.

April 12th, 1721.—Memorandum that Sir Samuel Clarke's rents are not paid, and are to be allowed to the Overseers when paid.

In 1733.—ffor breaking up the church 6/8

June 16th, 1721.—Agreed upon that 2/- shall be spent at the assessing of the land tax; that the Churchwardens pay for ringing on the 28th day of May, being the birthday of King George, 6/8; and upon the 29th day of May, the Restoration of King Charles, 6/8; and upon the 5th day August, the King's Proclamation Day, 6/8; and upon the 20th day of October, the Coronation Day, 6/8; and for ringing on the 5th November, 6/8; and for ringing on Christmas Day and New Year's Day, 3 ; and that the Churchwardens be allowed to pay upon accidental days what shall be reasonable, not exceeding 6/8. That there be allowed going to the Visitation at Walsall, £1—1—0; and at the Triennial Visitation at Litchfield, £1—5—0; and for going to Shenstone, 2/6 and the court charges. And that the Churchwardens give noe money away to any without a note from under Mr. Rann's hand. That the Constable shall not invade the Supervisor's office, nor sett up any stumps at all.

That the Constable give noe money to any vagrants. And that he give but 4d. to any hiew and cry, and that he set down the day of the month whence the hiew and cry came and whither sent. And that he be not allowed to give or spend any of the Parishe's money upon the traine souldiers or any other persons upon rejoicing days. And that the Constable buy what timber shall be needfull for the Parishe's use, and to give an account of whom bought. . . . . And we doe not think fitt to allow 1/- for the giving the oath to any officer at the entrance of his office. And that the Supervisors give an account of whom they buy their stumps, and that they be allowed noe more for them than they are really worth, and that they sett them up in the most convenient places. And that the Head-borough be allowed nothing for ale tasting.

Feb. 21st, 1723.—It is also agreed that the Churchwardens provide a Master of Arts hood.

April 23rd, 1724.—It was agreed that the Supervisors of the highways doe allow to every teame three pence a day for every day that they come in, and noe more; and likewise that every labourer have three half pence a day for every day, and noe more. Accounts are allowed by John Lane and John Dolphin, His Majesty's Justices of the Peace for the County of Stafford.

March 26th, 1731.—Agreed upon that the Minister goe this present year prossessioning in our Parish of West Bromwich.—John Turton, J. Rann, &c.

Nov. 9th, 1725.—It was then agreed upon at a publick meeting by us, whose names are hereunto subscribed, yt any person who shal bring ye heads of a dozen of sparrows to ye Churchwardens of West Bromwich shal receive for them two pence, and for any greater or lesser number proportionably, if catcht within ye said Parish.—Thos. Scott, for ye Earl of Dartmouth.—Wm. Wyley and Job Reeves, Church Wardens.—Jno. Rann, John Lowe, John Turton, John Jesson, Tho. Brett, Richard Sheldon, Edward Walthew, John Culwick, William Smith, cena., Jos. Hawkes, Job Hildick, James White, Job Simcox, William Smith.

Nov. 23rd, 1733.—Agreed upon that the ringers shall have 6/8 for ringing on Christmas Day and New Year's Day.

January 24th, 1734.—Agreed that there shall be a house fitted and prepared with such necessaries thereunto for the setting of the poor of the Parish of West Bromwich on work, and for the relief of the lame and impotent of the said Parish, and for the defraying and payment of the charges of the said workhouse it is alsoe agreed that the same shall be paid by the usuall four penny levey of the poors rate, and such leveys to be collected in manner hereafter named. That is one levey in this present yeare, and to continue the collection of two leveys yearly afterwards more than the charges of the maintenance of the poor, untill the expenses above said be fully satisfied and paid.—Signed by John Lowe, Jesson Lowe, Thomas Jesson, &c., &c.

April 8th, 1735.—Whereas an entry was made on the four-and-twentyeth of Jany. last past, for erecting a workhouse in the Parish of West Bromwich. Wee, the freeholders and tennants within the said Parish whose names are under written, do oppose the erecting of such workhouse as a thing that will be of great damage and pernicious consequence to the said Parish of West Bromwich,—Signed by John Turton, Ralph Moor, and others.

This last entry is taken from Overseers' Accounts at the end of the Burial Registers, No. 5. In these are also recorded protests against the erection of a workhouse, on April 18th, June 13th, 9th July, 22nd August, 1735.

Money collected for a fire in Willinbrow in September, 1738:—

	£	s.	d.
The Right Honble. Earle of Dartmouth	1	1	0
Samuel Clarke, Esq.	2	2	0
Mr. Tho. Jesson	0	2	6
Mr. Jesson Lowe	0	2	6
Mr. John Lowe	0	1	6
Mr. Rich. Witton	0	5	0
Mr. Turlton	0	1	6

		£	s.	d.
Mr. Bayley Brett	.	0	2	6
Mrs. Mary Brett	.	0	2	6
Collected in Church, &c.	.			

Total £4 19 0

18th March, 1738.—It is agreed at a Vestry Meeting . . . that ye Churchwardens shall assert and maintain ye Parishes right to the Seat in the Church now claim'd by Mr. Tho. Jesson and Mr. Jesson Lowe, in case Mr. Tho. Powell's right to it be disalowed, at ye cost and expence of ye Parish.

Sept. 26th, 1735.—Wee, the inhabitants whose names are subscribed, do hereby protest and declare against the erecting of a workhouse, buying any lands or buildings for that use, or that the poor shall be kept in any workhouse or otherwise than usuall, at the perill of the officers; or that the money which hath been granted be applyed to any other use than the relief of the poor as usual, and not putting them into a workhouse.—Edward Horn, John Turton, &c., Edward Rider. . . .

West Bromwich, March ye 19th, 1737.—The Overseers of ye Poor give notice to the inhabitants of ye Parish to meet them att ye house of William Morris, on Fryday next, att four a clock in ye afternoon, to consent upon the agreement that was made at Joseph Gutheridg's, and then to determine whether or not ye law charges expended on each side shall be raised by levys and laid upon the inhabitants, and applied to pay boath parties in the manner as is particularly sett forth in the said agreement. Agreed at the meeting that no law charges or expenses of either side shall be allowed to the Overseers in their account over and above such as are for the immediate reliefe of the poore.

April 24th, 1739.—The minister (Mr. Rann) nominated Joseph Wall, and the people Richard Sheldon, Churchwardens. Hitherto minister and people elected both, as they did once again in 1740.

1740.—For breaking ye Church, 3/4.
1743.—For breaking ye Church, 3/4.
1744.—For breaking the Church, 6/8.

Peter Jones, Minister.

January 3rd, 1746.—It was agreed upon by the megority that Jeremiah Wright and Josiah Stevens, present Churchwardens, shall pay 2d. per dozen for sparrow heads. March 31st, 1752.—Signed by William Jabet, Curate, under ye Sequestration.

April 24th, 1753. Henry Saunders, Curate, and in 1754, and April 1st, 1755, also April 20th, 1756.

March 27th, 1754. Vestry Meeting adjourned to the House of Richard Reeves—and it was there agreed to have the Workhouse put in good and sufficient repair at or before, or soon after Easter next ensuing the date hereof, for the reception and convenient lodging of all the poor in the said parish, and for providing all things necessary for the use of the poor—and that such Parish rates shall be made by the present and future officers of the said parish to raise such a sum or sums of money as may be requisite fully to carry on this order of Vestry into execution.—Ralph Moore and Joseph Stephens, Churchwardens.—Signed by Jesson Lowe, Samuel Lowe, &c. . . . ,

April 12th, 1757, Edward Stillingfleet, Minister.

1758.—Three Burials in Church . . 0 10 0
      For Breaking up Ye Church . 0 3 4

Nov. 29th, 1765.—Meeting for electing a Governor of the Workhouse. After taking the votes of those who paid the Church and Poor Rates, Joseph Sanders was found to have the majority. Edward Stillingfleet—Thomas Bagnall, John Turton—Samuel Lowe—William Turton—1767.—William Whyley—John Turton—John Wright—Richard Jesson, J.P., Philemon Parkes.

At a Vestry meeting held this 26th day of April, 1773, in the Parish Church of West Bromwich, pursuant to a notice given in the said church, on Sunday, the 25th instant, for the parishioners then and there to meet to consult and agree about enlarging the churchyard, in consequence of a gift of a piece of land to the said parish by Jervoise Clarke, Esq. for that purpose :—it was agreed that the Churchwardens shall build a wall to enclose the said land at the expense of the said parish.—Signed by, Edward Stillingfleet, Minister; Edward Elwell, and Richard Jesson, Churchwardens; John Wall, John Wright, Joseph Jesson, &c.

At a Vestry meeting held 21st March 1774.—It was agreed to enlarge the workhouse, as it was insufficient to receive the Poor applying for relief; and also all necessary workshops should be built, &c.

April 3rd, 1775.—Agreed at a Vestry meeting held at the Workhouse, that the parish's right to all the sittings in the gallery shall be maintained at the expense of the parish, and the Churchwardens are hereby desired to support and maintain that right. And whereas certain persons have, without proper leave and license from the parish, taken away one of the seats in the upper part of the said gallery, containing nine sittings or more, and also made other alterations, the Churchwardens are hereby

desired to take care that the said seat be again put up, and that everything be restored to the same state it was in before such alterations. And whereas certain persons calling themselves singers and others, have hindered and molested some of the parishioners in coming into the seats, and made other disturbances in the church, it is hereby agreed that if any person or persons shall hereafter offend in like manner, they shall be prosecuted at the expense of the parish, and the Churchwardens for the time being are desired to carry on a prosecution against them.
—Edward Stillingfleet, Minister.

June 22nd, 1783.—It was resolved that an alteration in the Church was absolutely necessary for the more decent worship of God and the better accommodation of the parishioners, and that the same might be carried into effect it was also resolved that the work must be completed by private subscriptions. At the same time we, the under-written, engage to contribute the following sums.—Present: Abraham Elton, Minister: Edward Elwell, Walter Brinton, Churchwardens.

	£	s.	d.
John Wright	50	0	0
Ed. Elwell	50	0	0
Rich. Jesson (for a New Church)	100	0	0
Philemon Parkes	50	0	0
Joseph Jesson	30	0	0
Wm. Bullock, senr.	50	0	0
James Bullock	50	0	0
&c., &c., &c.			

At a general Vestry held April 22nd, 1785, "For the purpose of coming to some resolutions with respect to the alteration of the Church, it was resolved that the work should be completed by private subscription, and that the parish at large would be satisfied provided the builder gives sufficient security that he will execute the work according to his estimate, so that the parish may with certainty be exempt from any share of the burthen. At the same time it was resolved that Mr. Whyley, Mr. Elwell, Mr. Wall, Mr. Wright, and Mr. R. Jesson, should constitute a committee for the management, inspection, and direction of the work." A. Elton, Minister, &c.

July 17th, 1786.—At a general Vestry held July 17th, 1786, resolved "that a Vestry shall be erected at the expense of the parish, and under the direction of Edward Elwell and William Whyley the present Churchwardens."

The first entry in the second of the Churchwarden's books is—" Notice is hereby given that a Vestry meeting will be held in this Parish Church on Monday, the twenty-sixth day of November instant, for the purpose of making allotments and appropriating the new-erected seats, pews, and sitting places within this Parish Church, and the parishioners, and particularly those who were subscribers, and all persons interested in the said seats and sitting places are desired to attend at the hour of eleven of clock in the forenoon.

November 25th, 1787.

The above notice was read in the Parish Church of West bromwich on Sunday, the said 25th instant, after Divine Service.

At a Vestry meeting held in the Parish Church of West bromwich, this 26th day of November, one thousand seven hundred and eighty seven. . . . we, whose names are hereunto subscribed, do resolve and agree that the new-erected seats, pews, and sitting places within the Parish Church

.... ought to be appropriated and allotted to and amongst the subscribers towards building and erecting the same, in proportion to the sums which they have respectively subscribed and paid. And we do therefore hereby allot and appropriate the several seats, pews, and sitting places respectively marked or numbered.

(1) Situate and adjoining the Clarkes reading desk and opening into the south isle, to the Rev. Abraham Elton, Clerk, the present Minister or Curate of West Bromwich aforesaid, and to his successors, Curates of the said parish for the time being. The seat marked No. (2) situate and adjoining the said seat alloted to the Rev. Abraham Elton, and opening into the said south isle, to William Whyley, of the Oak House. The seat marked No. (3) situate and adjoining to the said seat alloted to William Whyley, and opening into the said south isle, to John Wright. The seat marked No. (4) situate and adjoining to the seat alloted to John Wright, and opening into the said south isle, to Richard Jesson. The seat marked No. (5) situate and adjoining to the seat alloted to Richard Jesson, and opening into the said south isle, to William Bullock, the elder. The seat marked No. (6) situate on the south side of the south isle unto Joseph Jesson. The seat marked No. (7) situate on the said south side of the said south isle, and adjoining to the seat alloted to Joseph Jesson, to William Bullock, the younger, and to James Bullock. The seat marked No. (8) situate and adjoining a seat belonging to Jervoise Clarke Jervoise, Esq., and opening into the north isle, to Edward Elwell. The seat marked No. (9) adjoining to the seat alloted to the said Edward Elwell, and opening into the north isle to Isaac Hadley Reddell. The seat marked No. (10) adjoining to the seat alloted to

Isaac Hadley Reddell, and opening into the north isle, to Elizabeth Lowe, for the use of them, the said William Whyley, John Wright, Richard Jesson, William Bullock, the elder, Joseph Jesson, William Bullock, the younger, and James Bullock, Edward Elwell, Isaac Hadley Reddell, and Elizabeth Lowe, and their several and respective families now residing or hereafter to reside, inhabit, or dwell within the parish of West Bromwich aforesaid. To sit in and use the same during the time of Divine offices within the said Parish Church. And we do hereby allot and appropriate the seats, pews, and sitting places in the new-erected gallery within the said Parish Church, to wit, those several seats, pews, or sitting places marked or numbered 11, 12, 13, 14, 15, 16, and 17, situate on the north side of the gallery to Jervoise Clarke Jervoise, Esq., for the use of himself and his tenants, occupiers of certain houses within the parish of West Bromwich aforesaid. The several seats situate on the south side of the gallery marked 23, 25, 26, 27, to the Right Honorable William, Earl of Dartmouth, and his tenants, occupiers of certain houses within the parish of West Bromwich. The seat marked No. (18) situate on the north side of the said gallery to Thomas Penn. The seat marked No. (20) situate on the west side or front of the said gallery to Joseph Barrs. The seat marked No. (21) situate on the west side or front of the said gallery to Charles Jevons. The seat marked No. (22) situate on the south side of the gallery to John Blake. The seat marked No. (24) situate on the south side of the gallery to Daniel Whitehouse.—Signed by, Wm. Whyley, Jos. Jesson, Churchwardens; Ed. Elwell, William Fieldhouse, Willm. Turton, William Bullock, Sen., William Bullock, Jun., James Bullock, Willm. Hardware, &c., &c.

It was agreed at a Vestry meeting held July 16th, 1788, that the sum of £180, then due upon altering the church, should be borrowed by the Churchwardens, Joseph Jesson and Wm. Whyley, upon the security of the parish, to be repaid by levies upon the inhabitants.—Signed by, John Wright, Richard Jesson, J. P., Ed. Elwell, Wm. Whyley, Jos. Jesson, J. Clarke Jervoise.

July 16th, 1788.—Agreed, that Richard Stanley shall be Biddle for the present year; also, that John Perkin, the Clerk, shall be paid one shilling per week for cleaning the church.

1796.—Agreed, that John Perkin, the Clerk, be paid one guinea per year, for taking care of, and winding up, the church clock.

At a Vestry meeting of the principal inhabitants of the parish of West Bromwich, in the county of Stafford, on Monday, the 12th of March, 1798, the Rev. William Jesse in the chair: It was resolved unanimously—"That whereas the French have obstinately rejected every overture for peace, and have openly threatened to invade this country, for the avow'd design of overturning the religion, the laws, and the constitution of this Kingdom; . . . That whereas the French have made, and are making, great preparations to put their threats into execution; That whereas it can be no longer doubted that the design of our enemies is to erect their standard of devastation, of carnage, and blood in the heart of this Kingdom of Great Britain, to pillage and destroy the inhabitants of this country, to ruin our manufactories, our trade, and commerce, to annihilate the power and independence of this nation, and to subject Great Britain to the insolent control, to the despotic authority and barbarous domination of the French

Directory; Therefore extraordinary exertions are necessary on our part to be opposed against the malicious and violent exertions of our enemies; That in order to make and support these extraordinary exertions it is become necessary that all parties unite, and that every individual lend his helping hand in the common cause; That it is become necessary that all persons of every rank and ability in proportion to every one's several ability should engage in a general and voluntary contribution in aid of Government for the defence of the country; That a book be immediately opened in the Vestry room to receive the contributions of the inhabitants present at this meeting; That a committee be appointed to promote the end of this meeting, and particularly that the committee do go from house to house to receive the contributions of the parish at large, and that they receive even the smallest contributions with respect from those whose abilities are not equal to their zeal; That the following persons be of the committee:—Rev. William Jesse; Edward Elwell, junr., Thomas Hadley, Churchwardens; Joseph Jesson, Richard Jesson, Richard Wright, Thomas Blakemore, Edward Elwell, Isaac Hadley, Samuel Read, Joseph Barrs. The following sums were subscribed at the Vestry meeting held the 12th day of March, 1798:—

	£	s.	d.
Richard Jesson, J.P.	100	0	0
Joseph Jesson	50	0	0
Edward Elwell	50	0	0
Thos. Blakemore, and to cover assessed taxes	100	0	0
Isaac Hadley	2	2	0
Joseph Hadley	3	3	0

	£	s.	d.
Edward Elwell, jun.	20	0	0
Samuel Read	1	1	0
Joseph Barrs	1	1	0
Richard Wright	100	0	0
W. Jesse	20	0	0
Total subscribed	£447	7	0

That these resolutions, with the amount of the sums subscribed, be inserted in the *Sun*, the *Star*, and the *Birmingham Gazette*."

Under the above on the same page is—Memorandum, 1st September, 1815.—"That the collections from house to house in the parish of West Bromwich (by order of the Prince Regent) for the relief and benefit of the families of brave men killed, and of the wounded sufferers in the signal victory of Waterloo, on the 18th of June, 1815, and in other battles of the present campaign amounted to the the sum of   which I have this day received of the several collectors, to remit to the Treasurer of the Committee of the Waterloo Fund, in London."—Chas. Townsend, Minister.

August 26th, 1807.—At a Vestry Meeting held this day, in the Parish Church of West Bromwich, for the purpose of taking into consideration several petitions to obtain licenses for selling ale, &c., in this parish :

It was the opinion of the Minister, Churchwardens, and other principal inhabitants present, that there are already sufficient and more than sufficient public ale houses in this parish, and therefore request His Majesty's Justices of the Peace that no more new licenses be granted until the present number be reduced, or without evident necessity to be signified in a proper petition for such purpose.—

W. Jesse, Minister; Jos. Hately, Jos. Halford, Churchwardens; Henry Hallam, Thos. Jesson, Walter Brinton.

At a Vestry Meeting held 10th October, 1809—Resolved "That the present Churchwardens do forthwith proceed in a legal manner against all persons and companies who refuse to pay, to enforce the payment of all church levies now in arrear, or to be granted by the next levy." (The Birmingham Canal Co. had not paid their levy.)

Sep. 16th, 1814.—At a Vestry Meeting on the same subject as above: "We, the Minister, Churchwardens, Overseers, and other Inhabitants of the Parish of West Bromwich ..., beg respectfully to represent to your Worships that there are already a sufficient number of Ale Houses in this Parish, and more than sufficient for the accommodation of the public, and that an increase thereof would only tend to promote idleness and disorderly and vicious habits. We therefore request you will be pleased to refuse granting to any other house a License for Selling of Ale or Liquors in this Parish without the consent and signature of the Minister, Churchwardens, and Overseers of the Poor for the time being, and of other respectable householders and inhabitants.—W. Jesse, Minister; James Smith, Edward Elwell, Churchwardens; T. Jesson, John Brinton, Thos. Winter, Jos. Barrs, T. P. Blakemore, E. W. Jackson.

	£	s.	d.
1815.—To cash received from Miss Holmes for Dole	2	10	0
To 50 Psalm Books in the hands of Thos. Ault, at 1/-	2	10	0
To 130 Psalm Books in the hands of Mr. Jacques, at 1/-	6	10	0
To 194 Psalm Books in the hands of the Rev. C. Townsend	9	14	0

Churchwardens' Books.

At a Vestry Meeting held on Wednesday, the 29th of July, 1818.—To take into consideration the propriety and the means of enlarging the Church. Resolved, "That the following gentlemen do constitute a Committee to ascertain the amount of subscriptions that may be raised in the parish towards the erection of a New Church, and that they do report of the same at a meeting that shall be called for the 8th day of August next. And the same gentlemen do also agree to subscribe towards the erection of a New Church, the sums affixed by them to their several names:

	£	s.	d.
John Salter	100	0	0
Jos. Hateley	100	0	0
Wm. Robbins	100	0	0
W. Bullock	100	0	0
James Bullock	50	0	0
Edward Elwell	30	0	0
Saml. Whitehouse	50	0	0
Revd. Chas. Townsend	100	0	0
Total	£630	0	0

At a meeting held in the Church Vestry, Aug. 8th, 1818 the Committee report that the following persons had agreed to subscribe as follows:

	£	s.	d.
Brought down	630	0	0
Lord Dartmouth (1st Subscription)	500	0	0
Thos. Jesson	150	0	0
Saml. Dawes	100	0	0
Willm. Izon	100	0	0
J. P. Blakemore	100	0	0

	£	s.	d.
Joseph Halford	100	0	0
William Turton	100	0	0
William James & Co.	100	0	0
Joseph Barrs	52	10	0
John Dawes	50	0	0
Joseph Hadley	50	0	0
Thomas Bullock	50	0	0
Henry Hunt	50	0	0
Thomas Tickle	50	0	0
E. W. Jackson	25	0	0
George Salter	25	0	0
Ephraim Bullock	25	0	0
Benjamin Haynes	25	0	0
Richd. Shenstone	25	0	0
Edwd. Woolfe	20	0	0
Roger Hardware	20	0	0
James Bullock, jun.	20	0	0
Silvanus Mayberry	10	10	0
Thos. Wynter	10	10	0
Edwd. Kenrick	10	10	0
George Wilkins	10	0	0
James Negus	10	0	0
Joseph Cooper	10	0	0
Arthur Gilbert	10	0	0
J. E. Sutton	10	0	0
Saml. Holloway	10	0	0
Willm. Coldicott	10	0	0
Geo. Silvester	10	0	0
Chas. Starkey	5	0	0
Mrs. Sowerby	5	0	0
Jas. Hately, junr.	5	0	0
Miss Jessons	2	0	0
&c., &c., &c.			
Total	£2639	7	0

Resolved—"That it appears from the above report that the building of a New Church or Chapel of Ease is practicable and may be effected with the aid of Parliament under the provisions of the late act passed for building new churches, and that the Rev. Mr. Townsend be requested to apply to the Rev. Dr. Outram, one of the Commissioners appointed under the said act, in order to learn from him the regular mode of making the above application for a grant of money under the said act."

Next follows a vote of thanks to Lord Dartmouth for his subscription and for his offer of endowing the Living of which latter there is a plan, but we do not put it in here in its entirety, as it was not finally settled as at first proposed. The promise of Lord Dartmouth to cause the sum of £7500 to accumulate for the benefit of this Living was thankfully accepted and finally adopted. It is mentioned that the legal sum paid by his lordship to the Perpetual Curate was £20 per annum. For the provisions of the act see the last part of the chapter in the Stanley Trust.

In addition to the previous subscriptions, James Smith, Esq., £100 or £200 towards enlarging the Old Church.

At a Vestry Meeting, 14th October, 1818.—Resolved, "That the following gentlemen be appointed a Committee to conduct all the business connected with the building of the New Church or Chapel, proposed to be erected in this parish, and that five of them be competent to act. Also, that if either of them be absent from three successive meetings, another person shall be appointed by the Committee in his place.—Messrs. Jas. Smith, Saml. Whitehouse, Thomas Jesson, Joseph Hately, Joseph Halford, William Robbins, Edward Elwell, James Bullock, William James

John Salter, William Bullock, Thomas Tickle, John Blakemore, William Turton, William Izon; the Earl of Dartmouth and the Rev. Charles Townsend to be honorary members of the committee. That Joseph Hately, Esq., be requested to undertake the office of Secretary. That the following advertisement be inserted in the London papers, and in *Aris's Birmingham Gazette*, viz.:—' West Bromwich New Church.—Any person who shall be disposed to offer plans and estimates, and to contract for the building of a new stone Church in this parish, in a plain style of Gothic architecture (! !) and sufficiently spacious to contain 2,000 persons, may obtain the requisite information on application by letter to the Rev. Chas. Townsend, or Joseph Hately, Esq., West Bromwich. The acceptance of proposals will be kept open until the 14th day of Nov. next.' That the parish do agree to petition Parliament for the passing of the Bill referred to in the minutes of the last meeting."

At a meeting held 22nd February, 1823.—For taking into consideration the contents of a letter received from the Society for promoting the enlargement and building of Churches and Chapels. The Rev. Mr. Townsend having communicated to the meeting a letter lately received from the committee of the above Society, resolved:—that Mr. Townsend be requested to answer the same to the following effect: "That it would be inexpedient to commence any alterations in the present church until the new church shall be opened for Divine Service, which may possibly be within eighteen months from this time; the peculiar circumstances connected with the bankruptcy of the contractor must render this in some degree a matter of uncertainty. That if the accommodation which shall be afforded by the two Churches shall prove insufficient for the reception of those who shall wish to attend the Church Service, any grant which the Society ... shall be pleased to make for the enlargement of the Church will be very thankfully received, but the subscriptions that have been lately paid for the erection of the new Church must for some time preclude the expectation of any considerable sum, by rate or otherwise, from the inhabitants of this place, towards the accomplishment of the said object " . . .

At a Vestry Meeting held May 23rd, 1823. Resolved: " That the very crowded state of the present Burial Ground makes it necessary that an addition should be made to the same, with as little delay as possible. That the thanks of this meeting be presented to the Earl of Dartmouth for the readiness with which he has consented to accommodate the parish with a portion of ground from his land adjoining. That the offer his lordship has made through Mr. William Pearce of one acre of the said land at the east end of the churchyard at the price of eighty pounds be accepted, and that four pounds per annum be paid to Mr. John Woodhall as an equivalent for his interest in the same until the expiration of his lease (added in pencil) which Mr. Woodhall says will be in 7 years from Lady Day 873. That the churchwardens be requested to get the additional ground walled in with good and sound materials, and that the work be commenced as soon as convenient."

At a meeting held June 25th, 1823.—It was agreed to grant the churchwardens a double levy towards defraying expenses of the purchase and inclosure of the additional Burial Ground.

Memorandum 23rd May, 1823 :
Mr. Bell agrees to serve good Bricks at 2/- per M.

Mr. Woodhall agrees to fetch the same at 10½ per M.
Do.   do.   to fetch Lime from } 7/- per Ton.
    Walsall & Hay Head at
—Wm. Salter.

At a meeting held September 24th, 1823.—A second double levy granted towards defraying the expenses of enlarging the churchyard.

At a meeting held April 17th, 1827.—Resolved: "That an organ which has been purchased (by private subscription) for the use of this Church be forthwith erected in the centre of the west gallery, under the direction of the Minister and Churchwardens, and that the expenses attending the putting up of the same and its future reparation and the salary of the organist be payable out of the church rates."

April 21st, 1829.—At a meeting held for the purpose of electing churchwardens for this Church, and the new Church or Chapel lately erected in this parish, &c. "I, William Gordon, Minister of the new Church or Chapel in this Parish of West Bromwich, do elect Mr. Joseph Hately to be one of the Church or Chapelwardens for the said new Church or Chapel for the present year." The people elected Mr. Edwin Bullock.

The estimate for the New Ground and Wall amounted to £345 2s. 11½d.

FROM THE VESTRY ORDER BOOK.

At a Vestry Meeting on October 3rd, 1828, held to authorise the Churchwardens to raise a sum of money for inclosing the Burial Ground of the New Church, resolved: "That it was necessary to take measures for inclosing the scite and burial ground, and to provide for the consecration of the Church. (2) To authorise the Churchwardens to borrow a sum of money upon the credit of the Church Rates" &c., &c.

Remark: Every person present at this meeting agreed to and signed the resolution except Mr. Kenrick.

At a Vestry Meeting 16th October, 1828:—Henry Sheldon having declared himself unable to render the Parish that effective assistance in collecting the money, noticing team duty, and nuisances, which he has hitherto done, resolved: "That in consequence of his past services, and for such assistance as he is still able to render he be allowed the sum of ten shillings per week."

April 21st, 1829.—Resolved "That Isaac Richards and John Wilson be appointed beadles of the New Church, and that they be allowed a complete suit of clothes every second year, and a great coat every fourth year." Resolved also "That from the representation made of the ruinous state of the Poors' House, the Churchwardens of the Old and New Churches and the Overseers, together with Messrs. Ephraim Bullock, John Nock, and James Male be appointed a committee to procure one or more plans and estimates for building a New Poors' House upon the land belonging to the Parish," &c.

15th Oct. 1830.—At a meeting held to determine on a petition to Parliament relative to the Emancipation of Slaves in the British Dominions. Resolved "That the petition presented by the Rev. P. G. Harper be approved, and that proper measures be taken to obtain signatures to the same."

Some of the following items, from a list entitled "Disbursements on account of the New Church," may be interesting:—

	£	s.	d.
Jan. 19th, 1829.			
To Cash, four constables, three beadles, and clerk	2	0	0
,, Singers	4	7	0
,, Cakes	0	3	0
,, Collation at Hardware's and wine at Church	6	1	0
,, To Cashmore, attending three days	0	7	6
,, Mears for large bell	152	12	0
,, Frame and fittings	35	4	0
,, Small bell	57	17	4
,, Frame and fittings	20	0	0
,, Communion table and chairs	16	0	0
,, Commandments, Prayer, and Belief	36	13	0
,, Lettering and numbering the seats	12	15	0
,, Copper gutters to windows	9	17	0
,, Gangways along roof	10	16	0
,, J. Dickenson, pulpit and vestry furniture	16	0	6
,, Borini, looking glass	0	6	6
,, Candlestick, &c.	0	3	9
,, Bateman, communion plate	61	12	0
,, Gas apparatus for lighting, as ordered by the Bishop	110	0	0
,, Bebb and Mallin, beadles' cloth	10	0	3
Dec. 29th.			
To Evans and Cashmore, assisting to keep order	1	2	0
April 20th, 1830.			
To Mr. Bebb, beadles' coats	5	7	0

The total sum amounted to £1,998 19s. 8d., and there was a balance in hand. But further levies had to be granted to meet the current annual expenses.

The Parish of Christ Church was not legally separated from the Old Church until 1837.

6th April, 1831.—Resolved "That William Barton be allowed five pounds per annum instead of one pound as formerly for his salary as parish clark at the Old Church. That James Cashmore be allowed one guinea per annum, and Isaac Richards and John Wilson ten shillings and sixpence each, in addition to the clothing now allowed, as a remuneration of their services as beadles."

21st Sept., 1831.—Resolved "That it is the opinion of this meeting that the lamentable increase of crime, and the existence of a class of persons in this Parish who live without any visible means of subsistance are sources of vice and debauchery, and strongly call for a more efficient police. 2nd.—That in the opinion of the meeting the condition of the police in this parish is very defective, and that the inefficiency of the executive arising from the want of a sufficient resident magistracy calls for immediate attention. That a committee of gentlemen be appointed to adopt such steps as they may deem advisable; to report the result of their deliberations to a general meeting."— Appointed on the Committee: Rev. James Spry, Rev. William Gordon, Mr. Izon, Mr. Kenrick, Mr. Hunt, Mr. John Dawes, Mr. Botteley, Mr. Bate, Mr. Edwin Bullock, Mr. Matthews, Mr. Hately, Mr. John Bagnall, Mr. Hood, Mr. Dorset.

Sep. 14th, 1832.—At a meeting held to receive a statement of the present expenditure of the Board of Health, and to grant a further sum of money to the Board for the purpose of carrying the Cholera Act, and the orders of His Majesty's most Honourable Privy Council—it was resolved "to adjourn to the Schoolroom at Hall End," where it was resolved "to place at the disposal of the Board of Health the sum of £250, to be paid out of the Poor Rates."

Dec. 10th, 1832.—Resolved: "That the Surveyors and Committee appointed to assist them be requested to have a plan of all the highways in the parish made by Mr. William Salter, showing the width of such highways throughout, and distinguishing such of them as were set out by the Commissioners under the West Bromwich Inclosure Act—and also showing all encroachments upon the same, and the extent of such encroachment, with the names of the parties encroaching," &c.

Feb. 26th, 1833.—At a meeting held for the purpose of determining what Stipendiary Parochial Officers shall be in future employed in this Parish, and to fix their respective salaries—Resolved: "That a House Governor and Matron be appointed; the duties of the Governor to be to ascertain the settlement of all paupers applying for parochial relief, to have the general care of the poor house, &c., &c., his salary to be £70 per annum. A Collector to be appointed to collect Poor, Highway, and Church Rates, his salary to be £60 per annum. That a general Clerk and Accomptant be appointed—salary £60."

Sept. 6th, 1833.—Resolved: "That the Surveyors be strongly recommended to cause steps to be taken for the immediate removal of a certain building standing upon a part of the Highway adjoining the Turk's Head, and that they be desired to have hand bills posted up throughout every part of the Parish, apprising all persons who have encroached, by the fences or walls, upon any of the said highways, that notices will be levied upon them to remove the same immediately, and that it is the determination of the Parish Officers to resist future encroachments of every description, whether of building or fences. That it be specified in the handbills the width which every road shall be required to be kept."

Resolved at a meeting held August 5th, 1835, "That the Churchwardens be requested to wait upon the Right Hon. The Earl of Dartmouth to state the necessity of taking some effectual steps to prevent tippling in the public and beer houses on the Sabbath Day, and to solicit his Lordship's assistance to accomplish this object."

At a meeting held April, 1841, Resolved: "That the employment of a police force is uncalled for and unnecessary," and the meeting expressed their hostility to their farther employment and maintenance.—The same meeting consented to an alteration in "Sandy Lane," described as "the diversion as intended on the right hand side of the road leading from Stone Cross to Walsall—in consideration of the road being increased in width and the improved ascent to the bridge over the Lane."

At a meeting on July 8th, 1842,—For the purpose of considering the utility of a certain road called Temple Street, leading from the Turnpike Road, opposite the Heath Terrace, towards or ending at or near the Windmill in Tantany Lane. Resolved "That the said road is not of sufficient utility to be taken into the highways of the Parish liable to be repaired by the parishioners."

At a meeting held July 29th, 1842. Resolved nnanimously, "that the following memorial be presented by Major Chetwynd to the Court of Quarter Sessions :—' The undersigned officers and ratepayers of the Parish of West Bromwich believing that the constables, watchmen, and other officers are quite sufficient to keep the peace and protect the parish, and being convinced, after a trial of nearly three years, that the police officers stationed in the Parish are unnecessary, a vexatious burden upon the poor rate, and of no service whatever, more particularly at this time, for great numbers in the parish are without any employment, and bordering on want, and quite unable to pay their levies. Your petitioners therefore respectfully solicit your Worships to discontinue the Police force in their parish, and to relieve them from contributing to their maintenance.'" Eleven signatures follow—none of importance.

At a meeting on October 8th, 1847.—To consider among other things the "Diverting of a certain public highway, situate between a certain canal bridge called Pershouse's bridge at Golds' Green and the Eagle Furnaces." Resolved: "That the Messrs. Bagnall having consented to the alteration, and proposed to make the diversion at their own expense, on the condition that they may not be called upon for a Highway Rate for the period of three years, that the proposition be acceeded to by this meeting."

February 2nd, 1849.—"Resolved to pay out of the Poor's Rates the debts incurred for enlarging, improving, and repairing the workhouse."

At a meeting 26th Sep., 1856.—Consent given to the Guardians of the Poor selling a "Piece of Land, situate in Sandwell Road and near the Cronehills, alloted for the use of the Poor House by the Commissioners under the West Bromwich Inclosure Act, containing about 4 acres."

The last list of men qualified to serve as parish constables is in 1872.

In 1842 the Rev James Spry elected Mr. James Bagnall, as one of the Wardens of St. James' Chapel.

At a Vestry meeting April 9th, 1844.—Resolved: "That the

appointment of Chapel Wardens for S. James Chapel, Hill Top, be postponed until after the consecration, when it will be made a district Church.—Francis P. Socket, Chairman; James Bagnall," &c., &c.

At a Vestry meeting held Oct. 14th, 1853.—Moved by George Frederick Muntz, Esq., M.P. (Sandwell), and carried unanimously:—"That it would be of great public advantage if the Parish of West Bromwich were sufficiently paved, drained, lighted, cleaned, and otherwise improved, and a Local Board of Health established therein; and whereas the said purpose cannot be effected without the authority of Parliament, it is therefore the opinion of this meeting that the necessary steps should be immediately taken for obtaining a Local Act for the Parish of West Bromwich in the ensuing session of Parliament." A committee was appointed consisting of above forty of the inhabitants, among them George Frederick Muntz, M.P., Rev. James Spry, Rev. James Bradshaw, Rev. Benj. Willmore, Thomas Jesson, Henry Dawes (Charlemont), Thomas Davies, William Salter, John Chance, Charles Bagnall, &c.

At a Vestry meeting held January 5th, 1855.—Resolved "That this meeting do consent to the sale to the Guardians of the Poor of the West Bromwich Union of the land allotted for the use of the poor." The land is described farther on as "a piece of land formerly part of a croft in the Parish of West Bromwich, containing a frontage of thirty yards or thereabouts next the road to Lyndon, and the like frontage next Stoney-lane, together with a dwelling-house and buildings erected thereon, used as a poor house and called the West Bromwich Workhouse."

At a Vestry meeting held April 26th, 1859.—It was proposed by Mr. John Nock Bagnall, and seconded by the

Rev. Isaac Bickerstaff: "That the best thanks of this meeting be accorded to the Earl of Dartmouth for his liberal gift of an acre of land to enlarge the churchyard of this parish." Two Sidesmen were first elected in this year. —June 24th, 1859—William Barton, the Parish Clerk, having resigned, the Rev. James Spry appointed Henry Wilkins to that office.

At a Vestry meeting April 22nd, 1862.—Resolved: "That as Mr. Thomas Jesson has decided upon declining the office of Churchwarden, the meeting beg to express their deep debt of gratitude to him for the very faithful and conscientious manner in which he has invariably discharged the office for the last 25 years."

Mr. Bickerstaff left for Bonsall in 1863, and Mr. Kyrke was appointed Curate-in-charge. In 1865 the Rev. Edward Lloyd Edwards was in charge until August in that year, when the Rev. James Spry died. The chair was taken by Mr. Edwards, in the absence of the Rev. Frederic Willett, the newly-appointed Perpetual Curate, on 12th April, 1866. Four Sidesmen were then elected.

December 8th, 1870.—A Vestry meeting was held "To adopt plans, and to apply for a Faculty for the restoration of the Old Parish Church."

The Vicar having produced and explained the intended plans to the meeting assembled, it was proposed by Mr. Arthur Wright, seconded by Mr. Richard Bagnall, and carried: "That the following gentlemen be appointed a committee to examine more particularly the said plans and to report thereon to the Vicar at an early date."— Arthur Wright, Charles Jaques, Thomas Salter, Thomas Jesson, Joshua Fellows, Henry Duncalfe, and Richard Bagnall.

April 28th, 1871.—Resolved: "That the committee appointed by Vestry on December 8th, 1870, having recommended the erection of a North Aisle, and that the Vestry and Tower be left intact, and plans in accordance with this recommendation having been been placed on the table; and as well amended plans placing the Aisle on the South side; that the amended plans be adopted."

In 1872, eight Sidesmen were elected and two lay representatives at the Ruridecanal and Archidecanal Conferences.

November 1st, 1872.—At a meeting, resolved: "That the meeting having heard from the Vicar the proposed improvement of the north-west corner and west wall of the churchyard, hereby sanction any arrangements that may be made between the Vicar and Churchwardens on the one hand, and the West Bromwich Improvement Commissioners on the other, for the proposed improvement; and further sanction the application for a Faculty to carry out the same."

Twelve Sidesmen were first appointed on April 17th, 1876.

At the end of the first book are the following entries:—

May 14, 1682.—Collected there in the Parish of West Bromwich the sume of one pound four shillings eight pence for the reliefe of distressed protestants driven out of ffrance, subscribed, Samuel Addenbrooke, Minister; Job Simcox, John Carles, Churchwardens; Jan. 29th & 30th, 1689.—Collected in the Parish of West Bromwich, from house to house by virtue of a letter patten for the fire in the Town of Bungay, the sume of one pound six shillings & two pence, subscribed by Samuel Addenbrook, Minister; Thomas Darby & Willm Birch, Churchwardens.

ffebruary 12th, 1689.—Collected then in the parish of West Bromwich, for a fire in Alresford in Hampsh., the sum of ten shillings, subscribed by Samuel Addenbrook, Minister; Thomas Darby & Willm Birch, Churchwardens. Jan. 24, 1690.—Collected then in ye parish of West Bromwich for a fire in Surry, in ye County of Southwark (Sic.), ye Sum of 18^s, Subs^{d.} by Sam. Addenbrook, Edward Blakemore, Ragger Southall. Jan. 18, 1690.—Collected then in the parish of West Bromwich for a fire in East Smithfield, in Middlesex, ye sum of twelf shillings & two pence halph-peney. Sepr. 24, 1694.—Collected there in ye parish of West Bromwich fro house to house for the french protestants, the sum of £4—16s.—4d., paid unto the Archdeacon ye ffirst of October, at his visitation, subscribed by Sam. Addenbrook, Minist.; Rich. Hodkins, Will. Dudley, Parish Wardens.

May 19th, 1695.—Collected in the parish of West Bromwich for ye fire at Warwick, the sum of nine pounds & two pence half-peney, Subs^{d.} by Samuel Addenbrook, Minist.; Nath. Wiley, Edward Whitehouse, Churchwardens. Two more collections from house to house, the object not named. July 7th, 1689.—Then collected from house to house, in the parish of West Bromwich by virtue of a letter patten for distressed protestants coming out of Ireland, the sum of fourten pounds four shillings sixpence. April 25th, 1690.—The sum of three pounds eleven shillings nine pence (for the same object).

Oct. 30th, 1692.—Collected fro house to house in the parish of West Bromwich, by virtue of two letter pattens, one for ye redemption of   & for a fire at Cayford, ye sum of one pound one shilling sixpence.

CHURCHWARDENS OF WEST BROMWICH.

The following list of Churchwardens, compiled by C. H. Bayley, Esq., the Town Clerk, will be read with interest.

- 1678 William Turton, Richard Wheeler.
- 1679 Richard Bun, William Hadley.
- 1680 Richard Sterry, William Stamps.
- 1681 Joshua Whyley, John May.
- 1682 John Carless, Job Simcox.
- 1683 John Wiley, Samuel Allins.
- 1684 John Hadley, Moses Bird.
- 1685 Samuel Westwood, Richard Allen.
- 1686 Nehemiah Bague, Bayly Bratt.
- 1687 Richard Fisher, Humphry Roe.
- 1688 Christopher Uppton, William Undrell.
- 1689 Thomas Darby, William Birch.
- 1690 Edward Blakemore, Roger Southall.
- 1691 Thomas Jesson, John Grafton.
- 1692 Joseph Worseley, Humphry Dudley.
- 1693 John Cullwill, Jeffrey Dudley.
- 1694 Richard Hodgkins, William Dudley.
- 1695 Nathaniel Wiley, Edward Whitehouse.
- 1696 Edward Dudley, William Collins.
- 1697 Benjamin Lowe, Edward Horton.
- 1698 John Blakemore, Richard Marsh.
- 1699 William Medley, Henry Frith.
- 1700 Simon Partridg, Henry Partridg.
- 1701 Humphry Hemmins, William Smith.
- 1702 John Hawkes, John Richards.
- 1703 John Jesson, John Roe.
- 1704 William Sterry, Samuel Collins.
- 1705 William Stampes, Josiah Brookes.
- 1706 William Selvister, John Horton.

1707	William Simcox, Joseph Harris.
1708	Henry Freeth, John Mayow.
1709	Robert Capper, William Wiley.
1710	Thomas Dudley, Mathew Dudley.
1711	Benjamin Lowe, John Cullet.
1712	ditto John Culwick.
1713	Joseph Freeth, Thomas Brett.
1714	ditto. ditto
1715	Isaac Wyley, Joseph Hawkes.
1716	Joseph Freeth, Richard Jesson.
1717	ditto ditto
1718	ditto ditto
1719	ditto ditto
1720	Robert Capper, William Wyley.
1721	Joseph Freeth, Henry Freeth.
1722	John Jesson, Joseph Hopkins.
1723	John Westwood, Joseph Wright.
1724	Edward Walthew, Thomas Follis.
1725	William Whiley, Job Reeves.
1726	John Oakley, Henry Cole.
1727	Thomas Powell, Richard Sheldon.
1728	ditto ditto
1729	ditto ditto
1730	John Marsh, Edward Baker.
1731	ditto ditto
1732	Nathaniel Whiley, Job Reeves,
1733	ditto ditto
1734	Thomas Jesson, Thomas Dudley.
1735	John Parks, Edward Osborne.
1736	Job Reeves, John Marsh.
1737	ditto ditto
1738	Thomas Green, Edward Gibbons

Churchwardens' Books.

1739 Joseph Wall, Richard Sheldon.
1740 Joseph Wright, Nathaniel Whyley.
1741 Nathaniel Whyley, James Whitehouse.
1742   ditto   ditto
1743 John Selvester, John Meakin, jnr.
1744   ditto   ditto
1745 Jeremiah Wright, Joseph Stevens.
1746   ditto   ditto
1747 James Whitehouse,   ditto
1748   ditto   ditto
1749 Joseph Baker,   ditto
1750   ditto   ditto
1751 Ralph Moore,   ditto
1752 Thomas Willson,   ditto
1753 Ralph Moor,   ditto
1754 Thomas Ford, Thomas Wilson.
1755   ditto   Richard Sheldon.
1756 Benjamin Partridge,   ditto
1757   ditto   Joseph Wall.
1758 Thomas Wilson,   ditto
1759 George Cowper, William Fieldhouse.
1760   ditto   ditto
1761 Isaac Whitehouse   ditto
1762   ditto   ditto
1763   ditto   ditto
1764 William Bullock,   ditto
1765   ditto   John Wall.
1766   ditto   Joseph Jesson.
1767   ditto   ditto
1768 Nathaniel Freeth,   ditto
1769   ditto   Richard Jesson.
1770 Richard Jesson, John Stampes.
1771   ditto   William Fieldhouse.

Extracts from Papers in the Vestry.

1763.—9 pence received for windo tax.

Henry Hubbard will engage to cure the Vestry chimney for £3 13 6. No cure, no pay.

A paper is signed by Lord Dartmouth, dated February 5th, 1829, requesting the Churchwardens to summon a meeting of the Earl of Dartmouth and the Stanley Trustees, to elect one of the two Clergymen whom the Earl had chosen to be the Minister of the new church, his power being given by an Act of Parliament.

"Sir,—You will perceive by the enclosed bill that I have expended 5/- more than I received on account of the proceedings and advertisement of the two men for disturbing the Rev. Mr. White, &c.

"Wm. Coldicott, Jan. 1st, 1819."

"Birmingham, 11th Dec., 1824.

"Dr. Sir,—I have perused the resolutions of the Inhabitants of West Bromwich assembled in Vestry of the 19th May, 1819, and carefully considered the question how far you, as Churchwarden, are justified in paying the salaries of the seven special constables appointed by the Vestry meeting. I do not think the special constables can be considered as your assistants for all the purposes mentioned in the resolutions. For instance, they are 'To suppress the disorderly proceedings of any persons publickly assembled together on the Lord's Day without lawful occasion.' Now it is no part of your duty to suppress the disorderly proceedings alluded to, unless they take place in the church or churchyard. The Constable of the Parish is the proper person to preserve the peace and suppress the disorderly proceedings alluded to.

"By Resolution 2—'The Assistant Constables are to see that the public houses are not kept open during the hours of Divine Service on the Lord's Day, nor after 9 o'clock at night, nor for the purpose of tippling during any part of the day.' The Churchwardens as well as the Constables are by Statute (4 James II, 5, s. 7) and their oaths required to prevent tippling as well on Sundays as other days. Whether the Magistrates have ordered all public houses in your parish to be closed at 9 o'clock at night or not, I think it is the Constable's duty and not the Wardens' to see that they are closed at that hour.

"The 3rd Resolution is, 'To see that the butchers, hucksters, and other shopkeepers do not keep open their shops on the Lord's Day after 9 o'clock in the forenoon.'

"The 4th Section requires 'The Assistant Constables to assist the Churchwardens in clearing the church yard and church porch of all idle persons loitering there during the time of Divine Service.'

"CLEMENT INGLEBY.

"James Smith, Esq.,
  "Hall Green House."

"SIR,—I, Daniel Howard, do agree to take down the old stone of the parapet wall of the church, and re-build the same with Gornal stone for £35.

	£	s.	d.
To make four Pinnacals complate	16	0	0
,, ,, new figers at £4 each	8	0	0
,, ,, coping for do, at 9d. per foot, soposing to amount to	6	0	0
And to take of the top of the tower stare case, and to work and set a new doore	1	6	0
17th March, 1824."	66	0	0

"Gentlemen i hope i shall not offend you with a few lines which I now present to your consideration concerning sweping the church and making the fires: we have but one shilling a week alowed for sweepin the church and this was i believe the pay many years ago when there was no fires made. We have now made fires 6 years without any more alowance, if you please to alow us any more i shall take it as a great favour.   "I am, gentlemen,
                        "Your humble servant,
"March 28th, 1815."   "THOMAS AULT.

Dr., the Parish of West Bromwich, to James Smith.

	£	s.	d.
Bird, one urchin	0	0	4
Sheldon, one do.	0	0	4
Harrison, sparrow heads	0	0	4
Fones, „ „	0	0	4
Tom Wallis, 2½ doz. „	0	0	10
The Clergyman's expenses at Visitation	1	1	0
The Assistant Constables	8	15	0
Tom Wallis, sparrow heads	0	0	4
Davis, one urchin	0	0	4
Tom Wallis, sparrow heads	0	0	4
Edward Fones, one urchin	0	0	4
Harrison, sparrow heads	0	0	6

EXTRACTS FROM THE PARISH REGISTERS.

The Stranger that died at John Sabin's was buried the 8th day of August, 1614.

Robert Middlemore, gent., was buried 17th January, 16¼¾.

John Haickley buried the 22nd of January, 162⁰⁄₁.

Richard Wains, gent., buried August 27th, 1621.

Sampson, son of Samuel Gower, gent., baptized 12th Dec., 1621.

Robert ffoster, gent., was buried the last daye of Sep., 1626.

William Blackmore and Winifred Dolphin married May 27th, 1627.

Mr. Willobey had a son buried Nov. 2d, 1636, unchristened.

Thomas, son of Thomas Willoughbye and Elizabeth his wife, baptized 28th June, 1638.

Mary, the daughter of a poore woman, was buried the second daye of May, 1645.

There was one of Darleston buried the 14th of february, 164⅞.

Edward Cotterell, a Beggar, was buried 26th April, 1655.

Robert Vames, Wednesbury, ffordgman, was buried Oct. 11th, 1656.

Martha, daughter of Henry Avery, of the Rod Mill, and Mary his wife, born Nov. 21, 1656.

Danniel, the sonne of John Kilham, cole w^r (worker ?), and Ann his wyfe, was born 3rd July, 1657.

Henry Stone, the Parliamentarian, signed several Marriage Registers in 1655, &c. Sir John Wyrley (Hamstead), signed others, also Mr. W. Smith, Maior of Walsall.

Anne, the daughter of John Kirtland, phisitian, and Mary, his wyfe, was born the 20th day of April, 1657.

Samuel, son of William Truford, of the Forge, born Feb. 27, 165⅞.

John, the sonne of Henry Frith, of Sandwell, was borne the fourth daye of Sep., 1659.

———, the daughter of Mr. Richard Careless and ———, borne 13th Feb., 164⅞.

Elizabeth, wife of Mr. John Simcox, was buried 30th April, 1662.

Thomas Simcox was buried the 24th of August, 1663, the son of Mr. John Simcox.

Abigail, the daughter of Mr. John Simcox, was baptized 23rd Oct., 1664.

Mrs. Gage was buried the 23th day of July, 1666.

Mr. Ilford was buried the 29th day of August, 1666.

Gervase, the son of Mr. Walter Nedham, was baptized August 23rd, 1667.

Mr. Walter, son of Mr. Walter Nedham, was baptized Sep. 29, 1669.

Mr. Walter, son of Mr. Walter Nedham, was buried —— day of Oct., 1669.

James, the son of James Turner, a stranger, was baptized the 28th day of June, 1669.

Miss Elizabeth, daughter of Mr. Walter Nedham, was baptized 12th November, 1670.

John Walton, the sonne of William Walton, of Wardeind, in the parish of Aston, was born the 5th day of January, 1649, and this eyer being 1670, 21 eares old.

The Bishop's Visitation the 17th day of Nov., 1676.

Mrs. Stone was buried 18th January, 167⅞.

1679, October the 2nd, was the Bishop's Visitation.

John Doley, who came from Tamworth, was buried in woollen only, the 16th of Sep., 1680.

John Rider, a child so named, was buried in woollen only, 18th January, 16⅞.

1682, Sep. the 12th, was the Bishop's Visitation at Lichfield.

Mary, the daughter of John Hadley, was born the 28 day of ffebary, at a levn of the cocke at naight, and was baptized the 6 day of Aprell, 1686.

Mr. Jeremiah Addenbrook, of the parish of Kingswinford, and Mrs. Sarah Ropear, of the parish of King's Norton, were married Nov. 21, 1693.

Dillee, the daughter of Mr. Charles Louther, baptized the 30th June, 1694.

Mr. William Bach and Mrs. Jane Addenbrook married January 7th, 169⅔.

A certificate that Jonathan Brooks was free from his master and father to serve any other person, was subscribed under the hands and seals of the Minister and Churchwardens the 6th April, 1696.

Mary, daughter of Mr. Josiah Simcox, was baptized Nov. 29, 1707.

Mr. John Gilpin was buried October 10th, 1709.

John Spilsbury Witton, son of Richard Witton, born Jan. 3d, 1724, and baptized 14th Jan., 1724.

Richard Sergeant Witton, son of Richard Witton, born August 8th, baptized Aug 18th, 1726.

Mrs. Freeth was buried Feb. 1st, 1729.

Mr. Allen was buried June 12th, 1729.

Mr. Joseph Rann was buried Oct. 7th, 1735.

Mrs. Silvester, widow, was buried July 15th, 1743.

A woman that died on ye rode was buried July 28.

John, the son of Mr. Fledge Mattox, was buried Feb. 1, 1745.

Marye, daughter of Mrs. Abney, was buried June 28th, 1747.

Mr. Joseph White was buried July 15th, 1752.

Mr. Henry Hunt was buried May 21st, 1761.

Mary, daughter of the Rev. Thos. and Mary Davenport, baptized Aug. 16th, 1765.

Mrs. Mary Abney was buried June 2nd, 1770.

Amey, an old woman out of the workhouse known by no other name, was buried Oct. 16th, 1773.

The Rev. Mr. Howell was buried Feb. 14th, 1776.

Mrs. Phebe Flower was buried Aug. 27th, 1781.

The Rev. Luke Booker, L.L.D., of Dudley, and Ann Blakemore, of this parish, were married Jan. 5th, 1796.

John Lewis Moilliet, of Birmingham, merchant, and Amelia Keir, were married May 19th, 1801.

William Robbins, of S. Martin's, Birmingham, and Jane Blakemore, were married April 28th, 1801 (by L. Booker).

Mrs. Keir, wife of James Keir, Esq., was buried Nov. 25, 1802.

Ann, wife of the Rev. Luke Booker, was buried May 19th, 1806.

John, son of the Rev. Luke Booker, was buried June 15th, 1810; aged 14.

John Richard Booker died June 18th, 1810; aged 13.

James Keir died Oct. 11th, 1820; aged 85.

DOLES IN THE PARISH.—TITHE DOLE.

Sir William Whorwood, in the year 1614, gave, by will, £6 12s. 0d. to be paid equally to 33 poor inhabitants of West Bromwich, and such poor of Handsworth as dwell along the highway near Sandwell, viz., to every one a like portion as near as they can divide it, payable at West Bromwich Church on Christmas Eve and Good Friday for ten years after his decease; and after ten years, then £10 yearly for ever out of the tythes of West Bromwich. Lord Dartmouth now pays this dole.

BRICK KILN DOLE.

In 1635 Sir Thomas Whorwood, Knight, purchased land called the Brick Kiln Land out of the arrears of rent devised to the poor of West Bromwich by the will of Sir William Whorwood, deceased, and gave it to trustees for the poor for ever. First trustees—Edward Grove,

Thomas Grove, John Turton the younger, &c. 1691, trustees: John Turton, of The Oak, Thomas Jesson, John Lowe, Henry Hunt, John Turton, of Hately Heath. 1722, John Turton, Josiah Turton, &c., &c.

This dole was always given away in single shillings on S. Thomas' Day. In 1870 the Vicar, Churchwardens, and Trustees met together, and finally came to the conclusion to spend the money arising from the dole in blankets, to be divided among the ecclesiastical parishes. Instead of a shilling, spent and gone in a few hours, many a family is now yearly thankful for the comfort of a warm blanket.

With regard to this dole, among the Church papers is a notice, dated 1862, which says:—The land is situate at the back of the Lodge Grounds. The mines under this property have been sold to William Izon, Esq., and £6:9 1s. 4d. paid to the Official Trustee of the Charity Commissioners at the Bank of England, for investment in Government Securities.

PUDDING LAND DOLE.

William Turton, the elder, of West Bromwich (by indenture made May 10th, 1635), gave, granted, and confirmed to the following as trustees, William Turton, the younger, John Turton, and Thomas Turton, sons of said William Turton, and to John Jesson, one yearly rent of 40s. payable on one cottage, garden, orchard, and one croft situate in Lyndon, between land of William Stanley, Esq., and the lane commonly called Hargett Lane; also on one days earth of arable land lying in West Bromwich, in a common field there called Church Field, between a way there leading through the same field from Lyndon towards the Parish Church of West Bromwich of the one part, and the land late of William Orme of the other part; and also on all those leasows, meadows, &c., called Pudding Land, lying in West Bromwich, between land of William Stanley, in the occupation of George Kenrick, the King's highway leading from Birmingham towards Wolverhampton, and the lane leading from Greete Bridge towards Harvell's Oak, which premises the said William Turton purchased of one Wm. Colmore, of Birmingham, gent.

In 1643 there was a fresh appointment of trustees, also in 1680, when there were three William Turtons living in West Bromwich, viz., William Turton of the Oak House, gent., William Turton, of the Mill, gent., and William Turton, of Hateley Heath, gent.

Deed of appointment of trustees in 1680 is between William Turton, of Orgreave, son and heir of John Turton, the elder, late of West Bromwich, deceased, &c.

Deed, dated 8th February, 1722, appointing new Trustees, who were John Turton, of the Oak House, gent.; Samuel and Jesson Lowe, sons of John Lowe; Richard and Thomas Brett; Thomas Jesson; William Turton, son of Josiah Turton, of the Mill House,; John Jesson, &c., &c. There are several other deeds relating to this Trust.

"In the year 1701, Mrs. Eleanor Turton, of the Mill, in this parish, gave Five pounds per annum, chargeable on an Estate at the Mill aforesaid, now in possession of Josiah Turton, viz:—£2 10s. to the poor inhabitants of West Bromwich, and £2 10s. to the poor of Oldbury, in the county of Salop, to be disposed of at the discretion of the Minister and Churchwardens, on Good Friday, for ever."

This was afterwards called Abney's Dole.

The Dole is now paid by the Izon Family, whose iron-works occupy the site of "The Mill."

MOORE'S CHARITY.

Ralph Moore, and Phœbe, his wife, of this parish, by deed in 1761, gave to fourteen Trustees, for the use of the poor who do not receive collection from the parish, an House and Land rented at four pounds ten shillings per annum, to be paid on New Year's Day, and on Midsummer Day.

TERRIER, 1693.

A true note and Terrier of the profits allowed and given to the Minister, in the parish of West Bromwich.... Thomas Broom Whorwood, Esq., being Impropriator, alloweth to him that supplieth his cure there in money a salary of twenty pounds per ann., and a house to live in, with the garden and backside adjoining to the said house, and all the accustomed Surplice Fees of the parish aforesaid, for every burial in the church, one shilling; for every burial in the churchyard, fourpence; for every christening and churching, fourpence; for every marriage, with a license, five shillings; for every marriage, with open publication of banns, two shillings; and mortuaries according to the Statute in that case.

Besides, Walter Stanley, Esq., deceased, formerly Lord of the Manor of West Bromwich aforesaid, intrusted certain men as Feoffees with the disposal of the rents of thirty-two pounds thirteen shillings and fourpence, which Land is in the parish of Sutton, and in the parish of Aston, &c., &c., and in Wednesbury, in the county of Stafford, which rents the Feoffees hereafter mentioned, may, if they please, give to the Minister, if they approve of him, to preach a sermon in the Parish Church aforesaid every Sunday, or they can dispose of the aforesaid rents to another, as they think fit. The names of the present

Feoffees are as followeth :—John Shelton, Esq., John Turton, gent., Nehemiah Bague, Henry Hunt, Richard Shelton, &c.; subscribed by Samuel Addenbrook, Minister.

Mr. Rann's Certificate for Mortuaries.

"I do hereby certify that while I was Minister of West Bromwich, in the county of Stafford, I always received Mortuaries from housekeepers worth forty seven and upwards in moveable goods, according to the custom of my predecessors.—Witness my hand J. Rann; in the presence of Jos. Jesson, John Wright. 13 July, 1762."

West Bromwich, July 22nd, 1751.—A Terrier of the lands and profits belonging to the Church of West Bromwich:—

There is an house consisting of about two bays of building and a garden, about a quarter of an acre of land; Walter Stanley, Esq., gave certain lands, &c., &c. . . . ffrom which by timber sold there has since been purchased an estate in the parish of Wednesbury, which is lett at two pounds thirteen shillings and fourpence per annum. . . . The Impropriator, the Earl of Dartmouth, pays the Curate £20 per annum. Burying in the churchyard, sixpence; in the church, one shilling; in the chancel, two; registering, sixpence; marriages by banns, two shillings; by license, five shillings; mortuaries according to the Statute.—Peter Jones, Minister.

Delivered the Terrier the 4th of Sep., 1755.

SANDWELL HALL.

THIS House stands on the site of a Benedictine Priory, originally a Hermitage, founded by William, son of Guy de Opheni, about 1180.

The name "Sandwell" is from the spring on the lawn in front of the house, but not, as is popularly supposed, from "Sancta Fons," or Holy Well. Mr. Cox, writing on the subject, says, "I do not know any single place name that is a combination of Latin and Anglo-Saxon. Surely the first syllable, like scores of similar cases, is from the Anglo-Saxon "Sand" or "Sond"—our "Sand," (it was often spelt Sondwell in early days), thus making it the Sandy Well, or the Well sunk in Sandstone." No doubt this well was renowned in early days, and close by it the Hermitage was established.

Dugdale's account of this Priory will be given, taken from the 4th vol. of the "Monasticon," containing a copy of the charter of Gervase Pagnel, Baron of Dudley, confirming the founder's donation; also a short account from Shaw, and extracts from a small work on Sandwell by Miss Selwyn; also, as far as possible, a list of the Priors to the time of the Dissolution.

The property, as will be seen, at length passed to the Whorwood family, and eventually thence to the Earl of Dartmouth, whose descendent, the present Earl, now owns it.

Of this ancient Priory Dugdale* gives the following account:—"This little Priory was founded in the latter end of the reign of King Henry the Second, or the beginning of that of King Richard the First, by William, son of Guy de Opheni or Offney, in the hermitage in Bromwich, near the well called Sandwell. It was situated in the Parish of West Bromwich, and was dedicated to S. Mary Magdalen. Gervase Pagnel, Lord of the honor of Dudley, of which barony the lands at Bromwich were holden, confirmed the founder's donations. The possessions of this Priory are not enumerated in the taxation of Pope Nicholas IV., except that in the Church of Ellesborough (Elesberge), Bucks, the Prior of Sandwell is said to have two portions, one of the value of £1 13s. 4d., the other of £6 13s. 4d. per annum. This house was one of those which were suppressed, and given, in the 17th of Henry VIII., to Cardinal Wolsey, when it was endowed with spiritualities to the yearly value of £12, and temporalities to the amount of £26 8s. 7d."

The only Priors of Sandwell who have occurred are John, who was witness to a deed of Ralph Basset made to Canwell Priory, in Staffordshire, apparently about the time of Edward I.

John Tamworth, upon whose resignation (a pension of eleven marks being allowed to him),

John de Acton was appointed, Jan. 3rd, 1400. "Jure dom. Archiepiscopo Cantuar. devoluto."[1]

William Pruyne occurs Prior in the reign of Henry Sixth, upon whose resignation,

John Atton was elected "per viam Spiritus Sancti."

---

* Monasticon, vol. IV.,

[1] Ducaret's Extract from the Lamb Registers, vol. XV., p. 917.

He was presented for confirmation to the Abbot of S. Peter, Shrewsbury, April 4th, 1436.

The following is a copy of the charter of Gervase Pagnel :—

"Cartæ ad Sandwellense Cænobium in agro Staffordiensi spectantes.

"Carta Gervasii Paganelli domini Honoris de Dudley de Monasterio de Sandwell confirmando, nuper vocato Heremetagium de Bromwich. (Ex vetusto examplari penes Ricardum Shilton de West Bromwich in com. Staff., equit. aurat).

"Gervasius Paganellus dominus de Dudley omnibus anglis et alienigenis salutem et fidelitatem. Quia rationabiles dispositiones de rebus ecclesiasticis et earum possessionibus factæ sub plurium testationibus ratæ haberi debent, idcirco notum vobis facio Willielmum filium Guidonis de Offney, meum militem, quoddam heremitagium in Bromwich juxta fontem qui dicitur Sandwell scituatum monstrasse et monachis in eodem moraturis perpetualliter totum territorium circa predictum fontem et heremitagium donasse, et quosdam tenentes in Bromwich et Waueram in Honesworth cum eorum sequeeis, terris redditibus, et omnibus servitiis, sine aliquo sibi vel hæredibus suis retenemento, in liberam, puram, et perpetuam elemosynam, assartum de Ruworth, Duddesrudding, et solum inter Petulf Greene et viam regiam usque Wauer et le Burne, ecclesiam de Esselburgh cum manso quantum est de feodo nostro de baronia de Dudley, puteum apud Wich, molendinum apud Grete, decimas pagnagii, venationis molendinorum suorum panis cervisiæ, ferculorum de coquina domus suæ et hæredum suorum, lignum ad focum et ad omnia sua ædificia reparanda, pasturam ubique per totum manerium suum tempore anni ad omne genus animalium suorum et tenentium suorum, liberè pacificè et quietè imperpetuam. Quos quidem monachos et eorum successores benigne recipio in meam protectionem et defensionem, et omnes donationes de meo feodo eisdem collatas et deinceps conferendas, absque aliqua actione et clameo, in liberam, puram et perpetuam elemosynam, pro me et hæredibus meis concedo, et corroboro sigillo meo authentico. Hiis testibus, Dapifero de Parles, Osberto de Bosco, Johanne Albo, Petro Sacerdote, et aliis."

The following extract is taken from a little book intituled "Chronicles of Sandwell," by L. F. Selwyn, published in 1875:—

"In the King's Rembrance Office, Exchequer, are to be found the Letters Patent from King Richard II. to the Prior of Sandwell, made in the 14th year of his reign. This Monastery was in subjection to the Bishops of Lichfield, and many proofs still exist in the Archives preserved at Lichfield of the control exercised by the Bishop over the affairs of the community. The following is an extract from Records in the Diocesan Register at Lichfield, proving the jurisdiction exercised by the Bishops of Lichfield over the affairs of the Monastery.

"In the Diocesan Register of Bishop Roger de Northburg, 1322.58, p. 17, is found a document entitled: "Pro Priore et Conventu de Sandwell." It recites a Prior's complaints against persons unknown for various trespasses on the conventual rights and property, and requires the neighbouring Incumbents to denounce the crime and threaten excommunication.

"In page 9 is found a monition from the Bishop, as visitor to the Brethren, rebuking them for factiousness, in settling their common interests, bidding them appoint an efficient porter, and appeal to the conscience of a Brother, who was, as reported, minded to go to the Roman court to obtain a dispensation from his vows.

"Another monition requires all in the convent to be obedient to the Superior.

"Another recites the Prior's application to the Bishop, on visitation, to receive his resignation on account of age and blindness. The Bishop receives his resignation, and with consent of the Fraternity, makes provision for his comfort. He assigns him the new chamber adjoining the dormitory, with the shrubbery next the cemetery, and the stewpond and dovecot in the same. After his death these are to serve for the comfort of the Brethren in the infirmary. When he shall choose to dine at the Prior's table, the Prior to minister to him. When he prefers his own chamber he is to have the allowance of two monks, 20s. per annum for clothing, and a garçon to serve him.

"On page 137 is one entry entitled: Concerning the Prior and Convent of Sandwell, that they may not alienate their possessions indiscreetly. It also recites a complaint by patrons of waste, by neglect, by sale, and long leasing, and enjoins the Prior to desist from his proceedings under pain of excommunication.

"By the original deed of gift, copies of which are preserved by Dugdale, Gervase Pagnel, Lord of the Manor of Dudley, confirmed the founder's donation, granting to the Monastery perpetual possession of the lands situated near the well called Sandwell, the site of the former Hermitage, and also of several adjacent Manors, which are specified as the property thus made over to the Church. The Church was dedicated to S. Mary Magdalen, and its foundations can still be traced in the existing buildings. Remains also of a cloister can be seen, and an ancient doorway still remains; but the greater part of the original buildings being of wood, have long since disappeared, and such as were of stone having been demolished, the massive materials have been employed in building the present mansion, and the boundary wall of the Park.

"It appears from the records of the Parish of Ellesborough that in January, 1223, Thomas de Bardony was presented to the rectory by the Prior and Convent of Sandwell.

"This entry, and that of several other Rectors of Ellesborough presented to the living by the Prior of Sandwell, was made by the Rev. R. Armistead, who states that they were given him by Brown Willis, Esq., who collected them out of all the old records now extant.

"After the dissolution in 1524, the following entry occurs in the Ellesborough Registry, 'Robert Colmor, A.M., was presented, May 1st, 1532, upon the death of Kinnersley, by the presentation of the Prior and Convent of Shene." Observe—Sandwell was dissolved in 1524, and given to endow Cardinal Wolsey's College (Christ Church) at Oxford, on whose attainder King Henry gave Sandwell to Shene, now called Richmond.

"A stone coffin has been found among the remains of the Priory, and on the lawn front of the mansion the 'Sancta Fons,' or Holy Well, is still remaining, from which the Priory derived its name.*

"The following remarkable entries are found in Bishop Stretton's Register, A.D. 1361 :—

"'Brother Henry de Kyderminstre, Monk, inducted into Priorship vacant by death of William del Ree. Henry

---
* See page 143.

de Kyderminstre, being sole surviving Monk, had the sole right of election of Prior. This he ceded to the Bishop, who thereupon appoints him Prior over the empty cells of the Priory. A letter from the Bishop to the Prior elect, explaining the circumstances, is entered in the register.'

"2nd entry, April, 1379.—'John de Kyngeston having resigned the Priorship of Sandwell, he and William de Dunstable were the sole members of the Convent. They conceded their right of election to the Bishop, who thereupon appointed Richard de Westbury, Benedictine Monk and Priest, to the Priorship, with a very touching charge to him to labour for the revival of the Convent.'"

From the extracts Miss Selwyn took from the Episcopal Registers, it would appear that the list of the Priors of Sandwell given in Dugdale's "Monasticon" is not quite accurate. The Priory does not seem to have been very flourishing, and its dissolution in 1524 was a wise step according to the plans of Cardinal Wolsey—which were to merge small and almost useless Priories, and apply the funds thereof to other church purposes. The appropriation by the King was a very different affair.

The entry respecting Sandwell in the taxation of Pope Nicholas IV. is as follows :—

"Bromwych appr. pr. et conv. de Sandwell, vi. Marc'. viii. s. A.D. 1291

"Taxaco bonorum Temporalium Prioris de Sandwell, Prior de Sandwell habet apud Sandwell in Decan' de Tamworth tres carucat' terre et valet caruc' p ann. x. s. Et habet ibm de prosicuis staur' p. ann. cum pastur' x. s. Et habet ibm de prato. p. ann. dim' Marc'. Et habet ibm de duobus Molend' p. ann. x. s. Et de reddit' assis. p. ann. xl. s. Suma iiii. l. xvi. s. viii. d. Inde Dec, ix. s. viii. d."

The following transcript is taken from Dugdale:—

"Transcript from Survey, temp: Hen: VIII., in the Chapter House, Westminster, as to the Site and Buildings.

'SANDWALL, IN COM: STAFF:

'The chauncell there is in length xlj. ffote and in brede: xviii. ffote, and syled ov: and covd wth shyngull, and in dekay.

'Itm, iii. glassed wyndouez, cont: x paynez of imagerie worke, w^t a litle wyndow glassed.

'Itm, a tabull of the high awter.

'Itm, to imagez, one fully gilded and thother but paynted.

'Itm, the seyte in ye chauncell.

'Itm, the chauncell is pavyd w^t bryk.

'Itm, the iron of the glassed wyndow.

'Itm, the belframe standing bet: the chauncell and the church whiche and cont: xviii. fote in lenght, and xvi fote brede, w^t a litle sanct^n bell in the same, and covd w^t tyle and shyngull,

'The church cont: in lenght lvii. fote, and in brede xviii. ffote, w^t an ile on the south side the church, cont: in length lvii. ffote and brede ix. ffote, which church and ile ben: covd w^t tyle, ptlie in dekay, and the tymber of it metlie good.

'Itm, v. glassed wyndowez w^t imagerie worke, cont: xv. paynez.

'Itm, the iron of the said wyndowez.

'Itm, v. imiges.

'Itm, a chapel on the north side the belframe, cont: in length xxvii. ffote, and in brede xviii. foote, selyd and covd wth tyle.

'Itm, iii. wyndowez glassed and two paynez of glasse.

'Itm, the ironwork of the same.

'Itm, iv. olde imagez.

'Which chapel adioyneth to the howse and ryght nessessare to stand pavyd.

Itm, a chapell on the north side the belframe cont: in length ... ffote, and in brede xviii. ffote, celyd bad, covd w^t tyle.

'Itm, iii. glased wyndowez of imagerie work, w^t a litle wyndow co ... payne, which iii. wyndowez cont: ix. paynez.

'Itm, the iron of the same.

'Itm, a tabull of the awt, w^t the awter clothez.

'Itm, a little bell.

'Itm, the fflowre pavyd with bryck.

'Itm, the cloyst: covd w^t tyle, and the tymb: thereof metlie good.

'Itm, a howse adioynyng to the church, cont: in lenght lxxx. ffote, and in brede xx. ffote, w^t iii. loo parlers and iii. upp chaumbrs, and oon chymney, which howse is covd w^t tyle, and ptelie ruinows for lack of tylyng and payntyng.

'Itm, the flore of the chaumber be verie cours

'The haull adioynyng unto the cloyst buylded chaumber wise cont. in lenght lvii. ffote, and in brede xxi. fote, and cover'd w^t tyle, and the wall on the north side the seid haull greitlie ruinows, which, if it be not newlie made, wyll shortlie be the distrucion of the haull.

'Itm, the haul fflore is borded and verie evill.

'Itm, a howse und: oon rofe on the west end of the haull cont. in lenght lx. ffote, and in brede xxi., wherein is the small kechyn, wel buylded, and divz low howsez adioynyng dekaid, w^t ii. upp chaumbz, and covd w^t tyle, which howsez and chaumbers may welbe spared save onelie the kechyn.

'Itm, the kyln howse cont. in lenght xxi. ffote and in brede xiiii.

'Itm, the howse is covd w^t tyle, and the tymber good, and the walls made w^t mort. verie evyll.

'Itm, a howse called a stable, on the west end of the church, cont. in length xlviii. ffote, and in brede xxi. ffote, covd w^t tyle, w^t a chaumb and a gatehowse, and in dekay for lack of tylyng.

'Itm, a barn there, cont: lxxii. ffote, and in brede xxiiii. ffote, and the tymber thereof good, and coverd with tyle.

'The seid barn is ruinows in wallyng, as in dawbyng and ground sillyng.

'Itm, the dors of the barn be verie cours.

'Itm, a hey hows adioynyng to the barn, cont. in lenght lxiiii. ffote, and in brede xxi. ffote, and in dekay in tymb., wallyng, and tylyg, howbeit it may welbe spared.

'Itm, there is a wat. myln[1] thacked, buylded w^t good substant. tymber, cont. in lenght xx. ffote, and in brede xv. ffote, which was wont to goo by the wat: of the pool, which be now dekaied, and w^t a litle cost wold be made to goo ageyne, for it hath suffic: wat: belongyng to it, if the hedds of the pool were mendyd.

'Itm, iii. pools[2] dekaied, with a fair spryng rounyng thoro theme.

'The said howse is compassed abowte with enclosours, which be the demesyn ground belongyng to the same, and haith all man: of profitt of let, and weif and streif that there shall happen, and haith libties from a place called Horeston unto a place called Brend Oke, which lieth w'owte the said closez.'"

---

[1] Now a saw mill, still worked by the water of the pool.
[2] Pools close to the present house.

Sandwell Hall.

	£	s.	d.
Staff., Brumwyche—Tithe Corn	8	0	0
Sandwell—Inclosures about the house	0	0	0
Mary Magdalen's Meadow	0	0	0
Walsted Fields	2	13	4
Barnfeld	1	6	8
Brumwichfield	2	0	0
A Meadow		10	0
Little Quarell Field		13	4
The Conyngree	0	0	0
The Horeston Close		10	0
The Tynyngs	0	0	0
Great Tynyngs Wood	3	0	0
West Brumwyche—A Barn	0	4	0
Meadow	0	3	4
Water Mill	1	3	4
Patchers Land	0	10	0
A Croft	0	1	0
Belfields	0	16	0
Close, and Wigmorefield	0	4	0
Cottage, 3 pounds of wax, or		2	0
Bardiche Close	2	0	0
Hemend Meadow	0	10	0
Cottage	0	10	0
A Cottage on Fynspath Hill	0	0	4
A Close	0	13	4
A Cottage	0	1	4
Colenscroft	0	0	3
Ball Hill	0	1	6
Croft	0	1	0
Staff., West Brumwyche—Hethcroft	0	0	4
A Messuage on Hen Hill	0	0	2

	£	s.	d.
Newland Close	1	13	4
Messuage and Close	0	14	0
Houndesworth—A Messuage	0	0	0
Brumwyche—Barkerfield	0	14	0
A Messuage	0	5	0
Four Closes	0	10	0
Brakensbutt	0	5	0
A House and six Closes	0	14	0
Mannyngs	0	8	0
A Croft	0	7	6
Staff., Brumwyche—			
Calves Croft	0	2	0
Turners	0	3	9
Halys' Land	0	2	0
Banksmiln Land	0	1	6
Worc'., Dudley—			
Lands	0	4	0
Hampton Tenement	0	1	0
Elburge—Parsonage Close	0	4	0
Half Tithe, Corn and Hay	8	0	0
The other half Tithe, Corn and Hay	6	0	0

Shaw gives the following account of Sandwell:—[1]

"There are charters belonging to this Priory in MS in Bibl. Bodl., Dodsworth, vol. lv (f. 47.)

"There are many instruments of the resignation of William Prayne, Prior, and the election of John Acton, Prior, A.D. 1436.[2] From a copy of an Inquisition, dated Oct. 4, 17th Hen. VIII, in the Cardinal's bundle (amongst other records in Chancery), it appears that John Bayley was the last Prior at the dissolution of this Monastery, and

---

[1] Vol. ii, p 128. [2] Nasmith's edition of Tanner.

that the Prior and Convent of the same, before its suppresion, and destruction, were seised in their domain and in fee, in right of the said Monastery, of one large messuage, with garden and orchard, and other appurtenances in Sandwell; likewise of a water mill in West Bromwich, with all tithes, oblations, and profits thereto belonging, and of 20 messuages, 1,000 acres of land, 100 of meadow, 200 of pasture, 300 of moor, 100 of wood, and 40/- rent in Sandwell, Dudley, West Bromwich, Tybenton, Great Barr, Little Barr, Horburn, Werrel, Toston, Womborn, Weddesbury, Houndesworth, and Feecham, Co. Stafford, valued at £30 per annum clear.

"Luna Clifford died seised of Sandwell, May 12, 1 Eliz."

Reeves gives in his History the following Letters Patent, enrolled in Chancery:—

"13th August, 1608.

By Letters Patent of this date, his Majesty granted to Henry Fenshaw, Knight, John Osborn, and Francis Gofton, Esqs., all that the Rectory and Church of West Bromwich, in the County of Stafford, with their right, members, and appurtenances, to hold to them and their assigns for ever.

17th February, 1609.

By Indenture of this date, the said Henry Fenshaw, John Osborn, and Francis Gofton, for the consideration therein mentioned, gave, granted, sold, bargained, and confirmed unto William Whorwood, Knight, the said Rectory and Church, with their right, members, appurtenances in as ample a manner as the same was granted by his Majesty aforesaid.

3rd April, 1701.

By indenture of bargain of sale of this date, Thomas Brome Whorwood granted and conveyed the said rectory, and premises to the use of the Right Honourable William Lord Dartmouth, his heirs and assigns for ever."

The site of the Priory was, after the entire dissolution of Monasteries, granted to the Whorwood family, of Compton and Stourton Castle.

"Robert Whorewood, Esq., died October 13. 32. Elizabeth seised of the manor of Sandwell, with the appurtenances late parcel of the possessions of the Priory of Sandwell, a mill, and divers lands, &c., in West Bromwich, Barr, Hondsworth, and Tipton, held in capite by Knight's service, and the 100th part of a knight's fee. William Whorewood, afterwards knighted (his son), died July 1st, 1614, seized of the above, and the Fryer's park, containing four hundred acres of land, in West Bromwich, &c., Thomas being his son and heir."—(Dugdale).

List of the Priors of Sandwell.

John	Witness to a deed about time of Edward I.
William de la Lee	Instituted by the Bishop 1329, died in 1361.
Henry de Kyderminster.	Inducted A.D. 1361.
John de Kyngeston	Resigned in 1379.
Richard de Westbury	Appointed April 1379.
John Tamworth	Resigned in 1400.
John de Acton	Appointed Jan. 3rd, 1400.
William Prayne	Temp. Henry VI.
John Atton	Appointed April, 1436.

John Bayley last Prior at the Dissolution—1525.

As we have already mentioned the site of this Priory was granted finally to the Whorwood Family—Robert Whorwood seems to have been the first of the family who lived at Sandwell. He died in 1590, and was succeeded by his son William—a Knight. This latter William it was who died in 1614, and was buried in the Parish Church—and in whose memory the chapel was built, now used as a vestry. Some years ago the writer remembers seeing extracts from Sir William Whorwood's will, wherein he left directions for the building of the said chapel, which was to resemble "that of Mr. Stanley on the north side of the church." Sir William was Sheriff of the County; he died suddenly in London July 1st, 1614. His bequests to the poor are given on page 138. His son, Thomas Whorwood, knight, according to Shaw, was "much troubled about his commanding a bailiff to kill another man at King's Norton, and very ridiculous for his many base acts and penury. He died a little time before he was to have been censured in the Star Chamber, about 1634, at London." His elder son Thomas Brome Whorwood, who was "married about a day before his father's death," was the last of the family who resided at Sandwell.

The said Brome Whorwood suffered for his loyalty in the Civil Wars, and paid £872 composition.

The will of William Whorwood, of Tipton, who died July 4th, 1614, is at Somerset House. In his will he mentions his sons William and Gerard, and his wife Elizabeth, and his daughter Elizabeth. He bequeaths his portion of the Rectory of Tipton to his family. He mentions Sir Thomas Whorwood.

Arms of Whorwood:—" Argent, a Chevron between 3 stags' heads caboshed Sable."

The large vault under the vestry was no doubt the burial place of the Whorwoods, but there are now none of their coffins remaining.

The vestry was used, as has been said, as a pew for many years.

A Mrs. Mary Whorwood was buried in 1618. Perhaps she was Sir William's second wife; his first wife died in 1599.

The burial of "Mr. Field Whorwood," on August 1st, 1658, is recorded, and with the exception of "a female child of Thomas Brome Whorwood," on October 6th, 1687, there are no other entries in the registers of this parish concerning the family who lived at Sandwell upwards of a century.

(For Whorwood pedigree see Appendix.)

The present house is well known; it was the residence of the late Earl of Dartmouth. The present Earl has never lived there since his succession to the title, but after his father's death he eventually generously allowed Sandwell Hall to be used as a charitable institution for the education of poor children.—In time, also, arrangements were made for a ladies' school, and for the reception of ladies in reduced circumstances. This Institution was for many years under the management of Miss Selwyn, sister of the late Bishop of Lichfield, with the valuable assistance of Miss Martineau.

The following are the only entries in the registers which relate to the family of the Earl of Dartmouth:—

Robert, son of the Rt. Hon. the Earl of Dartmouth, baptized July 21st, 1716.

Robert, son of the Rt. Hon. the Earl of Dartmouth, buried December 19th, 1716.

Sir Lister Holte, and Lady Ann Legge were married October 9th, 1739.

Charles Duncombe, Esq., of Helmsley, and Lady Charlotte Legge (a minor) were married at Sandwell by special license 24th September, 1795.

Henry, son of George, Earl of Dartmouth and Frances his wife, baptized October 29th, 1803.

Frances Elizabeth, daughter of William and Frances, Earl and Countess of Dartmouth, baptized Oct. 16th, 1829.

Louisa Jane Cecil, daughter of William and Frances, Earl and Countess of Dartmouth, baptized Jan. 21st, 1831.

George Barrington, son of William and Frances, Earl and Countess of Dartmouth, baptized Feb. 28th. 1832.

Beatrix Maria, daughter of William and Frances, Earl and Countess of Dartmouth, baptized May 12th, 1833.

MISCELLANEOUS.

The Oak.

THIS old house was formerly for several generations the abode of the Turton family. Its present condition is thus described in the *Building News*, for Oct. 12th, 1877, which contains some most interesting drawings of the house. "This old mansion is a good specimen of the half timbered work of the 16th century, though now sadly out of repair for want of attention. The brick part seems to have been added subsequently, as the brick work is built on the face of framing. The plan is simple, consisting of porch, hall, three sitting rooms, and kitchen, &c., with bedrooms over. The lantern tower, which gives the house its picturesqueness, is approached by a steep staircase from landing. The interior is but slightly altered from its original state, most of the rooms still retaining their ancient panelling, and quaintly moulded chimney pieces." Reeves says in his History:—"This place takes its name from an ancient oak tree that stood on the green in front of the house, it was hollow, and was destroyed by fire about thirty-five years since. Formerly a great many of these oaks grew upon the estate. The late Mr. Turton would not fell any of them, but he advised Mr. Whyley to do it, and accordingly in the year 1768 many of these 'kings of the forest' were felled to make lock gates for the navigation then being first made through this parish. There have been several falls of timber on the estate since, and some of the trees were of great magnitude."

The extracts from the family deeds will throw considerable light on the Turton family—an inspection of them was allowed to the writer through the kind courtesy of Dr. Percy. the author of "Metalurgia," whose wife at present owns the Oak House.

It will be seen that the Oak passed from the possession of one brother to another of the Turton family, in the year 1634, and that it eventually came into the Whyley family.

The Turtons came from Dudley to West Bromwich, but they were descended from the Turtons, of Turton Tower, in Lancashire. In 1592 William Turton purchased two Mills from one Thomas Cowper, or Piddocke. These Mills were "The Mill" (as that is called, where the Messrs. Izon's Works now stand) and Bromford Mill. the latter being probably a Blade Mill. Both the pools belonging to these Mills are to be seen still; Bromford pool is near the Bromford Iron Works.

The first mention of "The Oak" in connection with the Turtons is in 1634; we do not know anything of its previous history; but that it had one is a fact beyond dispute, as the style of its architecture proves the house to be at least 300 years old. As far as we are able to judge from information obtained, Thomas Turton was the first of his family who owned "The Oak," as his father bought the two Mills already mentioned, and they were later in the possession of his eldest son William. Extracts from Simon Rider's MS. in the "William Salt Library" which relate to the Mill property, as also the heads of Richard Turton's will, who died in 1685, are given, as they are interesting.

Mrs. Eleanor Turton, who died in 1701, was sister and heir to Richard. She left a dole to the parish of 50/. After the death of Josiah Turton in 1735, "The Mill" and Bromford Mill came to a family named Abney, but by what means has not been ascertained. A Miss Abney married one Roger Holmes, and they left two daughters, who both died insane at Lichfield, and therefore intestate.

In the course of time three separate claimants appeared to this property. After a lengthy suit in Chancery, these claimants at last submitted their claims to a solicitor for arbitration. The claimant who was apparently the nearest of kin was one Edward Holmes, a labourer in Plymouth dockyard, and on him the property devolved, but with mortgages upon it for the benefit of the other two parties. As, however, the mines, which were thought to be very valuable, have proved not to be so, the ownership of it cannot be very profitable.

In the course of this history it will be observed a John Turton, of Cop Hall, is mentioned, as also a William Turton, of Hateley Heath. The latter is connected with the branch belonging to The Oak in a pedigree kindly lent by Arthur Sparrow, Esq., of Preen Manor, but John Turton and Humfrey Turton, who lived at Cop Hall, cannot be identified so far.

"Heads of the will of Richard Turton, of West Bromwich, gent., proved 17th July, 1685:—To his sister, Eleanor, his messuage called The Mill, in West Bromwich, and all his lands in the Parish of Oldbury; to his kinsman, Joseph Turton, a rent charge of 40/- upon his lands in West Bromwich; to his cousin, Mary Brown, 20/- for a ring; to his cousin, William Turton, of Orgreave, 20/-; to his cousin, John Turton, and Ann his wife, 20/- each; to

Miscellaneous.

to his cousin, Phillip Turton, and Mary his wife, 20/- each; to his cousin, Mary Yates, 20/-; to his cousin, Elleanor fflynt, 20/-; to his sister, Mary Freeth, £10; to the children of Mary Freeth, Joseph and Phœbe, a legacy. The residue to his sister, Eleanor, whom he left sole executrix. A codicil mentions, among others his cousin Joseph Simcox, and his sister Elizabeth, 10s. each."

Extracts from Simon Rider's "Hypomnema:"—

1592.—Thomas Cowper, *alias* Piddocke, of King's Bromley, conveyed to William Turton, the elder, of West Bromwich two mills and one meadow, called the Floodgate Meadow.

1602.—Copy of a writ of procedendum brought to the Court of West Bromwich, in which the name of William Turton appears.

1603.—Thomas Hadley sealed and delivered a deed to William Turton, giving possession of the croft near his house.

1599.—Paid to William Turton for rent, land in new leasowe.

1600.—Received from John Turton his rent at his entering.

1601.—Paid to William Turton his whole year's rent.

1602.—Paid to William Turton, the elder.

1602.— ,, ,, the younger.

1621.—Paid William Turton, senior, his rent due for an acre of land in the new leasowe.

Paid Anne Turton my rent for tieth hay at Oldbury for Sir Thos. Littleton.—19th Oct., 1621.

DEEDS ORIGINALLY BELONGING TO THE TURTON FAMILY.

Indenture of bargain and sale of land between Henrie Hand and Phillipp Orme:—Mentions two cottages, two gardens, and one croft in West Bromwich, and three pastures of land there, two called Tonky's land or Luttleys, and the 3rd pasture lyeth near the oake called Harvyls Oke, in Bromwich affores^d; also six dayes earth of land in the common field there, called Stycroft, and Churchfield. Made May 4th, 23rd Henry VIII. (1531.) Copy made by William Turton, 5th Feb., 1629.

Indenture dated 24th August, 27th Henry VIII. (1535), between Phillip Orme, of West Bromwich, and John Lutley, gent., Wm. Lutley and Roger Lutley, sons of John.

7th June, 37th Elizabeth, 1595.—Lease of Land called Turhills, in Rowley Regis, to John Turton, of West Bromwich, Naylor.

Indenture dated Sep. 30th, 13th James 1st (1615), between Thomas Orme, of West Bromwich, yeoman, and William Orme, of Longdon, his brother, wherein s^d Thomas gives, sells, conveys, &c., to Wm Orme, all that meadow called Hampson's Pool, all that close or pasture called Sharpeling's land—sometymes Lytley's—in West Bromwich; also a meadow called Over Huckleys alias Braynford Bridge, now in the tenure of Frances Symcoxe, sonne of Richard Symcoxe, deceased. One other meadow called White's Croft alias Gorstie Crofte in West Bromwich, now in the tenure of William Tey.

10th December, 1617 (15 James 1st).—Sale by William Orme, of Longdon, gent., to John Turton, of West Bromwich, yeoman, of a cottage and barn and 5 closes of land called Slowe's Land, lying in length and breadth between the land of Wm Stanley, Esq., land of Thos. Turton, land late of Richard Smalbrooke and the layne called Oxley's Lane, and the Common Heath of West Bromwich, called West Bromwich Heath. Another pasture called over Lutleys alias Bromford Bridge Leasow, between land of the s⁴ Thomas Turton, land of William Turton, the elder, the lane called Tinker's Lane, and the lane leading from West Bromwich Heath towards Oldbury.

10th June, 22nd James 1st (1624).—Marriage settlement by John Turton, the elder, yeoman, on the intended marriage of John Turton, his second son, with Elizabeth Hawe, sister of George Hawe, of Caldmore, mentions land at King's Norton.

Indenture made 10th September, 1625, between William Orme, of Longdon, and John Turton, of West Bromwich, yeoman, and John Turton, the younger, son of the said John Turton, for sale of lands, &c., and all that cottage or tenement with a garden and hempleck thereunto belonging, now in the tenure of one John Deeley and Edward Deeley, in West Bromwich, with all barns, &c. (Dagger Hall). "The above deed refers to, 1st, premises which in the days of Mr. Whyley were occupied by one Joseph Cullett, who was a butcher. He also at that time rented the fields, &c. These premises are those which now belong to Charles Cotterell, and are called the Horse and Jockey. Cullett lived in the house that looks down into Lyne. 2nd, to Dagger Hall, house and land. The 3rd refers to land which was called originally Tomlay's, and was bounded by the Heath and King's Highway. It also refers to part of the Oak Estate, then called Litley's; in another indenture, dated 3rd December, 1650, it is called Over Lutley's."

Indenture made 14th June, 3rd Charles 1st (1627), between Thomas Turton, of West Bromwich, and Symon Perkyns, of the city of Lichfield, tanner. In consideration of a marriage to be solemnised between William Turton, son and heir of Thomas Turton, and Judith Perkyns, daughter of Symon Perkyns, Thomas Turton grants as a jointure, part of certain lands, &c., called the Over Leaw, Tonke's Leasows, Well Meadow, Grove, Tinker's Lane Meadow, Rick Meadow, Glover's Grove, Clay Hay, all mentioned as late of the inheritance of William Turton, deceased, late father of Thomas Turton.

Indenture made 1st Oct., 10th Charles 1st (1634), between Thomas Turton, of West Bromwich, yeoman, and Alice his wife, and William Turton, son and heir apparent of said Thomas and Alice, of the one part, and John Turton, the elder, of West Bromwich, yeoman, of the other part. Witnesseth that s⁴ Thomas Turton, and Alice his wife, William Turton, and Judith his wife, with one assent and consent, for and in consideration of the sum of £350 .... have given, granted, sold, &c., to s⁴ John Turton .... all that messuage, tenement, or mansion house, with the appts., situate and being in West Bromwich, wherein s⁴ Thomas Turton doth now inhabit and dwell, with all barns, &c., and a croft of land to the same messuage belonging, and also 3 closes or pastures, &c. (mentioning same as in preceeding deed.)

Indenture made 20th March, 11th Charles 1st (1635), between John Turton, the elder, wherein, for the sum of £620, by John Turton, the younger, his second son paid, he gives to trustees all that messuage, tenement, or mansion house, wherein Thomas Turton, brother of the s⁴ John Tu ton, the elder, doth now inhabit, also meadows, lands, &c.—same as before—all which premises are amongst the lands and tenements John Turton lately had and purchased of Thomas Turton, brother of s⁴ John, and William Turton, his son, to have and to hold to the use of said John Turton, the younger, for his life, and then for his son

William (his grandchild), and his heirs for ever.

Indenture, date 31st October, 1635.—Between Wm. Cartwright, of Oldburye, within the parish of Halesowen, county Salopp, and Ann Turton, of Birmingham, widow, wherein Wm. Cartwright sells to Ann Turton, Brandford Leasow, in West Bromwich, between the river or water of Tame, &c.

To the Court Baron of Humble Lord Ward, holden at Rowley Regis, 10th June, 1651, came William Turton, of West Bromwich, gent., brother and next heir of John Turton deceased, in his own person and desired to be admitted tenant, &c., to house, &c., in Rowley.

Indenture, 8th Nov., 1655.—Between Richard Turton, of Hartlebury, county Worcester, and Ann, his wife . . . . and William Turton, the younger, of the Oak House, gent.

24th Dec., 1657.—Marriage Settlement on the intended marriage of William Turton with Elianor Paige of Leighton Stone.

Deed of purchase by Wm. Turton, gent., from Poultney . . . . of a cottage and lands in West Bromwich, called "The Greet;" date Feb., 1663.

14th November, 1674.—Sale of two closes or crofts lying near a messuage, and called Isabell Hill, alias Isabell Hull, and another meadow called the Hollowe Meadow, with a barn and a smithy standing on the same, all in West Bromwich.

Indenture, dated 22nd July, 1682, between William Turton, of the Oak House in the parish of West Brom[ch.] gent., and John Turton, gent., son and heir of said Wm. of one part, and George Devenish, of West Bromwich, gent., and Rich., of the Mill House, in the p[sh] of West Bromwich, gent., on the other part. Witnesseth that the s[d] Wm. Turton and John Turton, for the better enabling him, the sᵈ Wm. Turton, to make effectual provision for the payment of his debts, and raising portions for his younger children .... have granted, enfeoffed, and confirmed, &c., unto said George Devenish and Rich. Turton, all that messuage, corn mill, &c., in King's Norton; also, a house and lands in West Bromwich ....

Will of William Turton, of the Oak, 23rd July, 1682, mentions a house in the tenure of Nathaniel Wiley, a meadow called Pool Tayle (at Haytely Heath), one pasture called Over Leasow; mentions his eldest son John, and his son William, his son Robert to be a clerk or apprentice. He leaves to his "dear wife, Eleanor Turton, the bedd, bedstead, curtains, valances, chairs, stools, and furniture of all sorts which is now in the parlour where my cozen Devenish lodgeth, with sheets and other linen necessary for the furnishing of a room; and I also give unto her a bedd and furniture convenient for the lodging of a servant-maid; and I also appoint that my said wife shall have the use of six silver spoons, two silver porringers, and one little silver cup during her life." To his daughters, Elizabeth and Sarah Turton, he bequeaths "all the linen of all sorts that were their grandmother Turton's."

25th May, 1688.—Purchase by Isaac Wiley of West Bromwich, naylor, all the meadow called Wigmore Meadow, in West Bromwich, adjoining to a lane leading from Wigmore towards Penny Lane, on the North side, the land of Brome Whorwood, Esq., called Bellfields on the West side, and the land of John Shilton, Esq., called Ditch Land, on the South and East part; and two days' work of land in a field, called Churchfield, in West Bromwich, near to a place there called Penny Stile.

23rd March, 1705.—Lease by Dorothy Turton, widow

of John Turton, and John Turton, a minor, by his mother and guardians, of the Oak House, &c., to William Ward, Esq., of Willingsworth, in the parish of Sedgley.

2nd June, 1749.—Will of John Turton, of The Oak, leaves his property to William Whyley (his natural son). Mentions a messuage or tenement in the occupation of John Elwell. In default of an heir to William Whyley, then the property to go to William Turton, Esq., grandson of his uncle, Mr. William Turton, deceased, late rector of Standish. Nathaniel Whyley, of Wigmore, appointed guardian of William Whyley until he was of age.

14th November, 1777.—Indenture of this date between Jervoise Clarke Jervoise, Esq., Lord of the Manor of West Bromwich, of the one part, and William Whyley, of The Oak, in the Parish of West Bromwich, of the other part. Whereas, William Whyley is seized in fee of three closes or parcels of land called the Calves' Croft, Tillatt's Close, and Tinker's Meadow, which said lands formerly belonged to John Turton, gent., deceased, who was heretofore the owner of a certain mill standing near to the same, formerly called Turton's, but now called Abney's Mill, and of other lands there lying between the said mill and other lands of W. Whyley; and whereas a private road called Tinker's Lane was formerly made use of to and for the s^d mill through s^d closes, which road has been disused for upwards of fifty years; and whereas s^d Jervoise apprehended the s^d road to have been formerly a common and public road or way, and as such the ground and soil belong to him as Lord, and did some time since lay claim to the ground and soil as a part of the waste of s^d Manor, but is now satisfied of the contrary. Whereas William Whyley hath some time since, with permission of s^d Jervoise Clark

Jervoise, inclosed and fenced a certain piece of ground, part of the waste land of the said Manor, called Bromwich Heath, lying near to the dwelling house of Wm. Whyley, called The Oak, or Oak House; and hath also obtained permission to inclose another piece of the s⁴ waste land . . . . which two pieces so adjoining together are bounded on the south by the land of the s⁴ Wm. Whyley, lying before his house, used as a court, containing about 7 yds. in depth from the s⁴ house; other land of Wm. Whyley, called The Orchard, and by the cow-house, &c., fronting The Oak Green, and by a lane leading from Bromford Lane to The Oak Green. The s⁴ Wm. Whyley hath also inclosed another small piece of ground, part of a certain common or waste within the s⁴ Manor, commonly called Greet's Green. . . .

The following is taken from *The London Gazette*, No. 1134, from Thursday, September 28th, to Monday, October 2nd, 1676. Staff. Collections, W. Salt Library, vol. I., page 192:—" Stolen from Mr. William Turton, of West Bromwich, Staff^{shire.} Sept. 21st, 1676, a bright bay Mare, 8 years old, about 15 hands, with a black mane and tail doc'kt, having been a draught mare as by the collar marks appear; she hath a dry cloud in the right eye extending to blindness; she hath a bare place above the fetlock on the outside of the foreleg on the left side, where a wart hath been burnt and eaten off; she is full of hard knots within the skin of the neck, breast, and shoulders, as if she had been nettled. Whoever shall give notice of her to the said Mr. Turton, or to Mr. Edward Cranke, at the Swan, in Birmingham, Warwickshire, or to Mr. James Hicks, in the Post Office, London, shall have 20s. reward."

Some of the entries in the Registers relating to the Turtons:—

BAPTISMS.

Jobe Turton, the son of William Turton, junior, Dec. 14th, 1617.

Rychard, son of William Turton, the younger, April 18th, 1620.

Elizabeth, daughter of John Turton, junior, April 23rd, 1625.

William, son of John Turton, junior, Feb. 4th, 1626-7.

Sara, daughter of John Turton, junior, Nov. 4th, 1632.

Michaell, son of Thomas Turton, Oct. 14th, 1621.

John, son of William Turton, Dec. 13th, 1628.

John, son of John Turton, July 19th, 1629.

William, son of William Turton, April 14th, 1629.

Elizabeth, daughter of William and Judith Turton, Nov. 15th, 1640.

Sarah, daughter of Mr. William Turton, of The Ocke, and Sarah his wife. Born Oct. 8th, 1654.

John, son of Mr. William Turton, of The Oake, and Sarah wis wife. Born June 18th, 1656.

Elizabeth, daughter of Mr. William Turton and Eleanor his wife. Born May 24th, 1659.

William, son of Mr. William Turton, of The Oake, gentel., Feb. 5th, 1662-3.

Mrs. Sarah, daughter of Mr. William Turton, of The Oake, July 7th, 1667.

Mr. Robert, son of Mr. William Turton, Aug. 1st, 1673.

Mr. William, son of Mr. John Turton, of The Oake, Oct. 6th, 1687.

Richard, ye son of John Turton de Oake, March 11th, 1689.

John, son of Mr. John Turton, April 26th, 1692.

Mary, daughter of John Turton, Nov. 7th, 1693.

Sarah, daughter of Mr. John Turton de Oake, Nov. 11th, 1695.

John, son of William Turton, of Hack-le Heath, April 25th, 1668.

William, son of William Turton, of Hak-le Heath, March 12th, 1669.

William, the sonn of John Turton, of Cop Hall, was baptized the 11th day of August, and was just moonth old when it was baptized. 1685.

Ann, daughter of John Turton, Oct. 6th, 1687.

     Anne Whiley, single woman
William, son of Mr. John Turton, bap. Dec. 20th, 1735.
(sic)

MARRIAGES.

Bezahell Knight and Elizabeth Turton, July 23rd, 1626.

John Wolviston and Mary Turton, Feb. 25th, 1632-3.

Mr. William Turton, minister, of Rowley, and Mrs. Margery Grove, July 12th, 1659.

William Turton, of the Parish of Rowley, and Mary Winter, of this parish, October 7th, 1760.

BURIALS.

William Turton, the elder, Jan. 18th, 1627-8.

Thomas Turton, Jan. 14th, 1645-6.

———— of Mr. William Turton, August, 1656.

John, son of Mr. William Turton, Oct. 15th, 1656.

Mrs. Elnor, daughter of Mr. William Turton, of The Oak, Jan. 14th, 1664-5.

Mr. John Turton, Oct. 25th, 1672.

Mrs. Elizabeth Turton, widow, April 9th, 1680.

Mr. William Turton, April 1st, 1681.

William Turton, July 28th, 1682.

William, son of Mr. John Turton, of The Oak, June 13th, 1692.

Mrs. Elianor Turton, widow, Sept. 21st, 1696. Aged 61.
Master William Turton, of The Mill, buried Feb. 1st, 1655.
Mrs. Elianor Turton, of The Mill, May 7th, 1701.
Mr. John Turton de Oake, Dec. 8th, 1705.
Mrs. Dorothy Turton, March 9th, 1725-6.
William, son of Mr. Josiah Turton, April 17th, 1728.
Mrs. Turton, May 2nd, 1728.
Mr. Josiah Turton, May 5th, 1735.
Mr. Joseph Turton, May 15th, 1735.
Mrs. Sarah Turton, March 21st, 1745-6.
Mrs. Elizabeth Turton, Dec. 10th, 1748.
Mr. John Turton, August 3rd, 1768.
Miss Mary Whyley, Feb. 1st, 1784. Aged 20,
Mr. William Whyley, May 10th, 1800.
William Whyley, April 19th, 1806. Aged 20.

(For Turton pedigree see Appendix.)

OAKWOOD.

This house has been for above two hundred years, and still is, in the possession of the Jesson family.

Of this family Sir Bernard Burke, in his "Authorised Arms," 1860, says "Thomas Jesson, Esq., of Oakwood, descends from an ancient Staffordshire family, long settled at West Bromwich."

The name of the house may have been taken from the land on which it stands, which was called Oakley's Croft, or it may be from there having been a wood of oak trees on the spot in early times.

The house was built by Thomas Jesson, who purchased the land in 1679. Like most old houses in this parish the wood work is entirely of oak, and the rooms are most handsomely panelled with this beautiful wood, another proof that oak trees were very plentiful in this neighbourhood about 200 years ago, as in those days the wood most easily to be obtained close at hand was used.

A portion of the Pedigree of the Jesson Family will be found among other pedigrees of local families. George Jesson, who died in 1678, has left some curious papers, extracts from which will be found in the appendix.

DUNKIRK.

This property formerly belonged to a family of the name of Ryder, who resided upon it for many years. The accompanying extracts from the Title Deeds will throw some light on the history of this family. From the 'Hypomnema" of Simon Ryder in the "William Salt Library" already quoted, it appears that he—Simon Ryder —came to live in West Bromwich first in the year 1580. His occupation was that of a miller, and Dunkirk Mill was one of those three mills in near proximity to each other that were all worked by the water of the River Tame. The last Ryder who owned Dunkirk was Nicholas, who died in 1703, and after his death the state of the property was so unsatisfactory that a lengthy suit in Chancery was the result. A family of the name of Gutteridge lived at, and worked the mill for a good many years, and the mill is even now sometimes spoken of as "Gutteridge's Mill." This name and "Ryder's Green" perpetuate the memory of these two families. The estate was at length, in 1812, ordered to be sold, and Alexander Stainby became the purchaser, but he only actually paid one-third of the purchase-money, the other two-thirds being paid by Edward Blount, of Bellamour, and Thomas Whitgreave, of Moseley, who eventually became possessed of their share of the property. Alexander Stainby becoming bankrupt, his third of the property was sold by his creditors to Thomas and Henry Price; the latter died, leaving his brother his heir-at-law, in whom his share of the property became vested. In 1829 a Deed of Partition was made of the estate between Edward Blount, George Thomas Whitgreave, and the Price family. The latter portion has been sold to the Birmingham Canal Co.; this includes the old mill and water course. The writer is able to contradict a statement that a family named Whitgreave lived at Dunkirk at the beginning of this century, for on applying to Francis Whitgreave, Esq., of Burton Manor, near Stafford, for infomation on the subject, he says: "It is quite clear to me that no member of my family could have lived at Dunkirk Hall. The Thomas Whitgreave mentioned in 1700 was my great-great-great-grandfather. He lived and died at Moseley, and had not any brother. From him we pass, under date of June 18th, 1811, to Thomas Henry Francis Whitgreave. He was my grandfather, and had two half-brothers who both certainly died in their beds, and in England, and could never have resided at Dunkirk." (This is to confute the story told about a family of this name, one of whom is said to have been murdered, &c., but we have no wish to perpetuate it.) Mr. Whitgreave goes on to say: "George Thomas Whitgreave was my own father, who had no brother who survived boyhood, and who lived at Moseley and died in London. I had long known that we were connected with a family of the name of Rider, and I believe it was through another of the name of Palin, whose ancestor married a lady of our family, and I believe it was in this way that we became possessed of a share of the property at Dunkirk which I well remember my father selling a good many years ago. It was then very valuable mining property, and though small in extent, realized a large sum." Reuben Farley, Esq., is the present owner of Dunkirk Hall—now converted into a public house—and it is through his courtesy that we are enabled to append the following extracts.

Marriage settlement, dated 30th March, 1632.

On the intended marriage of Robert Rider, yeoman, grandson and heir of Symon Rider, with Joan Sydenhall, in which certain lands, &c., are conveyed to trustees, who are Charles Waringe, gent., Thomas Waringe, his son, of Solyhull, and Francis Rider, of West Bromwich, yeoman.

The property so conveyed is thus described:—"All that part of their messuage, dwelling-house, or tenement, now or late called or known by the name of the Parler, with the eight chambers over the same, the closet or study thereto adjoining, and the large buttery near unto the same, with all appurtenances, and the back side thereto adjoining, and the garden called the   garden, and two bays of the west end of the barne and the cowe-house, or close to the west bay of the s^d barn adjoining, with all appurtenances except and reserved unto the s^d Simon Rider and Robert Rider and the heirs and assigns of the s^d Robert, the usual gates and ways to and from the orchard and garden, &c. . . . with free ingress, egress and regress to and from the same. And also all that close, pasture, or parcel of ground called Newlands, and all that close . . . . called Blakehay, and all that close called Huckwalls, and all that meadow called Huckwall's meadow, situated between the land of John Woodward, the land of Edward Duddeley, the land of John Lowe, the land of John Foxall, the land of Richard Stone, and the lane leading from the King's Majesty's highway, called the Portway, towards the nether end of Greet's Green."

9th September, 1663.—Indenture made between Nicholas Rider, of Greet in West Bromwich, son and heir of Robert Rider, of Greet, deceased, of the one part, and Charles Waring of Berry Hall, in the parish of Solyhull, Esq., Thomas Palin, of Deamesdale, Co. Staff., gent., and Ann Palin, one of the daughters of Richard Palin, late of Deamesdale, deceased, of the other part.

It is witnessed that in consideration of a marriage then intended to be had and solemnized between the s^d Nicholas Rider and the s^d Ann Palin . . . . the said Nicholas Rider did grant, &c., to Charles Waring and Thomas Palin and their heirs . . . . all that messuage or tenement situated and being in Greet, wherein the s^d N. Rider and Joane Rider, mother of the said N. Rider, did lately inhabit and dwell, and also all the barns, gardens, out-houses, hemplecks, fold, yards, &c., and also all that water corn mill, commonly called Rider's Mill, and all the ponds, pools, fleams, streams, &c. . . . . also all the crofts, pastures, &c., called the Great Barn Field, the Little Barn Field, the Long Croft, the Peas Croft, the Great Stockwell Field, the Birch Hall, the Gersty Bank, the Broad Meadow, the Oat Leasow, the Cony Leasow alias Conbury Field, the Moor and the Mill Meadow, and all that close called the Little Stockwell Field; also all those closes called the Newlands, and those closes called the Blackheys, and that close called Luckwall's Leasow; also the Huckwall's Meadow alias the Long Meadow.

Covenant by said Nicholas Rider that he was lawfully seized and had good right to convey, free from incumbrances, except the estate for life of the said Joan Rider in some part of the said messuage, and in certain meadows.

August, 1691.—Mortgage by Nicholas Rider and his son Thomas to Joseph Moore, of the Huckwall Closes (before called the Newlands) and the Black Hayes, subject to redemption.

May, 1693.—Mortgage by the same to the same of the Great Barn Field, the Little Barn Field, the Peas Croft, and the Long Croft.

20th May, 1694.—Mortgage of Answorth Leasow, or Windmill Field, with the windmill erected thereon.

Bond, whereby Nicholas and Thomas Rider became bound to Joseph Moore in the penal sum of £60. Date 1st Nov., 1695.

Nicholas Rider was at his death indebted by bond to Thomas Bracegirdle, William Stanley, and Ann Cherrington, and several other persons.

His will is dated 21st September, 1702, appointing as his executors Thomas Whitgreave, Gilbert Merry, Thomas Palin, and John Pidgeon, directing that they should sell his real estates to pay his just debts, &c., and should divide the surplus amongst his children—Simon, Elizabeth, John, and Catherine Rider. Thomas died in 1702.

In Easter Term, 1708, the creditors of Nicholas Rider filed a bill in Chancery against the executors, and also against Isabella, widow of the testator, and against Joseph Moore, John Dolphin, and s^d Simon, Elizabeth, John and Catherine Rider, praying that the trustees and executors might come to an account of the real and personal estate, and that the real estate might be sold, and that all parties might join therein, and that the said trustees might execute their trust and pay the plaintiffs what was due to them.

Isabella Rider filed her cross bill against the creditors, trustees, and executors, to establish her jointure or dower, and both causes came on to be heard before the Master of the Rolls. The law-suit thus begun appears to have continued until 1812, when, after much litigation, the estates were ordered to be put up to auction at the Swan Inn, and were purchased by one Alexander Stansbie, who, however, only actually himself paid one-third of the purchase-money, the remaining two-thirds being equally paid by Edward Blount, of Bellamour, and Thomas Whitgreave.

In 1816 Alexander Stansbie became bankrupt, and his share of the Dunkirk estate was eventually sold to Thomas Price, of Bescot, ironmaster, and Henry Price, by trustees for the benefit of his creditors. A piece of land is mentioned called Church Work, being part of the Mill Meadow.

In 1816 Thomas H. F. Whitgreave died, leaving George Thomas Whitgreave his eldest son and heir-at-law.

In 1829, by a Deed of Partition, the estate was divided between Edward Blount, G. T. Whitgreave, and the Price family. The trustees of the Price family, of whom John Walker Turton was one, eventually sold their third part of the estate to the Birmingham Canal Co., who are the present owners.

CHARLEMONT HALL.

This house was built by the Lowe family about the end of the 17th century. Shaw mentions it in the 2nd vol. of his "History of Staffordshire," under the head of West Bromwich. He says:—"In the road leading from hence (the Manor House) to Barr, on the verge of the hill called Charley Mount, is a lofty, neat looking house of brick faced with stone, with iron palisades, &c., in front, and lately left by two maiden ladies, Miss Loyds (Lowes) in a singular manner to the Rev. John Hallam, D.D., Dean of Bristol. The adjoining valley is rich and pleasant, and the surrounding country picturesquely broken." The house has been considerably enlarged since the time when Shaw wrote the above description, and the road thrown further from the house; indeed, one of the walks in the grounds was formerly a public road. This walk, which, in all probability was altered at the time of the Inclosure Act, now leads round to the lawn behind the house from the front drive. Doubtless, the house, when first built, faced the old road, and it follows that what is now the back was then the front. Charlemont is a well-built and commodious house. The floors and staircases are of oak, and several of the rooms are panelled with the same. A new east wing was built by the present owner in 1855.

Very little is now known of the Lowe family, and there are no monuments or tombstones to assist in tracing their history. A large mound to the left hand of the centre path in the oldest part of the churchyard used to be pointed out as covering their vault.

The following facts are elicited from the parish registers, and incidental mention of several members of the family in deeds.

In 1689, John Lowe, who is described as an ironmonger, residing in Lyndon, married Elizabeth Jesson. They had five sons and four daughters, and were, we believe, the builders of Charlemont Hall. This is, however, only a surmise; the house may have been built by their son John or Samuel Lowe. In the year 1748, Elizabeth and Mary Lowe were living in the house in Lyne as tenants of Samuel Lowe; Jesson Lowe and his sister Sarah inhabited another house, probably Bustleholme, as Jesson Lowe worked that Mill at the time named, and Samuel Lowe was, in all probability, living at Charlemont, which eventually came into the possession of his sister Elizabeth.

Jesson Lowe died in 1758, and his death was thus announced: "Birmingham, June 19. On Monday last, died Mr. Jesson Lowe at West Bromwich, after a very long and painful illness." [1]

Mr. Jesson Lowe served the office of High Sheriff for this county in the year 1752.

Elizabeth Lowe, or as she was generally called "Madam Betty," survived her brother and sisters, and dying in 1793 left her Charlemont estates to her cousin Dean Hallam. A portrait of this lady is at Charlemont; and Colonel Bagnall has also the portrait of another member of the family, "Cornet Lowe," who, in 1715, shot two men dead, who, during a riot, were in the act of unroofing the old Meeting House. The Pictorial History of England, says, [2] referring to this time (1715) when many attacks were made by mobs upon the Meeting Houses of Dissenters:—"In Staffordshire, one of the least civilised and most tory counties, these excesses were greatest; and scarcely a Whig or Dissenter there could escape insult or more serious injury."

The men who were shot at West Bromwich were buried at Wednesbury, and the following is a copy of the register of their burial:—"Francis Gibbons, of Sedgeley, and Thomas Royston, of Wolverhampton, who were both of them shot to death at West Bromwich by those persons who defended ye Presbyterian Meeting House from being

---

[1] From Newspaper Extracts in the "W. Salt Library."
[2] Vol. 4, p. 309.

pulled down, which afterwards was effected and burned to ashes, July ye 14th day they were shot, and buried ye 17th, A.D. 1715."

Cornet Lowe, who was probably the eldest brother of Madam Betty, is again mentioned in 1744, as a leader in the riot of Shrove Tuesday.

Dean Hallam devised the property he inherited from his cousin to his son Henry, the well-known author of the "Middle Ages." Hallam Street derives its name from this family. Mr. Hallam, in 1807, settled the Charlemont estates upon Julia Maria Elton, whom he subsequently married, the daughter of the Rev. Sir Abraham Elton, Bart., of Cleeve Court, formerly Incumbent of this parish.

In 1812 other property in lieu of this was settled on Mrs. Hallam, and Charlemont was sold to Mr. Thomas Jesson in the following year.

Mr. Jesson planted a great number of trees and otherwise improved the estate; but one incident is handed down in reference to his residence there which nearly proved fatal to the house: One night on retiring to rest Mr. Jesson left his candle burning on a table covered with papers near his bedside. He fell asleep and the candle set fire to the papers, and the flames spread considerably. The fire thus kindled must have caused much damage, as several charred pieces of a beam, &c., were found when the new east wing was built. Mr. Jesson owned the Charlemont estates (though not resident latterly) until 1825, when he sold it to Mr. Samuel Dawes, of the Leveretts, Handsworth, from whose trustees, Colonel Bagnall, in 1854 purchased the house and three fields adjoining. Mr. Joseph Halford resided at Charlemont in 1836. A family named Price preceded him who were living there in the year 1822.

The latter have a sad history—it is said that they took off the roof of Tipton Old Church to cover their engine house, and that no good came to them afterwards. Their tombstone on the south side of the churchyard testifies to the early deaths of the children. One of the sons returning home intoxicated at night, and being unable to obtain an entrance into the house, lay on the lawn the whole night. He took cold and soon after died. Mr. Price was found dead with his throat cut in one of the bedrooms; and though the fact was hushed up and no inquest held, there is little doubt of its correctness.

Fire seems to be an enemy to this house, for in April, 1879, during the occupancy of the present tenant, J. H. Thursfield, Esq., a fire broke out, which, though fortunately extinguished, threatened to involve the whole building in flames.

From the Registers.
Baptisms.

John, son of Sawnders Loe, 26th Oct., 1628.
Alexander, son of Alexander Loe, 13th May, 1632.
Henry, son of Alexander Loe, 14th Feb., 1636.
Paul, son of Alexander and Sarah Lowe, 13th Nov., 1639.
John, son of John Lowe, Ironmonger, and Priscilla his wife, was born the 13th day of December, 1656.
Alexander, son of John Lowe, Ironmonger, and Priscilla his wife, was born the 15th of November, 1658.
Priscilla, the daughter of John Lowe, 17th July, 1660.
Sarah, the daughter of John Lowe, 17th Nov., 1663.
Joseph, the son of John Lowe, 6th March, 1665.
Benjamin, the son of John Lowe, 21st February, 1667.
Mary, the daughter of John Lowe, 10th August, 1670.
John, the son of John Lowe, junior, 19th October, 1689.

Samuel, the son of John Lowe, 4th Dec., 1691.
Abigall, the daughter of Mr. John Lowe, junior, born the 28th of May, and baptized the 16th of June, 1693.
Jesson, the son of John Lowe, 28th Feb., 1698.
Lizabeth, the daughter of John Lowe, 30th April, 1701.
Mary, the daughter of John Lowe, 2nd March, 1702.
Anne, the daughter of John Lowe, 28th January, 1706.
Benjamin, the son of John Lowe, 6th March, 1708.
Sarah, the daughter of Mr. John Lowe, 9th September, 1711.
William, son of Mr. John Lowe, 25th July, 1712.

MARRIAGES.

John, the son of Alexander Lowe and Priscilla Robins, the daughter of Mr. William Robins, of Bilson, deceased, 9th July, 1655.
Mr. William Loe and Mrs. Elnor Brett, 3rd June, 1661,
John Allen and Priscilla Lowe, 12th Feb., 1686.
Mr. John Low and Mrs. Elizabeth Jesson, 5th July, 1689.

BURIALS.

Sarah, the wife of Alexander Loe, 7th December, 1648.
Prastsillo, the wife of John Lowe, 2nd Sep., 1670.
John Lowe, senior, 25th April, 1702.
Anne, daughter of Mr. John Lowe, 24th Dec., 1711.

BUSTLEHOLME MILL.

Bustleholme is one of the most picturesque spots in the parish; hidden by the rising ground of Charlemont on one side, and by the canal on the other, no one would believe, as they gaze upon water wheel, garden, and the rural surroundings of a farmyard, that they were in a Black Country parish. The earliest mention found of Bustleholme is in a deed dated 20th February, 1594. It is again mentioned in a marriage settlement dated May 8th, 1626, also in a deed dated February 18th, 1663. From these latter it appears to have been the property of a family of the name of Simcox, a member of which family married Mrs. Alice Shelton in 1663, so that they were no doubt in a good position. Subsequently the property belonged to John Shelton, for in 1709 it appears he sold it to John Lowe, of Lyndon. The mill is described as "one Corn Mill, and one Slitting Mill joining together." At this date, and again in 1732, it is called "The Rod Mill and Oil Mill." At this latter date the mill was the property of Jesson Lowe, he having purchased it from his father—and proofs exist that the Rod Mill was worked by Jesson Lowe previous and subsequent to 1743, at which time he was supplying Mr. Thomas Jesson, of the Forge, with bars. A late partner in the old firm of John Bagnall and Sons, of Gold's Hill Ironworks, supplies the following facts: "Bustlehome was worked about 60 or 70 years ago by one Morris, whose father was with old Wilkinson;[1] afterwards by G. B. Thornycroft. Bars were supplied them from Gold's Hill to make into sheets. It stood idle for some years before Thornycroft took it, and having just learnt how to make sheet iron at the Hyde Works, near Stourbridge, I wanted to take it, but old Mr. Ingleby advised us to take Gold's Hill, which was standing at that time, and we did so. The first blast furnaces in West Bromwich were at Gold's Green, built by my father."

20th February, 37 Queen Elizabeth (1594). Indenture between William Comberford, of Wednesburie, and Humfrey Comberford, his son and heir, on the one part, and Walter Stanley, of West Bromwich, Esquire,

---

[1] Mr. Wilkinson who owned the works at Bradley.

on the other part. William and Humfrey Comberford release and quit claim to Walter Stanley and his heirs, "all their right, claim, and demand in all those fludgates standing and being in or upon the water of Tame in or near to a certain ground there called Bustelhome, *alias* Bustleholme, in West Bromwich, and of and in the soyle and ground whereon the said fludgates stand, and of and in all that parcel of ground, stank, or dam, containing in length 30 yards, and in breadth 15 yards, being in the Lordship of Wednesbury, adjoining to the said fludgates, and of and in all water, water courses, and fyshing of the water of Tame between the bridge called Tame Bridge and the said fludgates."

Marriage Settlement, date — May 8th, 1626. By Francis Symcox, of West Bromwich, on his marriage with Alice Hayteley, daughter of John Hayteley deceased. Gives to trustees "All that Mansion House wherein Johan Symcox, my mother, dwelleth . . . and one other Croft, near to the Stone Cross—adjoining to the lane leading from West Bromwich Church towards Walsall, and three closses lying together in West Bromwich, adjoining to the land of William Stanley, Esq., on the one side, and to a little layne there on the other side, and one Crofte called Longe Crofte—between the land of William Stanley on the one side—and one Little Croft adjoining to the layne leading down to Bustlehome Mill."

Indenture dated 18th February, 1663. Between John Simcox the elder, of West Bromwich, ironmonger, and Josiah Simcox, ironmonger—mentions lands called Bustlehome—"now in the occupation of John Simcox the elder." Also about 80 acres lying in West Bromwich, in a leet or common field there called Linedon Field.

17th June, 1709. Between John Shelton, Esq.—Mary, his wife, Joseph Shelton, gent., son and heir apparent of the said John—and Mary Shelton and Henrietta Shelton, two of the three daughters of the said John Shelton of the 1st part—The Right Hon. Sir John Holt Knight, Lord Chief Justice of Her Majesty's Court of the Queen's Bench, and one of the Lords of the Privy Council, of the 2nd part.—The Honourable Arthur Annesley and Vincent Oakley, of Wick, of 3rd part, &c. &c. —And John Lowe, of West Bromwich, ironmonger—Relating to the sale to said John Lowe of certain meadows called Smithy More, Wheatcroft, Little Meadow, and Dam Banks.

June 18th, 1709. Sale to John Lowe, ironmonger, by John Shelton, of "a Messuage—also one Corn Mill and one Slitting Mill—joining together called Bustleholme Mills, and also ten yards breadth of the cinder banks—being part of a meadow of John Shelton, called Smithemore Meadows to be measured from that part of the wall of the said mills that stands against the current of the pool belonging to said mills—and 49 yards in length of the said cinder bank —the same breadth all along the side of the mills as the water runs—being so far as the buildings of the mills—and a stone wall for supporting the troughs belonging to the mills now stands. Also all that close of land where the said buildings and mills stand—also two little closes adjoining—also another called Wheatcroft, also a meadow called the Floated Meadow, also the little meadow and one little leasow adjoining—and all ponds, pools, &c., and one half of the fishing in the pool belonging to the mills—and river running into the same from a place above the mills called Tame Bridge, down to the mills only.—Also a way for all sorts of carriages from the mills through the said Smithemore meadow, the next passable way that may be found to the said floodgates belonging to the mills . . . Also one way for all sorts of carriages and uses whatsoever from the said Close called the Wheatcroft, in and through a close of land of John Shelton called the Lower Stone Pitt Leasow, then in the holding of John Culwick, along the hedge side, the next way to the aforesaid meadow. Also one piece of land called the Little Ruffe, and also their right and title to the way leading from the mills to the road leading from West Bromwich to Tame Bridge, coming into the said road at Dead Woman's Burial Gate.—Also all that moor, called Woodin's Moor, lying near the mills, between the land then or late of Philip Foley, Esq . . . land of Mr. James Billingsley . . . All, excepting liberty at all times for John Shelton, his heirs, and assigns for ever hereafter to come upon the said premises at his and their wills and pleasure to fish with nets, or otherwise, in the said millpool or river, from Tame Bridge to the said mills."

22nd Dec., 1732.—Between Jesson Lowe, of West Bromwich, gent., and Robert Charwells, of Packington, gent., relating to sale by Jesson Lowe to Robert Charwells of "all that messuage, cottage, or tenement, situated in or near the Rod Mill and Oil Mill, commonly called Bustlehome Mills, in the Parish of West Bromwich, late in the possession of Moses Harpur; also all that close of land wherein the said mills and premises stand, and also two little closes of land adjoining thereto, also Wheat Croft Meadow, Floated Meadow, Little Meadow, Little Rough Moor, or parcel of moorish ground, commonly called Woodin's Moor, lying near said messuage, between the land late of Philip Foley, Esq., the land late of John Hodgetts, the land late of Mr. James Billingsley, the land late of John Stanton, the land late of John Shelton, Esq., commonly called Smithemoor Meadow . . . . and the river of Tame, running from Smithemoor Meadow to Jone Bridge, all which premises are near Bustlehome Mill, and now in the several possession of John Lowe, gent., William Hill, and Jesson Lowe." . . . Mentions also all houses, outhouses, stables, &c., which Jesson Lowe purchased of John Lowe, of Lyndon, alias Lyne, gent., father of Jesson Lowe.

LYNE, OR LYNDON.

That this is an old name will be seen on perusing some of the ancient deeds relating to the parish. In all probability the name was taken from the lime tree, or Linden. "Lyne was the centre of the parish till the close of the last century, and was the most populous part. Next in point of population was Mayer's Green, The Hollow, or Holloway, the Hall End, a few houses below Charlemont, with here and there a scattered house. Lyne once had its market. The market house, or ancient cross, has gone to decay nearly 100 years. The writer of this has conversed with some old people that could remember one of the walls standing in 1756. Originally a school was kept under the same. The cross stood in the corner as you go up Hargate Lane . . . . within a few yards of the cross was the prison. Tradition says that a distemper prevailing in Lyne, the market was removed to Stone Cross. The stocks stood in Lyne a little above the cross. Within the last twenty years many of the old half timbered houses have been taken down, and in taking some down opposite the Pearl, several old pieces of silver coin were found. The writer has a silver piece of Queen Elizabeth's found there. A large and respectable house, situate as you come out of Lyne towards the Workhouse, on your left hand, was taken down about sixteen years ago. It was formerly the property and residence of the Lowe family. Mr. H. Hallam, the last proprietor, had it taken down; a row of sycamore trees formerly stood in front of the same." [1] Allusion is here made to Lyne Pearl, a spring of excellent soft water, which has been lately bricked over, and from it the inhabitants can still obtain good water through a pipe; the water continually flows and seems inexhaustible.

FRIAR PARK.

Of this place Reeves says that it "was occupied by a society of begging Friars, and was a part of the establishment attached to the Priory of Benedictines at Sandwell; the original house stood in what is called the 'Moat Meadow,' within a quarter of a mile of the present house. A part of the moat is still to be seen. A chapel stood near, which was approached by a drawbridge, and I have been informed that the foundation was got up about seventy-two years ago. . . . The original part of the house was built at the time the first was taken down, and it is very likely with some of the materials. At the bottom of Sandy Lane, on your left, is the 'burial field' (so-called), it belongs to Friar Park Farm, and within the last twenty years human bones have been ploughed up." Friar Park is now the property of the Earl of Dartmouth. The mention of the 'burial field' seems a clue to that of 'dead woman's burial gate' in one of the old deeds to be found in the appendix. Reeves seems very clear in his own mind that a number of Friars

---

[1] Reeves, pages 54 and 56.

connected with Sandwell lived at this place but he does not give his authority.

STONE CROSS.

Is doubtless so named from the fact of there having been a stone cross there in early times, and in all probability this was one of the places where the gospel was read when the parishioners went perambulating this parish on the Rogation Days. Reference to this custom is made in an extract from the Churchwarden's books. A portion of the pedestal of the cross was in existence at the end of the last century, and is mentioned by the Rev. H. Saunders, in his "History of Shenstone," p. 210-11, he says: "I have seen one of these stone pillars in the road betweed Walsall and West Bromwich. They are of round polished stone, much like those upon which dials are placed .... but vastly higher."

OLD FORGE.

This stood in the lane now known as Forge Lane, leading from the Barr Road round Sandwell Park into the Birmingham Road. The pool on the left hand side of the lane was made for the purpose of working the water wheels which drove the machinery of the mill. About sixty or seventy years ago the Forge was worked by Wright and Jesson. The former member of the firm was Lord Dartmouth's steward, and lived at the Manwoods. The firm afterwards moved to Bromford, which was then an offshoot of the Old Forge. Subsequently the Baches worked it, being supplied with bars from Gold's Hill.

WIGMORE.

The name given to certain fields between Churchfields and Newton. There was a common field here also in early times. Near here is Lydiate field.

The lane leading to the new schools is now commonly called Penny Hill, but formerly Knapenny. The hill on which the Industrial Schools are situated seems celebrated for natural phenomena. About twenty years ago, at the back of the present Union chaplain's house, then a small inn, there was a large bath supplied by a natural spring of water, the water was considered medicinal and was much used.

A curious incident also is recorded of the same place. In the cellar of the house there was a natural flow of gas from the earth, which was utilized for lighting purposes; it was conveyed by pipes into the several rooms, and those who informed the writer on the subject have seen the gas burning.

Just below Wigmore the river Tame flows, forming the boundary of the parish; it is known at this spot as "Wigmore Brook."

With regard to the meaning and origin of the name "Wigmore," Mr. W. H. Duignan, of Walsall, who has most kindly assisted the writer by the loan of some ancient deeds, says "I have no doubt that the name is derived from the Saxon word "wig," a battle, and we may reasonably conclude that it means literally "Battle-Moor." From this we may conclude that some important battle of Saxon times was fought on this spot.

Near Wigmore, close to the road leading to Great Barr, stands a farm, now in the occupation of Mr. James Smith, which we believe to be "Jone Mill."

There has been a mill on the spot for many years without doubt, as the Tame has been diverted from its original course and the mill stream thus formed.

There is at present a water-wheel put in by the late Mr.

Beeson, but the diversion we speak of was made long before his time. The bridge, called "Jone Bridge," is, we also believe, the one over the Tame where that stream forms the boundary of the parishes of West Bromwich and Great Barr.

BLACK LAKE.

Or, as originally spelt, Blake Lake, is near Swan Village. Mr. Duignan says of the meaning of this name, "perhaps the Lake upon the Plain;" at any rate the name "Black" is more suitable than any other at the present time.

GOLDNS CROFT.

A name given in some old deeds to a field, is in all probability the site of Gold's Hill and Gold's Green Furnaces.

HATELEY HEATH.

Sometimes, as in the Registers, called Hak-le-Heath, probably took its name from the family of Hateley, whose name was sometimes spelt Haickley, as was also that of the place. Mr. Duignan thinks this place was originally called the "Longmor."

RIDGEACRE.

Formerly spelt Rugiaker. We do not know the origin of the name; but it was also a family name. The site of the present ironworks was originally a coppice, belonging to the Lords of the Manor, and well supplied with game.

CHURCH LANE.

Formerly Vicarage Lane from the old Vicarage and Schools standing in it, the site of which may still be traced in a field on the right hand side of the lane coming from the Cemetery towards Ridgacre, and nearly opposite a house now occupied by Mr. Woodhouse.

SWAN INN.

This house is said to be the oldest Inn in the parish, and the original part of it to have been built upwards of 300 years.

The parish registers bear testimony to the antiquity of the Swan in the following extracts:—

Richard, son of Richard Sterry, of the Swanne, and Alse, his wyfe, was born 16th Oct., 1655.

Alse, the daughter of Richard Sterry, In-holder, and Alse, his wyfe, born 19th day of Dec., 1657.

Swan Village, of course, takes its name from the Inn.

CAMP BANK.

On West Bromwich Common, between the Lodge and Cutler's End, was thrown up by the soldiers under Oliver Cromwell, when they laid siege to Dudley Castle, A.D. 1644, but this was too far for execution.*

THE OVER END.

Was probably inclosed about 1690 or 1700, it was waste land from the common; at that time there were not half-a-dozen houses within a quarter of a mile.*

SPON LANE.

Probably took its title from a family of this name who lived there. There used also to be a Spon Meadow, Spon Coppice, &c.

THE OLD END.

Is so called from being occupied by old huts, hovels, and houses from olden times.*

THE LING.

From the particular kind of heath which covered that portion of the common.

---

* Reeves.

Greet's Green.

Most probably "Great" Green originally.

Wood Lane.

From a wood on the right hand from Cutler's End to Greet's Green.*

Ridding Lane.

Near Hateley Heath, from "La Ruddinge," a field mentioned in deeds in early times; there is a lane of the same name in Wednesbury.

Witton's Lane.

From Mr. Richard Witton, a Dissenting Minister, who resided there.

Taylor's Lane.

From John Taylor, a poor man, who lived and had a school there.*

Marsh Lane.

From Merse (Saxon) a fen or watery place.*

Virgin's Inn, or End.

Is said to have taken its title from three women who sold ale at an old house there, sometimes called the Virgins.* This may be the meaning, but we are inclined to think the name may date much farther back.

The Three Mile Oak.

From an ancient oak tree that stood upon the left hand about two hundred yards from the public-house.*

Harvil's Hawthorn.

Originally Harvil's Oak. This is a corruption of Heronville. The Heronville's were Lords of Wednesbury, and their name is thus contracted in an old deed given in the "History of Wednesbury," page 21. The oak, no doubt,

---
* Reeves.

died, and its place was supplied by a hawthorn; but in old deeds Harvil's Oak is mentioned, not Hawthorn.

SINK HOLE.

Is the old name for the hollow below the two hills between Charlemont Hall and Newton Road Station.

SOT'S HOLE.

The name formerly given to what is now Church Vale.

CHURCHFIELDS.

The land lying immediately round the Church, as far as the Ten Score. There was a common field here, and also in Lyndon.

OLD HOUSES, &C.

The following extract relating to old houses in this parish, taken from Reeves' History, is interesting. He says " Many of the old houses and cottages, as some of the old people can well remember, were little better than a temporary hut, wattled with sticks, and plastered, in some cases, with mud, covered with branches of trees, straw, turf, and the like materials; most of these had but one apartment, some few with two. Some remains of these original dwellings may be seen in the Old End and Cutler's End. We have many houses yet standing which we may suppose were built about the reign of Elizabeth, and a little later; these are built with timber, and the interstices wattled with sticks (see some of this description in Lyne), while many of the old half-timbered houses are built in part brick, and have in general two or three upper rooms, these houses are getting less every year, and giving way to more modern edifices."

The Oak House, Bromwich Hall, Mr. Cotterill's (bottom of Stoney Lane), some houses opposite the late large house (still standing) and Mr. Blackshaw's in Lyne,* a few near the Holloway, and one or two near the Sheepwash Lane, are probably the oldest buildings in West Bromwich.

The waste lands were inclosed by virtue of an Act of Parliament in 1801, and what was before a wild heath was speedily transformed—houses were soon built, and thus a new town sprang up away from the original village. "Bromwich Heath" is now only a tradition of the past. The writer has heard it said that in the whole journey from London to Holyhead in the old coaching days, the bleakest and wildest part was over this heath.

The following bill was issued about the time of the Inclosure Act:—

"West Bromwich Common, County of Stafford.—Valuable Situations for Building, &c.—To be Sold by Auction, by Josiah Robins, at William Hardware's, the Bull's Head Inn, West Bromwich Common, on Saturday, the 14th of December next, the most elevated and cheerful parts of this very improving and populous situation, West Bromwich Common, adjoining the great Shrewsbury Road, and immediately opposite the ancient Lodge and Warren allotment made to Jervoise Clarke Jervoise, Esq., now the residence of Wastel Cliffe, Esq., all surrounded by the most delightful scenery of Dudley Castle and the Rowley Hills. . . . ."

The Bull's Head occupied the site of the "Dartmouth Hotel" of our day.

"The Lodge" was originally what its name designates, a lodge or hunting box, on the heath. It was enlarged by

---

* At one time the only butcher in the parish. This fact is in the recollection of the writer's grandfather.

the late Mr. Izon, who lived there for many years. The estate was sold after his death, and the house taken down, and upon its site the District Hospital now stands.

The following account of Walter Parsons, the giant blacksmith of this parish, given in Plot's History of Staffordshire, published in 1686, is interesting. It will be found on page 294, and is as follows. After speaking of some remarkably strong men, the author proceeds to say, "Not at all inferior to any of these in matters of strength was one Walter Parsons, of West Bromwich, in this county, though his was not so much to be admired as theirs, who were men but of a middleing ordinary size, whereas Parsons had a stature proportionable to his strength; being so very tall when he was a young apprentice, that they were forced to digg a hole in the ground for him to stand in up to his knees, when he struck at the anvil (for he was first a blacksmith) or sawed wood with another, that he might be at a level with his fellow workman. At length he became porter to King James the First, where he behaved so generously, that though he had valour equal to his strength, yet he scorned to take advantage to injure any person by it, upon which account we have but few experiments left us of his great strength, but such as were sportive, as, that being affronted by a man of ordinary stature, as he walkt London streets, he only took him up by the waistband of his breeches, and hung him upon one of the hooks in the shambles, to be ridicul'd by the people, and so went his way; and that sometimes by way of merriment, he would take two of the tallest Yeomen of the Guard (like the gizard and liver) under his arms, and carry them as he pleased (in spight of all resistance) about the Guard Chamber, where (if I am not misinformed) that is his picture which hangs at the end next the stairs leading down into the court toward White Hall Gate. There is another picture of him, as I have been told also by some, in the great room at the Pope's-head Tavern, in Pope's-head Alley, but whether they are true pictures of him or noe, it being uncertain that they were drawn in the just proportion, I took not the pains to have them measur'd, chusing rather to collect what his height might be from a true measure of his hand yet remaining upon a piece of wainscot at Bentley Hall, by which it appears that from the carpus to the end of the middle finger, it was eleven inches long, and the palm six inches broad . . . . . We may rationally conclude that Parsons must also be thereabout," *i.e.*, 7ft. 6in.

In all probability the blacksmith's forge where Parsons worked was near the church. In nearly all villages a blacksmith's forge is to be found in that position, especially in places where the church stands near a junction of two or more roads of importance, as in this case.

Mrs. Sarah Savage, a daughter of the Rev. Philip Henry, and sister of the Rev. Matthew Henry, the commentator, died, and was buried at West Bromwich in 1752. A small tablet to her memory is in the church. Mary, daughter of the Rev. Matthew Henry, married William Brett, of this parish. She was born in 1711. The name Brett is one of the oldest in West Bromwich, and there is no doubt it is the same as Bratt. Spelling was a matter of little importance in times past, and the alteration of one vowel is easily accounted for.

The father of the late Sir Rowland Hill kept a school at Hill Top, probably at the house known as " The Woodlands," and at this same house there lived at the beginning of this century, a Mr. Keir, the head of a then well-known firm—"Keir, Blair, and Playfair." Mr. Keir was a very clever man, and wrote the preface, containing an account of the minerals, &c., in the neighbourhood, for Shaw's History of this county.

APPENDIX.

The Manor.

THE following information from Colonel Wrottesley came too late for insertion under the head of "The Manor." "In looking over my notes I find that on the Subsidy Roll of 6 Edward III. William de Marnham is assessed at 6s., the highest rate of all the tenants in Bromwich. Roger Basset comes next with an assessment of 4s. 6d. I do not find a Devereux at all; and I have no doubt the Devereux parted with all their interest in West Bromwich and the Marnham's became sole lords of the manor. At the assizes of 21 Edward I. apud Stafford, Bertram, son of Richard de Marnham was tried for the murder of Richard, son of Richard de Marnham (probably his brother). He was acquitted, as the jury state he killed Richard in self-defence."

Sales of Land, &c., in different parts of the Manor.

20th July, 1655.—Sale by John Shelton, Esq., of West Bromwich, of Rea Hall, in Great Barr, to Henry Stone (the Parliamentarian.) Sealed in the presence of Robert Shilton.

Dec. 17, 1708.—Indenture of sale by John Shelton to Josiah Turton, ironmonger, mentions all that parcel of enclosed land called the Mill Closes, divided into two parts, near the dwelling-house of s⁴ Josiah Turton, called The Mill. Mentions the lane leading from Josiah Turton's Corn Mill towards Greet Bridge.

17th Dec., 1708.—Sale to W^m. Silvester, bricklayer, of a messuage in Lindon in West Bromwich; also three parcels of land lying dispersed in a common field in West Bromwich, called Lindon, alias Linefield, containing 3 acres; also one other close of land lying near Joan Bridge, called Joan Bridge Leasowe, containing 4 acres; also Joan Bridge Meadow, all which were formerly in the holding of Henry Penn, and then in the possession of Simon Partridge, commonly called Penn's Tenement.

17th Dec., 1709.—Sale by John Shelton, &c., to John Piddock, gent., of the Hermitage . . . . between the lane called Hermitage Lane, the lane leading from Sandwell Green towards West Bromwich Forge, and other land of s⁴ John Shelton.

July 18th, 1708.—Sale to John Mayoe Smith of a messuage and garden and 4 pieces of land, between the land of Job Simcox, and the land of John Jesson, and the roadway leading from Birmingham to Wednesbury; also 2 other closes of land called the Dry Leasows, between a certain common called West Bromwich Heath, the land of s⁴ John Shelton, called Cauldley Copy, and the land late of Mr. John Turton, in holding of Richard Jesson.

18th June, 1709.—Sale to Joseph Worsley of a cottage, barns, &c., and 3 crofts, situate in Lindon, &c.; also 3 closes to the same adjoining called Cornhill, alias Cronell, and Penny Crofts, situate in Nochells, within the Manor of West Bromwich, between the lane called Stony Lane, leading from West Bromwich Heath to Lyne, the land of John Shelton, the land of James Billingsley, gent., and the heath called Bromwich Heath; also 2 little parcels of land in West Bromwich, between the land late of John Turton, gent., the land late of Brome Whorwood, Esq., and then the Lord Dartmouth, in the holding of Job Wiggin, the land of John Grove, gent., and the land of James Billingsley, gent., then in the holding of Joseph Worsley: also a messuage and meadow, between the lane leading from a certain place in West Bromwich called the Hall End towards another place called Shepherd's Cross, other land of John Shelton called Rudgacre's Coppice, then in his own possession, other land of John Shelton then in the holding of Moses Bird, and the land late of John Hawe, gent.; also 2 pieces of arrable land lying in a certain field in West Bromwich called Knappenhill Field, alias Lydiatefield, containing 3 acres; also one other piece of arrable land lying in a field called Churchfield or Wigmorefield, containing 1 acre; another messuage; also 2 closes of land adjoining, called Broadfields; also 1 little piece of land, between the land late of Henry Hunt, other land of John Shelton, the land late of Thomas Parker, Esq., and the roadway leading from West Bromwich Heath; 1 other close of land, called Crook Hay, between the land of Wm. Stamps and the roadway leading from a place in West Bromwich, called Hateley Heath, towards Wednesbury.

18th June, 1709.—Sale to John Mayoe, of a messuage, &c.; also a meadow, called Mayoe's Meadow, containing 3 acres; also 5 other closes, called Mayoe's Closes (15 acres), between the land of John Hunt, gent., the land of John Shelton, called Rudgacre's Coppy, the lane there called Church Lane, and the roadway leading from Birmingham towards Wednesbury; 2 other closes, called

Bennett's Closes, late in the holding of John Blakemore (5 acres), between the land of Edward Shelton, gent., then in the holding of Sarah Sterry, widow, the lane leading from Blake Lake to a house then known by the sign of the Swan, and a lane called Billhay Lane.

Feb. 12th, 1709.—Sale by John Shilton, to Thomas Dudley, wheelwright, "all that parcel of land called Spann Coppice; also that other parcel of land called Spann Heath, containing 54 acres, between land now of the Lord Dartmouth, the land of Thomas Birch, land late of Joseph Simcox, called Squire's Croft, and a certain lane in West Bromwich called Spann Lane, &c., certain common called West Bromwich Heath.

VERY OLD DEEDS WITHOUT DATES.

Deed of John, son of Wm. Golde, of finchespath giving and granting, &c., to Randolph, son of Alexander, a certain Messuage—together with a house and curtilage, and garden . . . which belonged to Adam Faber de Finchespath—and six selions of land in Finchespath—four of which selions are adjacent to the land of Miles, son of the aforesaid Adam Faber, and the "Sinder hul," with all that pasture of mine the Sinder hul, and extends from the said curtilage to Cowecroft . . . and two selions in the field called la Rudinge . . . Witnesses Rich: Basset de Bromwich, Roger Yllori, William de Derlastun, Walter Musterel, Walter de Leager, Rich. Bonde, Rich. the Cleric.

Deed of William, son of William Suetman de Phinchespad, leasing to William de Phinchespad Miller—that piece of arable land in Phinchespad—lying between the land of Richard de——*(obliterated)* the land of Symon Miller, and the land of Richard de Bostun—and his own land, &c.

... Witnesses William de Wane—Richard Basset—Richard Bonde—Henry Godknowe—William Basset—Richard Golde—William ad Bostun de Bromwych—John de Ecleshulle—The seal has inscribed round it "William Sueteman."

Deed of Richard de Marnham, with the agreement and consent of Margerie, his wife—granting, &c., to William Miller de ffynchespath, for his homage, and eight silver shillings ... a messuage, with its curtilage, in finchespath—between the messuage adjoining Lecrosuayleye and the messuage of William Legemon—and between the country road which leads towards ffynchespath bridge and the land of William Byrrd. Witnesses William Lord of Derlaston—William Yllori (Hillary), Richard Baset—Richard Bonde—William Adbaston—William Deoyley—Ralph Musterel—William de la Cour—Richard the Cleric and others.

Deed of William, called Suetemon de Fyngespath—giving, granting, &c., to Walter, son of Robert de ———— one piece of land—lying between the land of the said William, called the Miller of ffyngespath, and Symon the Miller, situated at the boundary of the same gate ... for his service, and a certain sum of money .. to be paid at Wodensbury .... Witnesses William Symcok—John the Chaplain—William Golde—John Faber—William Miller—Walter Golde—Francis (?) the Cleric, and others.

Deed dated 3rd year of Edward III. (1329).—I, William, son of Richard de Marmham, Lord of West Bromwich, have given and conceded to Robert, son of Thomas de Darlaston and Margerie his wife, for a certain sum of money, a portion of land with its appurtenances, in my common at West Bromwich which lies between land called the Long Mor and another way which leads from ffinchpath to Birmingham—to have and to hold from me and my heirs, paying annually to me, my heirs, or assigns, 18 pence of silver in two annual payments, viz., on the Feast of the Blessed Virgin Mary 9 pence, on the Feast of S. Michael 9 pence, and in doing service at my court at West Bromwich, that is to say at my nearest court after the Feast of S. Michael. Witnesses: Roger Basset—Roger de Rugaker—John Faber—William Bracom—William de Lyndon, and others. Given at West Bromwich, on the Wednesday after the Crucifixion of Our Lord, in the third year of the reign of Edward III.

Deed dated 20th Edward III. (1346).—I, Michael, son of Richard ——— de West Bromwich, have given and conceded . . . to Philip Swift de ffinchpath, four—— of land, with appurtenances . . . in the waste field called the Heathfield. . . . Witnesses Richard Basset —Roger de Rugkaker—John de———William Swetkocks —John Dylow—Thomas Bolde, and others. Given at West Bromwich, on the first Tuesday after the Feast of S. Peter ad Vincula, in the 20th year of King Edward III. after the Conquest.

Deed dated 22nd Edward III. (1348).—Deed of conveyance by John Sarsone—Swetkoc, of Bromwych, to Richard Lovekyns, of the Wytheges in the parish of Tetenhall, six selions of land lying together in the fee of Bromwych, in the chief called Wyggmarefeld in length between the land of my Lord Richard, Prior of Sandwell, on the one part, and his own land on the other part, and in breadth between the land of Richard, son of Richard of Wyggemare, on the one part, and the land of William Gaychild of the other part. To have and to hold all the said six seliones of land, with all their appurtenances, to the said Richard and his heirs, or his assigns, of the chief Lord of that fee, fully, quietly, well, and in peace, by right and hereditarily for ever. The said Richard, his heirs or assigns rendering therefore annually to the chief Lord of that fee one penny of silver at the Annunciation of Saint Mary, in March, for all secular services, exactions, and demands . . . Witnesses Richard Bassat—Roger de Rugiaker—John de Salley—William de Luttelhay—John Doude—and others.—Given at Bromwych, on the Sabbath (Saturday) next after the Feast of Saint Benedict, Confessor and Abbat, in the 22nd year of Edward III.

Deed dated 6th Richard II. (1382.)—Conveyance of land by Richard Belle, of West Bromwich, to Roger Parteriche, of the same . . . six selions, with their appurtenances, which lie in Wigmare feld, between the land of Roger Bassatt and the land of William Sarsone of the other part —to have and to hold, &c. . . . of the chief Lord of that fee by the service thereof due, &c. . . . Witnesses John Marneham—William de Lyttelhay—William Sponne —John Symcoks—William in Haye.—Given at West Bromwich, Thursday next after the Feast of Saint John, at the Latin Gate, in the 6th year of Richard II.

Conveyance by Richard Gold—Bromwych—to Roger Partrich—of a moiety of a field called Goldnscroft—with its appurtenances as they are inclosed by hedges and ditches—to have and to hold, &c. . . . Witnesses John Marneham—William de Lyttulhay—William Sponne John Symcoks—William in Haye, and others.—Given at West Bromwych, on Thursday in the Feast of the Ascension of our Lord, in the 6th year of Richard II. (1382).

Deed dated 21st Richard II. (1388).—Conveyance from Roger Parterych and Agnes, his wife, to Richard, their son, and Joan his wife—of all their lands and tenements which they lately had of the grant and feoffment of John Huwet and William Wytteley . . . Witnesses John Marmham William Sponne—William Lyttelhay—Ralph Smyth—William Hayteley and others.—Given at West Bromwich on the day of S. Augustine the Bishop, in the 21st year of Richard II.

Deed dated 5th Henry IV. (1403).—Conveyance by Richard, son of Walter Smyth de Lyndon to William Hayteley de West Bromwych, of all his lands, tenements, &c., which he held in fee in West Bromwych; Witnesses, William de Sponne, John Symcoks, Thomas Symcoks, Richard Hikkeson, William Symcoks, and others. Given at West Bromwych, on Monday, 14th April, in the 5th year of Henry IV. (1403).

Deed dated 7th Henry VI. (1428).—An Indenture made between Christina, widow of Richard Wylkys, of ffynchespath, and Roger Hayteley de Lyndon, and Margerie, his wife . . . . the said Christina granting to Roger and Margerie all messuages, lands, and tenements, and app^{ts} which the s^d Christina had in ffynchespath and in all other places in the fee of West Bromwych. The s^d Roger and Margerie to pay to the said Christina during her lifetime 7 shillings and 7 pence annually, in two payments, viz.:—at the Feast of the Annunciation of the Blessed Mary, and Saint Michael the Archangel. If this rent was not paid within a month of the aforesaid feasts, Christina was to distrain for the amount due upon the goods and chattels possessed by Roger, in Lyndon. Witnesses, Nicholas Hayteley, Roger Hawkys, and others. Given at West Bromwych, in the feast of All Saints, in the 7th year of the reign of Henry VI., after the Conquest (1428).

As to Land at Hateley Heath, formerly called Longmore.

11th Nov., Feast of S. Martin, 25th Henry VI. (1446).—By deed of this date Thomas Swetcok gave, granted, and confirmed unto Henry Gesson two pieces or places of land within the fee of West Bromwich, at Vinspath, of which one piece was called Blak Lake, which lay between land of a certain Roger Hillary and land of John Whatcroft and a way leading to Birmingham, and another piece called Longmore, which lay between the lands of John Whatcroft on the one part, and the land of William Stony on the other part. To hold the said two pieces of land to the said Henry, his heirs and assigns, to be holden of the chief Lord of the fee.—Executed in the presence of John Whatcroft, Thomas Corbyn, Roger Hateley, John Herrying, and Richd. Kay.

Feast of All Saints, 14th year of Edward IV. (1474.)—Warranty of land from Thomas Parterych, of West Bromwiche, to William Staresmore, William Fyssher, William Pattyngham, John Lynde, and Roger Baker, of all his lands, tenements, meadows, &c., lying within the demesne of West Bromwyche.—Witnesses, William Herrynge, John Geele, John Hay, Richard Sareson, Thomas Heryng, and many others. Given at West Bromwyche in the Feast of All Saints, in the 14th year of Edward IV.

Dated 2nd Feb., 1474.—By indenture Henry Gesson, of West Bromwich, gave and granted to Henry Prest, of the same place, and Margery his wife, a croft of land called the Blake Lake, lying between lands of a certain Roger Hillary, Knight, and land of John Whatcroft, and another way leading towards Birmingham. To hold the said croft with the appurtenances to the said Henry Prest and

Margery his wife, and their heirs and assigns of the said Henry, from the Feast of the Purification of the Blessed Virgin Mary, for 99 years, yielding and paying to the said Henry Gesson four shillings and sixpence in silver. Sealed, &c.

19th Edward IV. (1479).—By deed of this date, Francis ———, of West Bromwich, granted and by his indenture confirmed to Henry Prest and Margery his wife, a certain parcel of land lying in Nether Findespath, in the fee of West Bromwich, lying from land of Master John Beaumont, in length near the Blake Lake, and in width towards a highway on the east part, and land of Henry Gesson, on the west part.

Deed of Conveyance dated 16th Henry VII. (1500).—Conveyance by William Staresmore, of Duddeley, and William Fisher, of the same, to William Malpas, of Tybyngton, and Margerie his wife, of all those lands and tenements, &c., which they lately had, together with William Patynham, John Lynde, and Roger Baker, while they lived, of the gift and feoffment of Thomas Parteriche, of West Bromwiche, while he lived, within the fee of West Bromwich, to have and to hold . . . . to the said William, and Margerie his wife, during the life of the said Margerie. —Witnesses, Thomas Patynham, Thomas Leylonde, Hugh Prestator, of Duddeley, Richard Rode, and Henry Byrame, of West Bromwich, on the Feast of the Invention of the Holy Cross in the 16th year of Henry VII, (1500).

5th May, 17th Henry VII. (1501).—By deed roll, John Gesson, of West Bromwich, husbandman, and Robert Gesson, son and heir of John Gesson . . . . granted and confirmed to William Lytley, gent., and John Lytley, his son and heir, one annual rent of four shillings and two-

Appendix.

pence, to have and to hold the same annual rent to the said William Lytley, and John, son and heir of the said Wm., their heirs, &c., for ever, at the Feast of the Annunciation and the Feast of S. Michael the Archangel, by equal portions arising out of one messuage called Blake Lake, situate in West Bromwich aforesaid, between the land of John Beaumont, Lord of Wednesbury, on the one part, and land of William Frebody, Lord of West Bromwich, called Ridgacres, on the other part, and extending in length and width from the land of the said William Frebody to another way leading from Wednesbury to Birmingham.

Indenture, dated 8th Henry VIII. (1516), between Henry Parterich Smyth and Thomas Parterich, his brother, and Johan his wife, witnesses that the s^d Henry hath granted . . . . and to farm, let to Thomas and Johan one parcel of land in Bromwich, with all erections thereon, lying there between the lane leading to the . . . . well, as far as the field called Guarpanell Field, of the one part, and the land formerly of William Parteriche, of the other part, in breadth, and extends, in length, from the ash tree growing on the land formerly of the s^d William Parteriche, up to the Manse of the Vicar of West Bromwich . . . . Given on Wednesday after the Feast of All Saints, 8th Henry VIII. —Witnesses, John Wylkes, William Aynesworth, John Repton, Robert Ryder, Thomas Syncocks, and others.

Deed, dated 9th May, 1*3th May*, 13th Henry VIII. (1521). —Conveyance of land at West Bromwich called the Grete Leasow, from Thomas Nasshe, John Brook, George Symecocke, and Thomas Merche de West Bromwich to Cecilia Stanley, gentlewoman, which they had by the donation and enfeoffment of Thomas Jennyns, of Wednesbury.

Deed, dated 1st March, 19th Henry VIII. (1527).—Thes indenturs maid the firste day of Marche, the 19th yere of the rayne of King Harrye the VIII., betwexte Wylliam Hogetts, of Dudley, baker, in the oon party, and Harrye Carvs, preste and vicare of the foresaid Dudley, on the other party, wytnessith that the said Wylliam haith grantede and to ferme letton oon pasture and a croft called sum tyme Crumpys Grond, lying in the parisch of Westbromwych, within the countye of Staford, with all maner of comodities and proffetts to the said pastur and crofte belonging, the wych pastur lyis between the hye waye ledyng from Robert Ryders to the town of Dudley, and on the other syide a closse longyng to a Chantrye of the Chirche of Walsaill, and the crofte meryth on the oon syd of the said hye waye, and on the other syide to another closse of the forsaid Chantrye, and at the nether end towarde Dudley a water called Tame, to have and to hold the said pasture and crofte to the forsaid Harrye or his assigns from the feste of the Annunciation of our Lady nexte for to come after the dait above wryten unto the end and term of XLti yerres then nexte following and fully to be complete; paying therefore yerly duryng the said terme, to the said Wylliam, his heirs or assigns, xiijs. and iiijd. of lawful money of Englonde by evyn porcions, that ys to say, at the feste of Sente John the Baptiste vjs. and viijd., and at the feste of Sente Michaell the Arkchangell vjs. and viijd.; also the said Harry schall pay ijd. to the chiefe Lord and keepe suyte of courte twys a yere, or ells when the said Wylliam doith a pay, to allowe him ij to his costs, and if yt so be that the said rent be note pay'd within the space of xiiij dais after the forsaid days of payment yf yt be lawfully asked, then it shalbe lawful to the said Wylliam to distreyne and it so to hold and kepe until he, his heirs, or assigns be fully contented and paid, and if so be that the s^d rent be not pay'd for the space of a month after that, if it be lawfully asked, that then the said Wylliam, his heirs, or assigns shall re-enter, and these endentures to stand void; also, the said Harry and his assigns shall crop and stook all maner of woods and browsments within the said pasture or crofte to the best usse that he or his assigns canne, except the hegrows, the wych shall not be fallen nor yete stoked duryng the said tym; also the said William hath resayvid on yer rent in hand, for the wych yers rent the said Wylliam, his heirs, or assigns, shall alowe the said Harry, or his assigns, too of the next yers insewing every yer iys. and viijd., and the said Wylliam by these presents graunteth to defend and warrant the said Harry and his assigns the forsaid pastur and crofte duryng the said tim, after the manner abovesaid, as an obligacion doith specifye.—In witnesse whereof the parteis abovesaid interchangble have sette their seales, these men beyinge wytnesse, Robert Clough, Fowke Malpasse, John Walker, of Dudley.

Conveyance of land 23rd Henry VIII., 1527.—By Johanna Hodgetts, widow—daughter of Richard Elis, otherwise called Richard Sadler and Walter Sutwyke, John Jukys—and William Phippon feoffees, to uses of the said Johanna—releasing to Richard Hodgetts all her right, title, estate, &c., in all lands and tenements being and lying in West Bromwich—lately called Crompes Ground.—Dated 14th March, 1527.

Conveyance 23rd Henry VIII. (1531.)—Conveyance by William Hodgetts, of Dudley, son and heir of William Hodgetts and Elizabeth his wife—to Richard Hodgetts, of

Segeley—all those lands, tenements—meadows, &c., which he had in West Bromwyche—called Crompes Grownde. Witnesses Thomas Schawe, of   John Stanley, of West Bromwyche, Esq., Wm. Nalle, of the same place, and others.—Given at West Bromwyche, 21st November, 1531.

Deed dated 34th Henry VIII.—(1542).—Confirmation of conveyance by Thomas Jennyns to Thomas Nasshe, &c., of a meadow, called the Greete Leasow, in West Bromwich, lying between land of Richard Hodgetts on one part, and the river called Tame on the other part—according to certain deeds between *Dorothy Stanley, gentlewoman, on the one part, &c.

Deed dated 20th Jan., 1555-6, 2 and 3 Philip and Mary— Conveyance by Francis Stanley, Esq., to Richard Hodgetts of one pasture or close in Greate, within the demesne of West Bromwich, lying between the land called Crompes ground and the water of the Tame, in width—and between the King's Highway leading from Greate Green to the town of Duddele—and land late of a certain Chantry of Tonge, in length.—Signed Franciscu Stanley.

20th April, 3rd Elizabeth, 1560.—By Bill of this date, under seal—George Lane, of West Bromwich, yeoman, held for   years ending
One croft, called the Black lake, lying in the fee of West Bromwich, whereupon was then built one house, or cottage, in which then one John Davys did inhabit, as by the lease of one Henry Jesson, bearing date the feast of the Purification of the Blessed Virgin Mary, in the reign of Edward IV. after the Conquest—for the term of 99 years— which lease was then conveyed to the possession and

---

* Mistake for Cicely.

Appendix.

hands of the s⁴ George Lane ... and the thereof was in one Richard Lutley, of the County of Salop, gent., —&c., &c.

8th May, 4th Elizabeth, 1561.—By Indenture between Richard Lutley, of Wollaston, in the parish of Gyson, in the county of Salop, gent., and John Lutley, his son, of the one part—and William Hunt, of West Bromwich, of the other part—Witness that the said Richard and John, in consideration of £50, will bargain and sell unto William Hunt, and his heirs, one Tenement, situated in the fee and Lordship of West Bromwich, with a garden and a croft thereunto belonging, then in the tenure and occupation of John Davys, for term of years thereof, by Indenture dated 20th April, in the 3rd year Elizabeth, with the rent, by the year, of 20s.; also the said Richard and John Lutley, for consideration aforesaid, did bargain and sell unto William Hunt one cottage, situate in the fee and Lordship of West Bromwich, with a garden—one croft, with a meadow situated together in West Bromwich, called Haytley Field, then in the occupation of Francis Jesson, tenant for a term of years thereof, by Indenture dated in the Feast of All Saints, in the 6th year of Edward VI.

1st April, 1571.—Indenture between William Hunt and Edward Davies, and Anne his wife.—Lease of the cottage, &c., described as being situated between the lands of William Orme, gent., in the tenure of George Hopkins—the lands of Winifred Stanley, widow—and the Queen's highway leading from Wednesbury to Birmingham, at the yearly rental of 30s.

4th May, 17th Elizabeth, 1574.—By deed roll, under seal, Winifred Stanley, of West Bromwich, widow—late wife of Francis Stanley, Esq., deceased—and Lady of the

Manor of West Bromwich—Reciting that William Hunt, of West Bromwich, had two cottages, &c., of the gift and grant of Richard Littlely, and John, his son—whereof one cottage, &c., was situated in the Nether Fynchpathe, within the fee of West Bromwich, called Blake lake, in length and in breadth between the lands of Thomas Ford, Gent., the lands of the said Winifred Stanley, and the Highway leading from Wednesbury towards Birmingham—and one cottage, &c., situated in West Bromwich, in length and in breadth between the lands of Winifred Stanley and the way leading from the Church of West Bromwich towards Wednesbury—all which were holden of the said Winifred Stanley, as of the manor of West Bromwich—by certain rents, services, &c. It is stated that the said Winifred, by her deed, did remise, release, and wholly, for her and her heirs, quit claim unto the said William Hunt, &c., excepting the suit unto the great Leete, or view of frankpledge within the said Manor.

Deed dated 12th June (1577).—Deed of sale by John Partridge, senr. and junr., to William Mucklow, of Halesowen, Salop, for the sum of £55, of land in West Bromwich, lying in length between the land of Winifred Stanley, gentlewoman, called Wall Way, the land of Henry Blakeweye, nigh the highway leading from Blake Lake towards Bromwiche Church, the highway leading from the said church towards Hateley Heath, and the land of the said Winifred Stanley, called Wall Moor Furlong, and also all that croft or close of land called Gold Croft, in West Bromwich, now in the occupation of John Partridge, in length and in breadth between the highway leading from Hateley Heath towards Bromwiche Church aforesaid, the field there called Knapeney Hill Field, the lane leading from Hateley Heath toward Jone Bridge and the land of William Wilks in all parts, and also 6 acres of arable land lying in West Bromwich in the fields there called Wigmore Field, in length between the head land there and the land of Robert Whorwood, Esq., and breadth between the land of the foresaid Winifred Stanley and the land of John Naylor.

Indenture dated 8th November, 1577.—Between John Hateley, of West Bromwich, and Thomas his son, leasing land, lying in Fynchespath in the lordship of West Bromwich, to Thomas Parkes, of Wednesbury, mentions the land of Wynyfred Stanley, widow. The rent to be paid at the Feast of the Annunciation of our blessed ladie the Virgine.

Lease dated 20th April, 27th Elizabeth (1584).—Between Thomas Hayteley, of West Bromwich, and Thomas Meir, of West Bromwich, for 20 years, of a croft or close of land being in Fynchespath in the lordship of West Bromwich, between the land of Michael Foster, gent., &c., and the highway leading from Wednesbury towards Birmingham. Sealed, &c., in the presence of Edward Grove and others.

13th June, 1584.—John Partridge, senr., of West Bromwich, yeoman, and John Partridge, junr., his son and heir, sell to William Mucklow, of Northfield, smith, one messuage or tenement, with a garden, orchard, and croft, and land adjoining it, called Gold Croft, and six acres or butts of land lying near.

14th June, 3rd James I. (1605).—By Indenture made between William Hunt, of Smethwick, and George Barber, lease of cottage and croft, and also one other croft or close of land called the Moore, lying and being in West Bromwich, being parcel of a ground there called Hateley

Field, between the land of Walter Stanley, Esq., the land of the said William Hunt, in the occupation of William Jesson and the highway there leading from Lydeatt towards the common there called Hateley Heath.

30th January, 1626.—Gift of land called Gold Croft and Wigmore Field, by William Hunte, of Smethwicke, to his son, John Hunt. These properties are mentioned as being in the tenure of William Jesson, and having descended to Wm. Hunt from his father, W'm. Hunt, who bought them of one Wm. Mucklowe . . . . and other lands, &c., of Richard Lutley and John his son, namely Blake Lake.

LANDS CALLED BARDITCH, BARKER'S FIELD, AND OAKLEY'S CROFT.

1594.—Indenture of sale between William Skeffington Esq., of Fisherwick, and Elizabeth, his wife, to Francis Symcock, of West Bromwich, of the land called Barditch, described as lying between the land of George Birch, deceased, and the land of William Whorwood, Esq., and the ancient way leading from Wolverhampton towards Birmingham, and the ancient way leading from West Bromwich to Smethwick.—Dated February 5th, in the 37th year of Queen Elizabeth.

1637.—Sale of land by John Stone, of Willenhall, to Henry ffoorde, of West Bromwich, mylner, mentions lands, called Barker's Field, house, &c., lying between the lane leading from Bromwich Heath towards Wednesbury, the land of Sir Rychard Shilton, and the land of Mr. Walsteede. Dated March 12th, 13th King Charles (1637).

Indenture made June 26th, 1638.—Between Sir John Garrard, of Lamer, son of Sir John Garrard, Knight and Bart., in the County of Hertford, Bart., and Thomas Oakley, of West Bromwich, nailor, wherein Sir John

Garrard sells to Thomas Oakley several crofts or meadows in West Bromwich, one called Two Crofts, another Wall Hayes, another Gorsty Close, one other meadow, about four acres, lying close to the house where John Newey now dwells, in West Bromwich, all which said premises late were the inheritance of John Nether Myll, Esq., deceased.

Deed in Latin, dated June 27th, 1638.—Same as above, On the back are the signatures of Nethermill Garrard, Radelphi Kendricke, John Turton, Simon Rider, Walter Grove, junior, Michael Turton. Mem.:—" This copie was taken and examined by Wm. Barnsley, of Trysull, gent., the original whereof with. . . . . several other deeds are in the custodie of Richard Sterry, of The Swan, in West Bromwich, who purchased the last of the lands within mentioned of Thomas Oakley."

Indenture made 2nd January, 1638-9.—Between Thomas Oakley, of West Bromwich, nailor, and Henry ffoord, of West Bromwich, milner. Wherein Thos. Oakley sells for £36 10s. 0d. the croft or parcel of ground lying in West Bromwich, over against the nowe dwelling house of John Newey, in West Bromwich, between the land now or late of Sir Richard Shilton, Knight, the land now or late of John Sparrye, gent., the King's Majesty's highway leading from Bromwich Heath towards Wednesburie, and a little lane leading from the said King's highway towards Bromwich Church, which said close the said Thomas Oakley lately purchased, amongst other lands and tenements, of Sir John Garrard, of Lamer, in the County of Hertford, Bart. —Sealed and delivered in the presence of Symon Rider, Robert Rider; mem. of peaceable possession, &c., witnesse, Humfrey Lowe, George Biker.

Indenture dated 11th Sept., 1661.—Sale of property at West Brom^ch. between Richard Hilton, of West Bromwich, and Joyce his wife, and Henry Ford of Winson Green, one part is mentioned as "lying between the Great Portway leading from Wolverhampton towards Birmingham, the land now or late of William Hunt, and the copy-hold land late of William Lane, deceased." Also, "another cottage with four meadows, between the said Portway leading from Wednesbury towards Birmingham, the land of Mr. Amphlett, the land of the said Henry Ford, in the tenure of Gregory Averns, the land of John Shelton, Esq., all which said cottage and premises were late part of the inheritance of Francis Wasted, Esq.. deceased.

Indenture of lease dated 12th August, 1663.—Between John Simcox, ironmonger, of West Bromwich, and Francis Harris, blacksmith, mentions four leasows or pastures called Barditch, and two days work of arable land in the common field.

24th March, 1670.—Sale of the property called Barditch, by John Simcox, the elder, to George Jesson, describes the land "as lying in West Bromwich, between the King's Majesty's Highway leading from Wolverhampton towards Birmingham, a certain lane, now or late called Smethwick lane, wh: leadeth from the way aforesaid towards Smethwick, the land now or late of Broom Whorwood, Esq., and the land now or late of Thomas Birch;" and also two parcels of arable land, containing about 2 acres, lying and being in a certain common field in West Bromwich called Wiggmorefield, one whereof lyeth adjoining the land of the said Broom Whorwood, on the one side, and the land of William Partridge, of Lyndon, on the other; and one parcel of land lyeth adjoining to the other side of the land of the said William Partridge."—Outside the deed is written: "Memorandum that before the sealing and delivering hereof it was agreed between the parties to the within written indre. that the money formerly paid to the Abbot of Sandwell, and now to Broome Whorwood, Esq., and his heirs, shall be as effectually excepted by this as if the same had been excepted in the indenture within written.—John Guest, Henry Ford, Francis Harris.

Sept. 10th, 1679.—Sale of Barker's field, situate in West Bromwich, between the Portway leading from Wednesbury towards Bromwich Heath, the land of John Shelton, Esq., and the land of Richard Amphlett, Esq.; also, all those pastures, &c., called Oakley's Croft, adjoining to the Portway and a lane leading from the Portway to West Bromwich Church, between Henry Ford, of Clifford's Inn, London, son and heir of Henry Ford, late of West Bromwich, deceased, and Thomas Jesson, of Sutton Coldfield.

Indenture dated November 3rd, 1658.—Sale by William Smallwood of the Middle Temple, London, gent., and John Gilpin, of Wednesbury, gent., of land lately the lands of inheritance of Francis Walstead, late of the Middle Temple, esquire, deceased, to John Hilton.

Indenture dated March 25th, 1660.—Between Brome Whorwood, esq., of Sandwell, and Thomas Nurthall, a lease for 21 years of land called Bald Hills, about 20 acres of the Hayes, abutting on lands held by Humphrey Dudley and Edward Mawdick, and the meadow called the Hayes Meadow, in West Bromwich. Reserving all quarries and mines of stone or cole; at a rent of £7 10s., to be paid twice a year, viz., at the Feast of S. Michael the Archangel, and the Annunciation of our Blessed Lady S. Mary the

Virgin, and also paying at the Feast of All Saints one couple of fatt capons.

April 5th, 1666.—T. Nurthall assigns the remainder of the lease to George Jesson.

Settlement by John Haitley, Nov. 6th, 1620.—To all Christian people. John Haitley, of West Bromwich, sendeth greeting in our Lorde God Everlasting. Know ye as well for and in consideration of a marreage shortly, by God's permission, to be had and solemnized between Walter Vale, son of Symon Vale, of West Bromwich, husbandman, and Elianor, my daughter, do for other good causes and considerations, me the said John Haitley, moving, I the said J. H. have given, graunted, enfeofed, and confirmed . . . . unto Symon Warde, of West Bromwich, yeoman, and Nicholas Rider, of the same parishe . . . . yeoman . . . . all that messuage, cottage, dwelling-house, or tenement . . . . wherein I the said John Haitley doe now dwelle, in finchepath, neare unto Wednesbure Bridge, and also all that cottage . . . . adjoining to the aforesaid dwelling-house, wherein one Elizabeth Parkes, widow, nowe dwelleth, and also all and every the houses, barnes, stables, buildings, out-houses, foulde, gardanies, orcharde . . . . and parcells of ground . . . . situate . . . . between the land nowe or late of Willm. Stanley, esquire, the land of Raphe Tomkys, deceased . . . . to the use and behoof of me the said John Haitley, for and during the terme of my naturale lief . . . . and after the decease of me . . . . then to the use and behoof of the said Walter Vale and Elianor my daughter . . . . Indented in the presence of . . . . Walter Stevens, Francis Brookes, Symon Rider, Nicholas Rider, and others.

Walter Vale and Elnor Haickley married the 23rd of November. *anno predicto* (1620)—(Register).

BRIDGE END CROFT.

Indenture dated April 25th, 1643.—Between Walter Vale, husbandman, and Simon Vale, his eldest son—and Henry Ford, of Birmingham, yeoman—For the sum of £50 have demised, granted, sett, and to farm lett all that messuage—cottage—dwelling house, or Tenement, with appurtenances, wherein the said Walter doth nowe inhabit in Finchpath—and also all that cottage or dwelling house, with appurtenances adjoining to the aforesaid house, in the tenure of George Bassett, lying between the land of Sir Richard Shilton, Knight—the land of Francis Tomkys—the land of Thomas Sheldon—the King's Majesty's Higheway leading from Bromwich Heath towards Wednesbury, and a little lane leading from the said highway towards the land of the said Sir Richard Shilton—At a peppercorn rent for 21 years.—Witnesses Thomas Smalbroke—John James—Thomas Grove and George Jesson.

Indenture dated October 16th, 1649.—Between Walter Vale and Richard Brooks of a lease, for 21 years, of the Bridge End Croft—on the payment of £30—and at the yearly rent of one Rose flower.—Richard Brookes, in 1652, assigned the remaining term of years of the above lease to his wife, Elinor, who, in December, 1658, for the sum of £19 paid her by George Jesson, assigned the remainder of the lease to Thomas Jesson, the son of George.

Indenture of lease between Walter, Elinor, and Symon Vale—granting to George Jesson—the land called Bridg End Croft—in consideration of the sum of £20—and a Peppercorn Rent—date 16th November, 1657.

Lease made over to George Jesson, yeoman, by Joseph Brookes, 7th June, 1658. The original lease mentions a piece of land called the Bridg End Croft, lying between the land of the Lord of the Manor, the land of Francis Tomkis, of Wednesbury, now in the occupation of Richard Selvister, and the land of Walter Ffale, which land is leased for the sum of £30 by Walter Ffale to one Richard Brookes for 21 years, at the yearly rent of one roase flower at or upon the feast day of S. John Baptist (if it be lawfully demanded).

Indenture bearing date Dec. 15th, 1658.—Sale by Walter Vale to George Jesson of houses and land in West Bromwich, lying together in Finchpath, near Wednesbury Bridge. Two houses, gardens, and orchards are mentioned —one house as the habitation of Samuel Higgins, the other a cottage, in the tenure of Joseph Morrice and Thomas Cashmore, " situated between the land of John Shilton, Esq., the land of Francis Tomkis, the land now or late of Thomas Sheldon, the road way leading from Bromwich Heath towards Wednesbury Bridge, a little lane leading from the said road way to the land of the said John Shilton." . . . .

DAGGER HALL.

Indenture dated 17th April, 13th Charles I. (1637.)—Between Mary Gibbons, of Oskote, widow, and William Gibbons, of Oskote, yeoman, of the one part, and Edward Grove, the younger, of West Bromwich, yeoman, of the other part. Witnesses that the said Mary Gibbons and William for the consideration therein named did grant, bargain, sell, enfeoff and confirm unto the said Edward Grove and his heirs, a cottage, garden, and hemplecke in Lyndon, also 4 crofts or closes of land or pasture in West Bromwich, also one acre or dayes earthe of errable land

and one lande with the appurtenances, which said cottage, garden and hemplecke doe lye between the land of Sir Richard Shilton, knighte, the land of Phillippe Parkes and the highewaye there called Hargate Lane. Two of the said crofts lye together between the land of Edward Grove, the elder, the land of the said Sir Richard Shilton, the land of John Turton, and the way there leading from the dwelling-house of the said Edward Grove, the elder, towards Birmingham. One other croft lyeth between the land of Sir Richard Shilton and the waste ground called Bromwich Heath, and the other croft is called the Monnynges, and lyeth between the land of Brome Whorwood, esquire, the land of John Turton and the lane there, and the said acre of land conteyneth four seliones of land, and lyeth in the comon feilde called the Churchefeilde, between the land of Sir Richard Shilton on both sides, and the other selione of land lyeth in the comon feilde called Stycrofte, between the lande of Edward Grove, the elder, on the one side, and adjoyneth to the lande of John Littley on the other side.

Indenture, 12th August, 1667.—Between Edward Grove, of Lyndon, yeoman, of the one part, and William Turton, of the other part, witnesses that the said Ed. Grove, in consideration of the sum of £5 paid by William Turton, did grant, bargain, sell, &c. .... to the said William Turton, and his heirs, all that piece of land, containing about 100 yards of ground ... being part of a close of land lately purchased by Edward Grove, from one William Gibbons, of Oscote, abutting on the south side thereof, upon a house and garden of the said William Turton, in the tenure of James Cox, known by the name of Dagger Hall, and on the west end thereof upon the lane leading from the said howse towards the church of West Bromwich; which said piece of ground is now marked and paled out from the greate gate post of the said Edward Grove, at the common entrance into the said croft, along by the north end of the said howse eastward to the angle or corner of the said garden belonging to the said howse, upon part of which said piece of ground William Turton, or his assigns have caused a draw-well to be made.

Indenture made 12th August, 1667.—Between William Turton and Edward Grove reciting last Indre; also stating that William Turton on the said premises had a draw-well, and intended the same for a pump. Then it witnesses that s^d William Turton did demise, set, and to farm, let unto s^d Ed. Grove the use of the s^d well or pump for the cattle of s^d Ed. G. that depastured there. To hold the use of the said well or pump to s^d Ed. Grove, and his assigns, from the date thereof for 200 years, under the rent of one peppercorn, payable on the 25th September, if demanded.

N.B.—Edward Grove had an only daughter, Mary, who married James Billingsley; they had an only daughter, Sarah, who married Charles Magenis. She survived her husband, and by her will devised all her lands in West Bromwich and Wednesbury to her son Constantine, and his heirs. Constantine died without issue, upon whose death the same descended to Charles Magenis, his brother and heir lately deceased.

"Sarah Magenis, widow, of Alcester, left by her will her lands at West Bromwich and Wednesbury to her second son Constantine, with a charge with him to pay on arriving at the age of 21 years, the sum of £125 to each of her four daughters. Constantine died before attaining his majority; the estate came to Charles Magenis, and we find a deed of release, date October 17th 1734, by William Mantell, who had married one of the four daughters, and Catherine his wife, to Charles Magenis, on the payment of £125 by him. A similar deed by Edward Watton, and Frances his wife; another by Richard Hawkesford, and Ann his wife; another by Henry Baddily, and Sarah his wife."

A copy of the will of Charles Magenis, date Ap. 3, 1745. Robert Aglionby Slaney and Richard Rann trustees; directions to sell his estates if necessary.

Sep. 30th, 1728.—Let to Saml. Lloyde two pieces of land a joyning to Dager Hall, in the parish of West Bromwich for five pounds ten shillings per annum, for twenty-one years from Lady Day next, and I do agree not to have more in tillage at aney time than one piece, and for the last three years of the term not to have aney parte of it in tillage, and the said Thomas Jesson promise to alow forty shillings for muck and to quick-set the dead gaps, and Saml. Lyde promises to cleane and weeade the same. —As witness our handes, Thomas Jesson, Samuel Loyd.

Indenture made the 22nd September, 1748.—Between Robert Aglionby Slaney, of Walford, in the county of Salop, esq., and Richard Rann, of Birmingham, gent., and Rebecca Magenis, widow, relict of Charles Magenis, late of Birmingham, merchant, of the one part, and Thomas Jesson, of West Bromwich, ironmonger, of the other part, witnesseth that the said R. A. Slaney, Richard Rann, and Rebecca Magenis for . . . . have bargained and sold . . . . unto the s⁴ Thomas Jesson . . . . all those two closes of land or pasture . . . . late in the tenure of John Worsley, situate in West Bromwich, and lying together between the land heretofore of Edward Grove, senr., Sir Edward Shilton, and John Turton, deced., but now or late of

Parratt, in the holding of one .... Smallwood, the land late of John Worsley, deced., in the holding of Saml. Lloyd, and the land of John Turton, gent., in the holding of the s⁴ Saml. Lloyd, and a lane leading from a house there called Dagger Hall towards Bromwich Church .... and also all that other piece or parcel of land lying in a certain field in West Bromwich called the Churchfield, and late also in the tenure of the said John Worsley, and lying between the land of the Rt. Honble. the Earl of Dartmouth, in the occupation of Nathaniel Whiley, the land of Mr. Jesson Lowe, and a road or way leading from the land of the s⁴ Jesson Lowe to other parts of the said Churchfield .... and also the use of the well or pump formerly granted by Wm. Turton, gent., to Ed. Grove, standing near the house called Dagger Hall .... yielding and paying therefore one peppercorn, at or upon the Feast day of S. Michael next ensuing the date hereof, if the same be lawfully demanded.—Signed, R. A. Slaney, R. Rann, Rebecca Magenis.

RELATING TO THE MANOR.

Inquisition post mortem. 19 Edw. I., No. 14.—Extenta feo-dorum militum que fuerunt Rogeri de Somery defuncti qui de Rege tenuit in capite.

(Among many others.)

Dimidium feo-dum quod Walterus Deverys tenet in Brumwyz quod extenditur ad ... x ti.

Dimidium feo-dum quod Ricardus de Marham tenet in Brumwyz quod extenditur ad ... x ti.

Inquisition post mortem 16 Edward II., No. 72.—Staffordia Inquisicio facta coram escuetore domini Regis apud Staffordiam vj, die Decembris anno regni Regis Edwardi sexto decimo ad inquirendum de feodis militum et advocacionibus ecclesiarum que fuerunt Johannis de Somery in comitatu predicto die quo obiit secundum tenorem brevis domini regis huic inquisicioni consuti per sacramentum Thome Hillarrii, Johannis de Wirle, Johannis de Bagre, Ade le Fremon, Roberti de Walshal, Willielmi atte Putte, Ricardi le Bedel, Ricardi atte Chircheheye, Ricardi de Offel, Johannis de Mollesle, Willielmi de Derlaston et Henrici de Aula Qui dicant per sacramentum suum quod. [Here occur the names and holdings of various owners in different localities.] Stephanus Devereys, tenuit de predicto Johanne (die quo obiit) dimidium feodum militis in West-Bromwich et valet per annum x x. s. Item dicunt quod Ricardus de Mar ** m tenuit de eodem Johanne dimidium feodum militis in eadem et valet per annum xx. s.

Inquisition post mortem. 30 Edward III. (1st n*) No. 53.—Inquisicio capta coram Johanne de Swynnertone escaetore domini Regis in Comitatu Staffordie apud Walshale xvij. die Junii anno regni regis Edwardi tercij a conquestu tricesimo virtute cujus-dam brevis huic inquisicioni consuti per sacramentum Johannis Dymmok, Willielmi Dymmok, Willielmi de Hervile,* Ricardi de Wavere, Johannis le Cook de Pelsale, Willielmi Sweyne, Roberti de Yelbrigg, Henrici le Bideles, Hugonis le Ridere, Thome le Bideles, Thome Barneville, et Willielmi de Rugacre qui dicunt super sacramentum suum quod Rogerus Hillary defunctus in brevi contentus tenuit in dominico suo ut de feodo die quo obiit de domino rege in capite per magnam serjantiam unum mesuagium, &c., &c. [Here follow various holdings in various localities.] Item tenuit apud Bromwych sibi et predicte Katerine (uxore sua adhuc superstite) conjunctim et heredibus ipsuis Rogeri ij mesuagia . . . .

---
* Heronville.

acras terre iij. acras prati ij. acras pasture x. solidatas redditus percipiend annuatim ad festa predicta de Johanne de Alrewas et Alianora uxore ejus ut de jure ipsuis Alianore per servicium militare et reddend per annum v. s. x. d. et valet per annum salvis reprisis xx. s. et ibidem tenuit conjunctim cum predicta Katerina in forma predicta unum mesuagium xij. acras terre ij. acras prati de Willielmo Devreux per servicium xj. d. pro omnibus et valet per annum ultra reprisam vj. s. viij. d.

Inquisition post mortem. 4 Henry IV., No. 36.—Inquisicio capta apud Wolvernehamptone die Jovis proximo ante festum exaltacionis Sancte Crucis anno regni Regis Henrici quarti post conquestum quarto coram Willielmo de Walshale Escaetore domini Regis in Comitatu Staffordie virtute brevis ipsuis Regis eidem Escaetori directi et huic inquisicioni consuti per sacramentum Johannis Mollesley senioris, Johannis Buffrey, Johannis Waryng, Johannis Symondes, Johannis filii Hugonis, Henrici Tommesone, Johannis de Mollesley junioris, Ricardi Chalener, Johannis Deykes, Willielmi Cartewrught, Johannis Cole, et Ricardi Jurdan, Qui dicunt super sacramentum suum quod Rogerus Hillary miles in dicto brevi nominatus tenuit die quo obiit de domino rege in capite per magnam serjantiam. [Here follows certain land in Kingswynford]. . . . Dicunt quod predictus Rogerus obiit sine herede de corpore Margarete uxoris sue procreato. . . . . Dicunt quod idem Rogerus tenuit die quo obiit conjunctun cum prefata Margareta uxore sua adhuc superstite duo mesuagia xx. acras terre iij. acras prati ij. acras pasture et x. solidatas redditus cum pertinentiis in Bromwiche de herede Alianore de Allerwas per servicium v. solidorum per annum pro omnibus serviciis et valent in omnibus exitibus per annum ultra reprisas xx.

solidos Et tenuit ibidem conjunctim cum prefata Margareta unum mesuagium xij. acras terre ij. acras prati cum pertinentiis de herede Johannis Deures* per servicium xij. denariorum pro omnibus et valet per annum ultra reprisas vj. s. viij. d. . . . Et dicunt quod predictus Rogerus obiit sine herede de corpore suo in festo Sancte Trinitatis anno regni regis predicti primo et quod Johannes filius Saeri filii Johanne unuis sororum predicti Rogeri Hillary et Elizabeth ux Johannis Russell militis filia Elizabeth alterius sororum ejusdem Rogeri sunt heredes propinquiores ipsuis Rogeri et quod predictus Johannes filius Saeri est etatis quadraginta annorum et amplius et predicta Elizabetha filia Elizabethe est etatis quinquaginta annorum et amplius.

Extracts from a manuscript of Simon Rider, called the "Hypomnema," in the William Salt Library:—

I. Simon Rider, born at West Bromwich, 8th April, baptized the 15th, 1558.

Married at Halesowen, 25th November, 1578.

My father died 24th May, 1579.

My son, Nicholas, born at Oldbury, 31st May, baptized at Halesowen, 2nd June, 1579.

I, Simon Rider, came to live at West Bromwich, 4th June, 1580.

My daughter, Joanna, born at Oldbury, 15th March, baptized at Halesowen, 18th March. 1580.

My son, Robert, born at Oldbury, 23rd December, baptized at Rowley, 1582.

I was elected Ale Taster 19th October, 1583, and Thomas Parsons was my associate.

---
* Devereux ?

My daughter, Margerie, born at West Bromwich, Friday, the 9th July, baptized at West Bromwich, 11th July, 1585.

My daughter, Anna, born at Oldbury, Saturday, 2nd December, 15—, baptized at Rowley, 3rd day of December, ——.

My daughter, Anna, born at West Bromwich, 30th April, baptized at West Bromwich, 2nd May, 1589.

My mother died 31st December, 1588, buried at West Bromwich, 1st January.

My son, Simon, born at West Bromwich, 4th day of October, baptized 8th of October, 1591.

My son, Francis, born at Oldbury, 24th January, baptized 25th January, 1593.

My daughter, Margaret, born at West Bromwich, 31st July, 1595.

My daughter, Maria, born at West Bromwich, 15th September, baptized at West Bromwich, 27th September, 1597.

My son, John, born at West Bromwich, 24th April, baptized 2nd May, 1600.

In the first day of October, anno 1579, Mistress Wynifrede Standley, the late wife of ffranncis Standley, Esquire, deceased, did keep a leete or great courte by her steward, William Booth, of Birmingham, the elder, gent., at which court I, Symon Ryder, was, and the steward demanded of me whether my land was harriotable and ought to pay harriott to the lady of the manor. I sayd it ought not, &c. . . . . and to confirm my saying I did shewe unto Maister Walter Standley there presently two deeds, ... the other deed containing only Huckwalls . . . . my chiefest for Sich field is yearly 4d.

It doth appear that one Margery Marnham in her widowhoode did grant unto Walter, the son of Nicholas Erdynton . . . . and the other deed doth com of the grante of Richard Marneham, being chiefe lord of West Bromwich, unto William, the son of John Erdinton, containing Huckwalls; and Maister Walter Standley demanded to have a coppy of the same deede, and the steward, at his desire, did copy them out.

Item the 25th day of October anno dom. 1580.— Mystrys Winifred Standley kept a leete at West Bromwich, when I, Symon Ryder, was to agree with her for my knight's fee, and my land being equally and undifferently . . . . was esteemed to be the tenth part of a knight's fee, for which I payd unto her yd. And whereas one of those deeds was granted by Margery Marnham to Walter, son of Nicholas Erdinton, for his homage and service, with distress at her charges, as in the same it doth and may appear, wherefore the steward doth say that I ought to do homage unto my chief lady, which I think I ought not to do, by cause it was granted to him only for his homage and service, and doth not say of his heirs. . . . .

When a free man shall do homage to his lord of whom he holdeth in fee, he shall hold his hands together between the hands of his lord, and shall say thus: I become your man from this time forwarde for life for membre and for worldly honor, and I shall owe you my faithe for the lands that I holde of you, saving the faithe that I do owe to our Sovraigne Lady Queen and to my other lords.—17 Edward II.

When a free man shall doe fealtie to his lord he shall hold his right hand upon a book and shall say thus: Heare you my lord R. that I, P. . . . shal be to you both faithful and true, and shall owe my fidelytie unto you for the lande that I holde of you, and lawfully shall doe such customes and services as my duty ys to you, at the termes assigned, so helpe me, God.—17 Edward II.—Robert Rider, arbitrator, 1571.

Item the 29th day of September, ann. 1572.—Payd unto Richard Jennens, of Wednesbury, yeoman, five pounds of currant english money to and for the use of Robert Byrom, late of London, bricklayer, in the presents of Syr Henry Blakemore.—Rychard Barker, Jhon Hawks, Roger Walton, Richard Bennet, Robart Wright, John Watt alias Comson, Jhon Hopkis, junior, &c. *(Side note)*—Paid in Bromwich Church Porch, by Robart Rider, my father—die et anno infra scripto.

Item the 23rd day of October, 1573.—I, Robert Rider, was at the sealing and delivering of a deede from Richard Jennens, of Wednesbury, to Jhon Jesson, of West Bromwich—the which deed contained three lands of arrable land lying in Monney feild—also I was at the sealing and delivering of another deed graunted by the aforesaid Jhon Jesson to Richard Jennens—conteayning one land of arrable land lying in the Churchfeild of Wednesbury—and I sawe livereye and season to these Deeds the daye and yeare above mentioned.

Item—the 14th day of November, anno domino 1575. I, Symon Ryder, was at the sealing of a Deed and liverye, and season of the same being done by William Orme, gent., to obtain feoffys, being in number 21, and these were present, but two of them, viz., Thomas Russell and Roger Colborne, to whom these deed was delivered in name of all the rest and to what use I do not know—The which deed did contein in yt a certain croft lying a little from Rowley Church on the south-west part where the livery was made, and whether it do conteine any more or not I do not remember.—These were witnesses to the aforesaid livery and season, and the sealing of the deed Jhon Nock Clarke—Thomas Geavons—Richard Handsaker—and Richard Hipkiss.

Item the 21st day of November, anno domini, 1575.—We, Robert Rider and Symon Ryder, were at a lyvery and season done in manner of forme following—first Jhon Parkshouse, of Hurst Hill, having a mortgage of certain land of Gregory Woodwarde, of West Bromwich, called Winses Ground—did . . . . his mortgage unto the aforesaid Gregorie Woodwarde, thereby setting him in full state of the aforesaid Winses—and then the aforesaid Gregorye did seale an Indenture of Mortgage to the aforesaid John Parkshouse . . . . and my father digged the turfe with his bill, and Gregorye gott a twigge of an oke, the which grewe over the water of tame . . . . These were witnesses . . , . William Greene, Clerke—John Garbet — Robert Ryder and Symon Ryder—with others.

Item the 5th day of November, anno domini, 1576.—I, Robert Rider, made an entry in a certain more called Saulley's Moore, and in a part of bircholt which I did with my landlord bissell upon a reasonable consideration, the which he would never (perform?) first I entered into that part of bircholt which is before Whersted and there I cut a bough of an oke and digged a turf and stucke the boughe in the turf, and did bid beare witness that here I entered in my owne right, and then I layd the bough and the turfe down upon the hedge. Then I went into Saulles more and there I did cut another bough and digged a turfe and stucke the bough in yt and sayd as

I did before, and I hanged that bough and turfe upon an oke which grewe in the sayd more, being in the presents of Nicholas Smith, Jhon Bridgman, and Robert Ward.

Item the 18th day of October, anno domini, 1577.— Hew Shelley, sonn and heire of Thomas Shelley, deceased, did make an entry in the meadowe at my father's house in his owne right in the name of all the lands which his father sold to Jhon Bissell, and of a gorse at (Birmicham ?) and there came with him his mother and two young men, and she sayd that the last yeare before he made his entrye in the aforesaid manner, &c., &c.

My daughter, Margeria, died 17th July, 1622. Buried at Rowley, 18th July.

My daughter, Anna, died 7th October, 1622. Buried at Madeley, in ecclia, 8th October.

My son, Nicholas, died 10th August, 1823. Buried at West Bromwich, 12th August.

My wife died 21st December, 1629. Buried at West Bromwich, 22nd December, aged 70, et post . . . . sine . . . . Annos, 51.

My daughter, Amy, died 5th March 1632. Buried at Canocke, 7th March.

My son, Francis, died 12th December, 1633. Buried the same day at Rowley Regis.

Robert Rider, son of Robert Rider, son of Nicholas Rider, born at West Bromwich, 30th March, 1636, and baptised 1st day of April.

Mr. John Shilton, of Birmingham, deceased, 8th March, 1601.

William Orme, of Rowley, deceased, 7th March. Buried the 8th March, at Rowley, 1616.

The 21st day of Marche, being thursday, and S. Benedict's Day, there was a wonderfull strong tempestuous winde, which began on the Wednesday night and continued until the Thursday with in night, which blew down many houses, tres, and over threwe steeples, chimneys, and other stronge and large buildings, to the great terrour of the people and losse of the realme. Anno 1594.

Richard Sheldon, of Wednesbury, died the ninth day of September, 1613.

Sir William Whorwood, Knight, died the first daia of July, about 6 of the clocke in the morning, Anno Domni 1614, att London, and was buried at West Bromwich.

Willm. Whorwood, of Tipton, died the 4th day of Julye, 1614, about 7 of the clocke att night, and was buried the 5th daia of July at Tipton.

Walter Stanley, Esquire, died the 8th day of Aprile, Anno Domni 1615, and was buried the tenth day of Aprile following.

Thomas Russell, co-heir of William Orme, died the 22th day of November, 1615, and was buried the 23th day of November, att Rowley Regis.

Paid to William Turton, the elder, for his land in newe leasowe. . . . 16 October, 1621.

Paid to Anne Turton, widow, my rent for tiath hay at Oldbury, for Sir Thomas Littleton, the 19 October, 1621.

Paid to Anne Turton, widow—the halfe-year's rent due for the meadow before my door at the Annunciation last past, the 10th day of April, 1623.—15s.

Itm. paid to my Aunt Rider her rent the 27 day of Marche, the which I paid to William Knowles, his boy, in presence of John Baker. Paid to my Aunt Rider her annuity 21 April, 1589.

Paid to Agnes Rider her annuity the 20th October, 1589.—6s. 8d.

Paid to Mr. Whorwood for my tithes the 1st of May, 1587—5d.

14th March, 1601.—A note of my son Nicholas his marriadge money.—A note how I bestowed the said marriadge money—....

(One Itim is) Paid to Thomas Grove, for the land in Newe leasow, the 19 daie of Aprill, 1602, 20s. Itm paid to Mr. Walter Stanley the 28th day of Maie £5.

20th day June, Anno dmni, 1586. Margaret Darby, daughter of William Darby, was baptised at West Bromwich.

(Richard Jennyn Clarke—mentioned 20th December, 12 Hen. VIII.)

The tenth daie of October, 1603, Mr. Symon Stanley was buried.—

The second daie of November, 1603. Sir William Walker Clerke was buried att hondesworth.

The fourth daie of September, 1636.—John Furnetbie, prebend and official at Lichfield, and parson of Handsworth and Aldrich, was buried at Handsworth.

(Mentions his son-in-law, John Chambers.)

Paid, per Wm. Hill, to my son Robert, in 1613.

My daughter Amye had a brasse pott, weighing twelve pounds.—22th day of Maie, 1615.

Willm. Hill had a bushell of seed corn, which my daughter Anne fetched.—15 October, 1613.

My daughter Joanne, her marriage goods.—The 20th September, 1601.

Itm. paid for her gowne cloath, the 20th September, 1601, 31s.

Appendix. 239

Itm. for baies to line yt, 7s. 6d. Itm. for the triming of it, 16s. Itm., her hat, 8s. 6d.

I accounted with my sonne, John Ryder, the eleventh day of february, 1636, and he was then in my debt five pounds for which he ys to find my grandchild's apparell of all sorts three years—daughter of my sonne Symon.

My son Robert Rider, my grandchild Robert, 1638.

My son John, 1630; my daughter-in-law Mary Rider, her rent of huckwalls, 1630.

My son Nicholas, Sep., 1630.

My son-in-law William Birde.

Itm. that William Turton, the younger, caused Roger Browne ? to shut eleven links to my dog cheyne.

21st April, 1612.—Mr. Wm. Whorwood, of Tipton, did seale and deliver to Rychard Jesson, of Brierly, a release and surrender of one closse, &c., medowe in Brierly, called Birchin Crofte, and presently after Richard Jesson, and his sonne Henry, sealed and delivered a lease and an obligacion to John Hawkes, of the same meadowe for sixteen years, which were executed upon the said meadows in presence of William Whorwood, gent., Richard Hopkins, stranger, William Fellowe, and me, Symon Rider, and Richard Jesson.

Paid to John Osborne, the 28th day of January, 1599, for three years, clerk's wages, videlicet for the year 1596, 1597, 1598, 6d. a year, in the whole 1s. 6d, Vicessimo secundo die Januarii, anno 1660, et anno Elizabetha 43, paid to John Osborne for clerk's wages for the years 1599, 1600, 12 pence, before John Partridge the younger, then churchwarden.

Paid to Simon Ward, the 17th day of April, 1621, for my Easter reckoning and my household, 3s.; for my mill,

2s.; for amercements, 16 pence; for my chief rent, 8 pence; in toto, 5s.

Item, the task of West Bromwich, 3s. 8d. armoury, wherewith the parish of West Bromwich was charged for the common armoury, 8th of March, 1596, by John Bowes, Edward Littleton, Edward Aston, knights, and Thomas Bagod, Esq., two corslets, with pikes, 1 musket, 1 culeever, 1 archer all furnished with sword, dagger, and girdle.

The following interesting and curious extracts are taken from old papers in the possession of the Reverend Thomas Jesson, and are in the handwriting of his ancestor, George Jesson, whose mother having married Mr. Thomas Grove as her 2nd husband, George Jesson was executor of his step-father, and also of his brother Edward Grove.

Probate of the will of Henry Grove, of Hondesworthe, yeoman, date 11th September, 1589, mentions his sonns, Edward and Thomas Grove, his wife Elene, bequeathing to her, among other things, "my best feather bedd with bolsters and pillowes and all other things belonging to the same." Mentions also his wife's son, William Cookes, and Henry Grove, his son Edward's son. "To cozen Robert Grove, one weyning calf."

Indenture of lease, 25th April, 1631.—Sealed and delivered in the presence of William Turton, John Turton, John Downes. A true copy examined by Thos. Grove, Henry Hunt, Thomas Jesson, senr., Thomas Jesson, junr., relating to land at Rowley.

Indenture of lease, date 17th October, 1638.—Lease granted to Thomas Grove and Edmund Darby, of land pastures and closes called Turhills.

Thomas Grove mentioned 1661.

Appendix.

The 19th day of Aprill, 1661.—Receved of Edward Grove for all his lands in West Bromwich, dewe at Saint Mary day last past, the some of three shillings and twopence for my owne lands and John Gills lands, I say receved.—Matthew Ruston.

Similar receipt dated 20th November, 1661.—For rent "due at St. Michall the Archangel last past."

Similar—" dewe at S. Mary day last past," 28th April, 1662.

Receipt from Edward Grove same as before, date Jan. 18th, 1677.

Rent received of Mr. Edward Grove Sep. 21st, 1668.

" Mary Grove, wife of Mr. Edward Grove, buried October, 1657."

" Mr. Edward Grove and Mary Persall married October 20, 1664."

" Mr. Edward Grove had a child buried 24th July, 1665."

" Mary, daughter of Mr. Edward Grove, baptised 22nd June, 1666."

" Mr. Edward Grove buried Jany. 5th, 1668-9."

" Mr. Thomas Grove buried 7th August, 1669."

" Thomas Grove and Amye Jesson were married the 12th of ffebruary, 163½." George Jesson, step son of Thomas Grove, executor to his will—he was executor to his brother Edward's Will.

A Bill of the funeral expenses of Edward Grove, whoe departed this life the 2nd day of January, 1668-9, as folleth—

	£	s.	d.
Payd to Edward Jesson for bread and cake		5	5	0
Payd to Sarah Thorne for ale			12	0
Payd for wine			6	0

	£	s.	d.
Payd for suger		5	0
1 quire of riting paper			5
Fine Incke			3
For ginger			6
A peare of hose for the child			6
For cloves and mase			9
For one quarter of veale		2	2
For fore capuns		4	0
For one gouse		1	6
For a peace of befe		1	0
For towe rabets		1	0
Payd to the Clarke		4	0
Payd to Ann Blumer		2	0
Payd to Thomas Briscoe		2	0
Payd to Robert Grice		1	6
Payd to Samewell Westwood			6
Payd for laying him out and windden him		1	6
Payd for tobackoe		2	0
Payd for tobackoe pipes			4
Payd to Edward Grove, Henry Grove, John Grove, and Thomas Grove, for carring him to Church, and layinge him in his grave, twelvepence apeace		4	0
Payd to my cusen John Grove for taking the Inventory and ingrossing it		5	0
Payd to George Jesson for copinge out the will		2	0
Payd for provinge the will and the commission for taking my othe		15	0
Payd to Mr. White for his funerall sermon and a mortorie, and for giving me my oathes		16	8
Payd to Thomas Belaingam for keeping the plompe which was due at Cristmas last		1	0

Appendix.

	£	s.	d.
Payd to James Cope for the starlings, the moles, and towards the making of the hedges		2	6
	£10	0	11

October 13th, 1669.—Received then of George Jesson for taking upp the seates when Mr. Edward Grove was buryed, and setting them down again the some of two shillings and fourpence —2/4

My cosens Tennants as followth—	£	s.	d.
John Osborne for his howse . .		16	8
And for the towe craufts . . .	1	0	0
Robert Grice for his howse and land . .	1	5	6
Robert Grice for the barne . .		2	6
James Cox	2	0	0
My Ante Grove		5	0
Rent due at Allhollowetide.			
Rafe Cullwicke—rent due at Chrismas .	6	10	0
Widdowe Baker . . .		19	0
The howse in line . . .	1	10	0
My ffather Grove received of his maid for a bolster		4	0
of Edward Dudley for line barne . .		12	0

A bill of what money my ffather Grove hath received of my Uncle Edward Grove

	£	s.	d.
Three tun of hay . . .	3	0	0
For boards which came from line . .	1	1	0
For one Cow	2	10	0
Received of Elizabeth Dawes for one coverlet and one box		11	0

	£	s.	d.
Received of Henry Lowe for pewter		13	0
,, of John Deely for one flichen of bacon		15	0
,, of James Bun for the cubert		11	0
,, of William White for one cofer and two blankets		7	6
,, Goody Large for one chaf bed and two blankets		6	4
For one coffer and one chaire		4	4
For one spade			4
Received of Thomas Simes for a peare of bedsteads		9	6

A note of my unkle Grove's debt, and whic money father Grove paid for my uncle Ed. Grove.

	£	s.	d.
Mr. Thomas Groves acquitance	2	0	0
George Jesson's ,,	2	0	0
To father Grove	5	0	0
Unkle Grove's funerall expenses	10	0	11
Paid to Mary Grove for keeping the child	1	10	0
Paid to the churchwardens		1	6
Paid to John Stamps for the poore		1	6

One quarter's rent was due to my Mother Grove for her dowry out of my father Grove's land at Oldbury.

MONEY TO BE ALLOWED ME UPON ACT.

	£	s.	d.
Paid for my father Grove's funeral expenses	11	12	1
The charge of housekeeping between my father Grove's death and my mother's	10	19	8
Mother Grove's funeral expenses	8	19	2

Legacies.

To his sister Coper		10	0

Appendix.

	£	s.	d.
To Thomas Coper	.	10	0
To Mr. Thos. Grove	.	2	0	0
To Cozen John Grove	.	2	0	0
&c., &c.			

	£	s.	d.
Imp: The cast Mettle Plate belonging to the Hall Fire	00	11	00
The Great Brasse Pann	00	19	00
One Spitt	00	01	00
The Truckle Bed	00	03	04
One Forme	00	01	00
The Axe	00	01	00
	£01	16	10

Received these goods above written in part of a Legasie given by Thomas Grove, lately deceased, by mee, George Jesson.

I sold to my Ant Grove these things under written—

One great kettle	0	10	00
A nurse chair, one fflichen of bacon	0	10	0
And the store pig	0	07	0
One joyned stule	0	1	10
One warming pan	0	02	0
Two little joyned stules	0	01	0
All the flax, and the woole, and the litle wheele	0	04	0
One chest, one coffer	0	06	6
Two smuthinge irons	0	00	10
One ffallinge table		1	0

One feather beed at seaven peence the poound cometh to one poound eight shillings and sixpence, and for kiping the cowe the some is besides . . . .

	£	s.	d.
Sold one kettle, 15 pounds weight, at 10 pence the pound, comes to	00	12	06
Sold three pewter dishes att 6 pounds, and one quarter, att	00	06	00
Sold one brasse chafinge dish, att	0	1	4
Sold one table with two tressells in the buletinge house, att		2	0
Sold one coppinge knife, att	0	0	6
Sold the little table in the hall	0	4	0
Sold one chafe bed, att.	0	2	10
Sold one chaire in the hall chamber, att.	0	2	0
Sold one coffer in the kitchen chamber to Will White, which he hath not paid for	0	3	0
Sold two peare of ould blankets to Will. White which he hath not paid for, att	0	4	0
The great chest, at	0	11	0
Sold one wine sheet, one bag, and one axe		5	0
One lume, not paid for, att			
Sold one hurdle to Thos. Briskoe, not paid for	0	0	4

Delivered to my Ant Grove one great kettle, one dabnet, one brasse mortar and pestle, one brasse limer, one brasse candlestick, one little kettle, two barrels, one burning lume, one skelle, one kimnell, one brasse pott, one churne, fiare shovle and toungs, two joyned chaires, one deske-stule, a nurse chaire, one flichen of baken, and the store pig.

Left with Mistress Selly 7 fowles, and fore guislings, and one patted woden bole.

To Thomas Simcox one bedsteds	0	9	6
One cofer	0	2	2

Appendix

To Humphrey Rowe the great brass poote at 9 the pound	1	16	0
One table boord	0	4	0
One corne showlle	0	1	8
One barill	0	3	6
To Thomas Simcox a peare of coberts	0	2	6
To William White a sacor	0	0	4

In the butrey, tenn shillves in the darke rume, seven shillves below the entrey, towe benches in the halle.

Goods receved at time unsold—One table and forme in the halle, one londwin (?) and bare of iorne, the screne, towe candlesticks, towe peare of beeadstides, six silver spownes, One jacke and wates, one coffer, one old bible, and a peare of gold waites, one little book, one cofer and linings, one smothing iorne, one dripin ponn and broache (spit), one fether beead and beead hillinge, one wate mill.

What shillves and benches are lafte in Mrs. Selly's rumes, as folleth : towe joyned beeds and cords, and mats, in the hall, one longe table, one joyne forme, towe joyne benches, one other bench, in the butrey, tenn shillves, in the dark rume seaven, belowe the entrey towe, one lous irn, one iorne bare, and geeale.

"The outmost boundes of the Parish of Wesbromwich, are these following :—From Brand forde Bridge downewardes the River of Tame doth divide that from Halesowen, Rowley, Tipton, Wednesbury, Barre, and Aldrich and Hansworth until that cometh unto Mr. Henry Cookes, his land, or Henery Osborne's meadowe, and thence forward the lane leadinge from Bromwich Forge to Whorston, at or neare Sandwell copey corner, and from thence along a wine Waye slantinge towards a guter wich poynted upon

George Alane, his Barne which stood in the uper cornor of his land towarde Hansworth, part of the barne in West Bromwich and part in Handsworth, as men sayd, and so from thence to the nether end of olde Wm. Hunte, his farme called the Street house, to a place in Smethwick Lane called Totmons Lowe, and from thence along the hedge rowe which partes Asprs More, in Smethwick, from the land of Thomas Birch, in West Bromwich, to Spane brooke, and so downe alonge the said Spane brooke to the river of Tame at Bramford Bridge aforesaid."

CATALOGUE OF FRUIT TREES PLANTED AT BROMWICH HALL.

"S. Clarke 1721." This Catalogue, or account of Fruit Trees, &c., sent from London to Westbromwich, must be carefully preserved for future informations: 1720. Layton Stone, 15th December, 1720. Sir Samuel Clarke.—I received your letter, and according to yo' order have this day packed up all the under mentioned Trees, &c., and thereunto have fixed Labels, numbered, referring unto each sort of fruite, for each Aspect in each of yo' two gardens, and have writt upon each Bundle or parcell what they refer to. They are all sound, perfect in health, larg, strong, well taken up, and sure in their respective kinds, viz.

For the South East Aspect, or against the House in the broad gravel walke.—

		The quantity of trees, or quantityes of trees.
No. 1.	White Muscadine Grape	3
„ 2.	Royal ditto	2

No. 3. Red July ditto . . . 3

Are 8 Vines to grow between the dwarfs or the Wall trees undermentioned.

No. 4. Newington Nectarine . . 2
" 5. Newington Peach . : 3
" 6. Scarlet Newington Peach . . 2
" 7. Early Newington Peach . . 2

Are 9 Peaches and Nectarines to goe between the above-mentioned.

ffor the South-West aspect, or the left-hand side coming from the house, being that side of the wall unto which the end of the barn reacheth :—

No. 8. Gorls Bury pears . . . 2
" 9. Diana Pears or Doyne pears . . 2
" 10. Done Pears . . . 2
" 11. Mapell plumbs . . . 2
" 12. Jonhatine Plumbs . . . 2
" 13. Green gage plumbs . . 2
" 14. Turkey Apricots . . . 2
" 15. Roman ditto , . . 2

    6 dwarf pears, 6 plumb trees, 4 apricot trees.

ffor the North West Aspect, or the upper end of the parlour garden which reacheth to the summer house from the East Ward.

No. 16. Bleeding Heart Cherrys . . 2
" 17. Lewkeward . . . 2
" 18. May Duke Cherrys . . 4
" 19. Swan's egg peare . . . 2
" 20. Summer Bon Cretien . . 2
" 21. Bury de Roy . . . 1

    8 dwarf cherrys, 5 pear trees.

For the North East aspect, or for the wall from the Pump

Court Door to the Summer House, in the Parlour Garden, viz.—

No. 22.	S. Catherine plumb	2
,, 23.	White Holland plumb	2
,, 24.	Orleance plumb	2

6 plumbs

,, 25.	Morella Cherry	2
,, 26.	Black Heart Cherry	2
,, 27.	Orange Burgamott peare	2
,, 28.	Imperial plum	2
,, 29.	Rosia peare	2

4 cherrys, 4 peares, 2 plumbs.

To be planted in the Kitchen garden, viz., ffor the South East aspect in the kitchen garden.

No. 30.	Mascaline apricot trees	2
,, 31.	Royall Orange ditto	2

4 Apricot trees.

,, 32.	Red Roman Nectarine	2
,, 33.	Arlbermarle peach	2
,, 34.	Vanguard peach—Trees—bad	2
,, 35.	Minion peach Trees	2
,, 36.	Bell Chevereuse peach	2
,, 37.	Newington Nectarine	1

ffor the South West aspect, or the right hand wall from the house, against which wall Nath^{ll} Walls house reacheth in the kitchen garden, viz.—

No. 38.	Old Newington peach trees	2
,, 39.	Turkey Apricot	3
,, 40.	Drab d'or plumb	1
,, 41.	La Royall plumb	1

Two peaches, and 3 apricots, Two plumb trees.

ffor the North East aspect, or the wall on the Left hand

Appendix.

from the house being that wall over against ye Slaughter house.

No. 42.	Early amber plumb	2
,, 43.	Pomegranette plumb	2
,, 44.	Early Blanquet peare	1

    4 plumbs, 1 peare.

ffor the North West aspect, or against the house in the Kitchen garden, vizt.

No. 45.	Bury de Roy peare	2
,, 46.	Jargonell peare	2
,, 47.	Amarell peare	1

    5 peare trees.

,, 48.	Standard peaches and nectarines	8
,, 49.	Vines to go between the others	7

These following trees are sent with the others, vizt., the Standards to be placed against the walls where John Thomas the gardner doth see proper, these Standards are marked with an "S" as well as with numbers, I mean the leads for them are so marked, vizt.—

No. 1.	Gross Blanquet Peare	1
,, 2.	Diana peare	2
,, 3.	Citron de Carini peare is Carmis	1
,, 4.	Burgamott de Rashea	2
,, 5.	Standard Roman apricot	2
,, 6.	Standard cheerys of various sorts	14

    6 Standard peares, 16 standards.

These other trees are alsoe sent with those before mentioned, vizt., these have no numbers, nor doe they need any.

Mulbery trees strong	3
Strong Codlins	20
ffine white Rasberrys is Rasberries | 100 |

Red and White Dutch Currants	100
ffine sorts of Goose Berrys	100
Philberds	100
ffigs	2

These Currants are for the dwarf wall or the Brest Wall in the Best garden—commonly calle the Parlour garden.

S^r which are all I have in my memorandum, excepting the 6 quinces, which shall goe along with the standards for the orchards, and the dwarfs for the parlor garden. I hope you will give John Thomas, your gardnor, notice of theire coming and the other needful instructions.—I am, S^r, Yo^r Hum. Servant, Adam Holt. Layton Stone, the 13th December, 1720.—Examined by S.C., and T. Elderton.

The 5 bundles of trees made up in mats have hoope stick talleys on them marked sc No. 1, 2, 3, 4, 5, and on the mats alsoe stand the marke sc with ink, the little bagg with the leads in it is marked with sc No. 6. These leads have numbers stamped thereon agreeable to Mr. Holt's numbers in his account; you will finde three leads with No. 1, for the three white Muscadine grape trees, and you will find 2 leads with No. 3c, for the 2 Muscadine apricot trees, and soe on for the rest; the spare leads that are not stamped must be carefully preserved for some other occasion; they are to be nayled on the wall with nails through the holes made in them; it's thought four-penny nails will be big enough.

London, the 21st January, 1720, sent to Westbromwich fifty and fowre standard apple trees for the two orchards, vizt.:—

No. 60.	ffrench peppin apples	2
,, 61.	English golden peppins	8
,, 62.	Jennetings	4

Appendix.

No. 63.	Kentish peppins	. . .	4
,, 64.	Holland peppins	. . .	2
,, 65.	pyles Russets	. . .	4
,, 66.	Summer gilly-flower	. .	4
,, 67.	Summer paremaines	. .	8
,, 68.	Winter paremaines	. .	4
,, 69.	Golden Rennetts	. . .	6
,, 70.	Wheeler's Russetts	. .	4
,, 71.	Non par Elles.	. . .	2
,, 72.	Bearnards apples, for baking	.	2

54 Standard apple trees.

,, 73	Black Damozeen plumbs	. .	2
,, 74	White Damozeens	. . .	2
,, 75	Black Muscle plumbs	. .	2
,, 76	Blew Violet plumbs	. .	2

8 Standard Apple trees.

,, 77	Catherine peare trees	. .	2
,, 78	English Winsors, is Windsors	.	2
,, 79	Early Bergamotts	. .	2
,, 80	Orange Bergamotts	. .	2
,, 81	Hamden's Bergamotts	. .	1
,, 82	Peppinger peare	. . .	1

10 Standard peare trees. 72 Standard trees.

Dwarf trees for the Borders in the parler garden, otherwise called the best garden, vizt.

No. 83.	Mapell plumb Dwarf trees	. .	2
,, 84.	Violet perdrigon	. .	2
,, 85.	Apricot plumb	. . .	2
,, 86.	Minion plumb	. . .	2
,, 87.	ffotheringham	. . .	2
,, 88.	White Damozeen	. . .	2
,, 89.	May duke Cherry Dwarfs	. .	2

No. 90.	Orleans		2
„ 91.	Morella		2
„ 92.	Carnation		2
„ 93.	Black Heart		1
„ 94.	Red Heart,		1
„ 95.	White Heart Cherrys		2

12 Dwarf Cherry trees.

„ 96.	Little Mus-catt Pear dwarfs		2
„ 97.	Citron de Carmis or Bouldon		2
„ 98.	Red Admirall		2
„ 99.	Jargonell		2
„ 100.	Summer Bon Cretien		4
„ 101.	Bury de Roy		4
„ 102.	Orange Bergamots		2
„ 103.	Hamden Bergamots		2
„ 104.	Autumn Bergamots		2
„ 105.	Vortc Lougee		2

24 Dwarf Pear Trees.

„ 108.	Spencer Peppins		4
„ 109.	Kentish Peppins		4
„ 110.	Holland Peppins		2
„ 111.	Pyles Russets		4
„ 112.	Summer Gilly flower		4
„ 113.	Summor Pearmaine		8
„ 114.	Jennettings		4
„ 115.	Golden Rennett		6
„ 116.	Wheeler's Russett		4
„ 117.	Non Parelles		2
„ 118.	Bearnard's Apples for Baking		2

102 Dwarf Trees in all, vizt.—
    12 Dwarf Plumb trees
    12 Dwarf Cherry trees

Appendix. 255

    24 dwarf Pear trees
    54 dwarf Apple trees

ffor the borders in the parlour garden and some other places as hath been directed. All of them strong, vigorous, hopefull, thriving trees, good bearers, and of the verry best sorts of the said severall kindes; and alsoe a bundle in which are the above-mentioned seeds, and somthing for Mr. John Thomas. All these things are sent away from London, the 21st of January, 1720-1, by Thomas Shears, wagoner, who is to deliver them in good condition and undamaged, at West Bromwich Hall, on fryday next.

London, 3rd ffebruary, 1721-2.—Mr. John Thomas, the gardener, this day went (*sic*) by Thomas Shears, wagoner for Birmingham, made up in a matt, which hath direction to me at Westbromwich hall, writ on parchment tyed to that mat, the following trees, vizt.

    2 S. Catherine Plumbs
    4 Kentish Pippin Apple trees
    4 Jennettings   ditto
    4 Russet Pippins   ditto
    2 Golden Rennetts ditto
    3 Orange Bergamott Pear trees
    3 Old Russet Bergamott Pear trees

sound, strong, hopefull, of the best sorts, and of the verry best bearers, 100 Artichoke plants of the best, strongest, and largest sorts. The eight trees that died must be supplyed with other eight trees of the verry same sorts in the same places, and the rest of the trees now sent down you must plant in such places of the orchard as you think most suitable and convenient.

Mr. John Thomas—London, 29th January, 1722.—I have received yor of the 9th instant, which acquainted me that six of the fruit trees formerly sent down from hence, which had been planted by you in the parlour and kitchen gardens, had miscarried, and are dead, in place whereof you desired me to send other six of the same sorts and numbers, and also one more to plant in the place of the old great Cherry tree which was taken down and did groe on the south-east wall of the kitchen garden. This day I did send by Samuel Gutteridge's wagon one bundle of trees and one box, both directed to my selfe at Westbromwch, which he hath promised shall be delivered on Satterday next, either at West Bromwich Hall, or else at the house of Mr. John Jesson, or Mr. Richard Jesson, whose houses lie in the road to Tipton. . . . . Then follows a list consisting of Apricots, Peaches, Plumbs, Cherries, Pears, and Apples,

The box contained Marrowfatt Pease, Admirall Pease, Spanish Pease, Portugall Onyon seed, Melon seed, White Turkey Cowcumber seed, and Cabbage seed, received from Russia in the yeare 1722.

Another catalogue follows of trees sent to Westbromwich from London, by Samuel Gutteridge's wagon, the 19th November, 1723. This contains Nectarines, Cherries, Pears, 2 White Figg trees, 1 Blue Figg tree, Red Heart Dwarf Cherry, 2 Ambroshea Pear trees, Amber Heart Cherry trees, 4 Cadiliack Pear trees, &c., the Norbury Portugall Vine layer, Hambro Grape Vine cutting, Le Mune ditto, Black Raisin ditto, Black Muscadine ditto.

London, 10th December, 1723.—Mr. John Thomas.— I told you that Mr. Adam Holt had sent Cherry trees insteed of Plumb trees in that bundle you received about sixteen days agoe. On Sunday last Mr. John Grove dined at this house, and desired me to procure for him the following trees, viz.: then follows a list containing Plums, Nectarines, Peaches (one Plum is named John Hatine), then another list of trees "for my own use . . . . and having on a parchment tyed to the bundle a direction to me at West Bromwich, which will be delivered to you at the Cross Guns on Saturday next by Gutteridge's servant to whom it was delivered this morning, and he promised to me myself to take particular care thereof. Now those five Plumb trees must be planted in such places in the gardens as you thinke most proper for them, altho' you should remove some Cherry trees into the orchards to make room for the Plumb trees, which we value more than the Cherry trees. I hope Mr. Holt has rightly packed up the fifteen trees above-mentioned, but if it should soe happen he hath committed any mistake, such mistake must fall upon Mr. Grove, for the five Plumb trees which I ordered for myselfe must be planted in my gardens without faile.

Trees sent to West Bromwich ye 24th November, 1724, to be planted against the back part of the parlour-garden wall in the new piece of ground taken out of the leasow called the Little Stockings, and leading from the back part of the summer house to the gate between ye new barn and ye Pump Court, vizt.: then follows a list of Peach, Nectarine, Plum, Apricot, and Mulberry trees. Next comes a list headed "an account of trees which have miscarried in ye gardens and orchards at West Bromwich Hall, Staffordshire, and are supplyed by the same numbers of trees of the same sorts."—London, the 27th January, 1728-9.

Then a list of trees planted in 1748-9, January—Plums, Peaches, Nectarines, Pears, &c. Then a list of trees planted in 1750, again including Plums and Peaches; then trees planted in 1751-53-54-56-58-60, among which are Plums, Peaches and Nectarines, and Apricots. The Catalogue ends in 1760 with 1 Indian Figg, and 1 Portugal Cherry.

THE END.

PEDIGREES.

STANLEY, OF WEST BROMWICH - - No. 1.
SHELTON - - - - - ,, 2.
CLARKE - - - - - ,, 3.
DESCENT OF THE MANOR - - - ,, 4.
WHORWOOD, OF SANDWELL - - - ,, 5.
TURTON - - - - - ,, 6.
JESSON FAMILY - - - - ,, 7.
LOWE, OF LYNDON, AFTERWARDS CHARLEMONT ,, 8.

No. 1.—STANLEY, OF WEST BROMWICH.

John Stanley, = Cecilia, daughter of William Freebody,
Died 7th October, 1584.   Died 1569.
Letters of Administration granted
to his widow at Lichfield,
Nov. 23rd, 1584.

┌────────────────┬──────────────┬──────────────┬──────────────────┬──────────────┐
Francis,   Winifred, daughter of   Roger   Catherine   Simon,   Elizabeth = Roger
Died 1587,   Thos. Middlemore, =   of Har-   daughter of =   Buried at   Littelton.
Aged 52.   Lord of Edgbaston.   borne.   —Combesford.   Wt. Brom
                                        Oct. 10, 1603.

┌──────────────┬──────────────┐
Gertrude, = Frances = John Wolverston. Jane = —Okell. Ryohard, Charles.
daughter of Sir   Died March,
Wm. Hollys.   1611, buried Barbara = John
                                                          at Wt. Brm.   Shilton.

Walter,   = Mary, daughter
Died 1615,   of George Grey, of
Buried at   Enville,
Wt. Brom.   Buried at West
               Bromwich, 1624.
William,
Et. 29, in
1614.

┌──────────────┬──────────────┬──────────────┐
Elizabeth,   Mary,   Francis,   Thomas,
Bap. 12th Jan.,   Bap. 1st Sept.,   Bap. 20th Feb.,   Bap. 20th Dec.,
1609, at West   1610, at   1615, at   1618,
Bromwich.   West Bromwich.   West Bromwich.   Buried same day,
Buried 1612, at   at West
West Bromwich.   Bromwich.

No. 2.—Pedigree of Shelton.

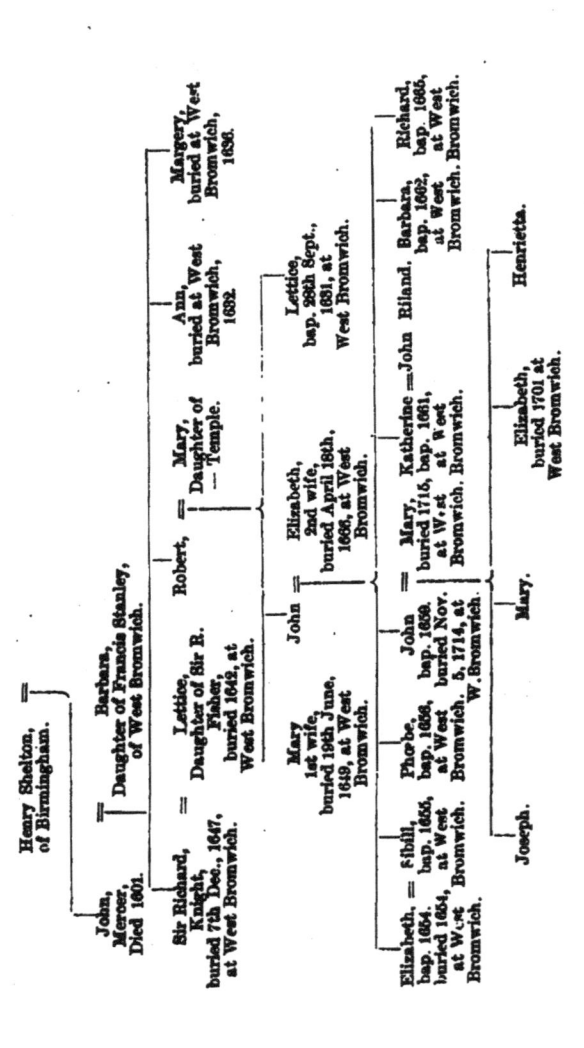

Henry Shelton, of Birmingham.

- John, Mercer, Died 1601.
- Sir Richard, Knight, buried 7th Dec., 1647, at West Bromwich. = Barbara, Daughter of Francis Stanley, of West Bromwich.
  - Lettice, Daughter of Sir B. Fisher, buried 1642, at West Bromwich. = Robert, = Mary, Daughter of — Temple.
  - Ann, buried at West Bromwich, 1682.
  - Margery, buried at West Bromwich, 1650.

John =
- Mary, 1st wife, buried 19th June, 1649, at West Bromwich.
- Elizabeth, 2nd wife, buried April 18th, 1666, at West Bromwich.

Children of John:
- Elizabeth, = Sibill, bap. 1655, buried 1654, at West at West Bromwich. Bromwich.
- Phœbe, bap. 1656, at West Bromwich.
- John, bap. 1659, buried Nov. 1714, at W. Bromwich. = Mary, buried 1715, at W. Bromwich.
- Katherine = John Riland.
- Barbara, bap. 1662, at West Bromwich.
- Richard, bap. 1666, at West Bromwich.
- Lettice, bap. 28th Sept., 1681, at West Bromwich.

Joseph. Mary. Elizabeth, buried 1701 at West Bromwich. Henrietta.

No. 3.—Pedigree of Clarke.

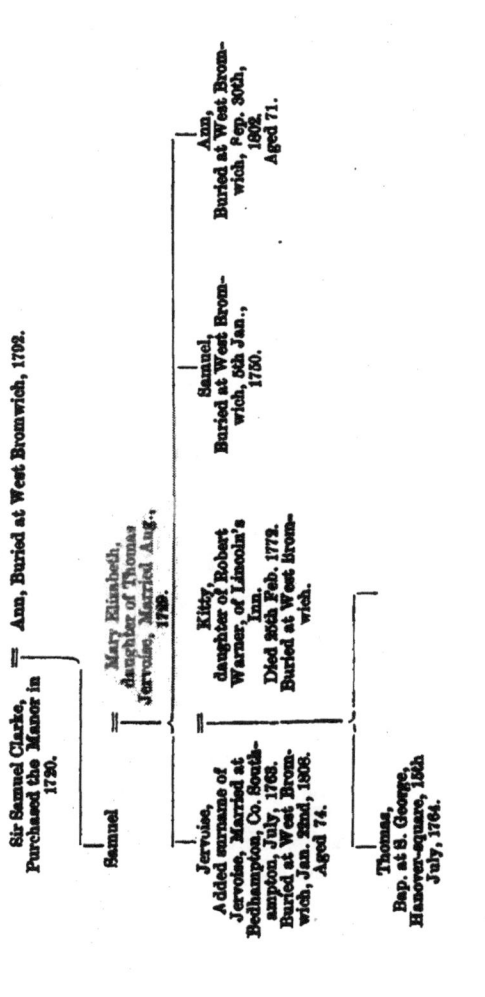

Sir Samuel Clarke, Purchased the Manor in 1720. = Ann, Buried at West Bromwich, 1702.

Samuel = Mary Elizabeth, daughter of Thomas Jervoise, Married Aug., 1720.

= Kitty, daughter of Robert Warner, of Lincoln's Inn. Died 26th Feb. 1772. Buried at West Bromwich.

Children:
- Jervoise, Added surname of Jervoise, Married at Bedhampton, Co. Southampton, July, 1763. Buried at West Bromwich, Jan. 2nd, 1808. Aged 74.
- Samuel, Buried at West Bromwich, 5th Jan., 1750.
- Ann, Buried at West Bromwich, Sep. 30th, 1802. Aged 71.

Thomas, Bap. at S. George, Hanover-square, 15th July, 1764.

No. 4.—Descent of the Manor.

```
Guy de Opheni = Christiana.
    1155.
         |
    William = Juliana.
    1180.
         |
    Richard = Geva
 (Surnamed Basset?)
  died before 1224.
         |
  ┌──────────┼──────────────┬──────────────┐
Margerie = Richard de    William,      Sara = Walter Devereux,
           Marnham       d. s. p.              d. 1291.
                         before 1255.
     |                        |
  Richard =               Walter =
  living in 1322.         living in 1292.    Stephen =
     |                        |              living in 1322.
  William = Alianora                              |
  living in 1375. | living in 1375.           William, =
     |                        |               living in 1356.    John.
   John,                   William,
   living in 1338.         living in 1388.
   a daughter m. to)           |
                         William Freeman
                         Gave the manor to his
                         daughter Alice, in Henry
                         VI. reign, before 1427.
                         Alice = William Freebody
                                 (of Dudley)
                                    =
                              William,
                           Lord of the Manor
                           in 1436, d. 1447.
                                    |
                                William =
                              21 years of age
                                in 1448.
                                    |
                              John Stanley, = Cicely,
                              d. 1534.      | d. 1552.
                                        Francis = Winifred
                                        d. 1557. | Middlemore.
                                              Walter = Gertrude
                                              d. 1615. | Hollys.
                                                   William = Mary Gray
                                                   Had issue.

Sir Richard Shilton, = Lettice Fisher.
Cousin to Wm. Stanley,
became possessed of
the manor in 1626.
d. 1647.
         |
    John Shelton, = Elizabeth,
    Nephew of Sir | Second wife.
    Richard.
    d. 1665
              John = Mary.
              b. 1659, d. 1714.

Sir Samuel Clarke = Ann.
purchased the manor
in 1720.
         |
       Samuel = Mary E. Jervoise.
              |
        Jervoise = Kitty Warner.
        d. 1808.  |
              Thomas.
```

No. 5.—Pedigree of Whorwood, of Sandwell.

John Whorwood, of Compton. == Elizabeth, Daughter of Rich. Corbyn, of Corbyn's Hall.

Children:
- **John, Died 1585.** == Joyce, Daughter of Sir Ed. Grey, of Enville.
- **Edward, of Compton. Pedigree continues in Shaw.**
- **Three other Sons.**

John == Dorothy, Daughter of Thos. Basset, of Hints.

Robert, of Sandwell, Died 1590. == Frances, Daughter of Walter Chetham, of London, Knt.

Children of Robert and Frances:
- **William, of Sandwell, Knt., J.P., Buried at West Bromwich, 1614, æt. 51.** == Anne, Daughter and heir of Henry Field, Died Oct., 1599.
- **Three other Sons.**

William and Anne's children:
- **Thomas, of Sandwell, Knt., Died abt. 1635.** == Ursula, Daughter and heir to George Brome. Married Nov. 1604.
- 2 William.
- 3 Robert.
- 4 Field, died 1658.
- 5 John.
- Frances.
- Ann.
- Elizabeth.
- Mabel.
- Isabel.
- Mary.
- Dorothy.
- Magdalen.

Thomas Brome. == Jane, Daughter and co-heir of Wm. Rider, of Kingston-upon-Thames, gent.

- **William, Student of the Middle Temple.**

No. 8.—Pedigree of Lowe, of Lyndon, afterwards Charlemont.

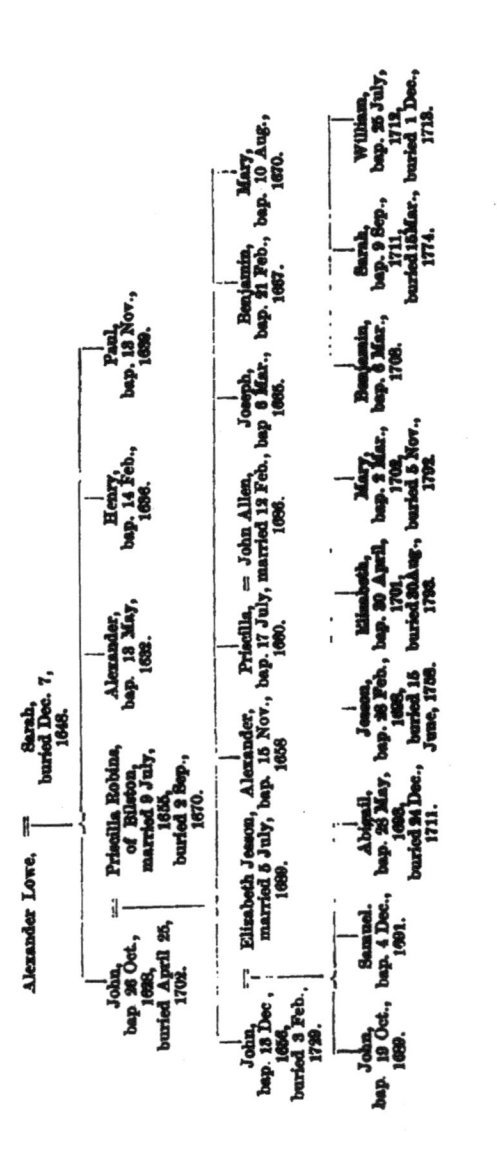

Alexander Lowe, = Sarah, buried Dec. 7, 1648.

John, bap. 26 Oct., 1629, buried April 25, 1702. = Priscilla Robins, of Elleston, married 9 July, 1655, buried 2 Sep., 1670.

Children of John and Priscilla:
- Alexander, bap. 13 May, 1652.
- Henry, bap. 14 Feb., 1656.
- Paul, bap. 13 Nov., 1659.

Priscilla, = John Allen, bap. 17 July, married 12 Feb., 1660. 1696.

Joseph, bap. 6 Mar., 1665.

Benjamin, bap. 21 Feb., 1667.

Mary, bap. 10 Aug., 1670.

John, bap. 13 Dec., 1656, buried 3 Feb., 1729. = Elizabeth Jesson, Alexander, married 5 July, bap. 15 Nov., 1689. 1658.

Samuel, bap. 4 Dec., 1691.

John, bap. 19 Oct., 1689.

Abigail, bap. 25 May, 1693, buried 24 Dec., 1711.

Joseph, bap. 26 Feb., 1695, buried 15 June, 1763.

Elizabeth, bap. 20 April, 1701, buried 20 Aug., 1762.

Mary, bap. 2 Mar., 1703, buried 5 Nov., 1762.

Benjamin, bap. 3 Mar., 1708.

Sarah, bap. 9 Sep., 1711, buried 16 Mar., 1774.

William, bap. 25 July, 1711, buried 1 Dec., 1712.

Lightning Source UK Ltd.
Milton Keynes UK
UKHW010641260721
387780UK00002B/476